THE MYSTERIES OF JESUS

A MUSLIM STUDY OF THE ORIGINS
AND DOCTRINES
OF THE CHRISTIAN CHURCH

RUQAIYYAH WARIS MAQSOOD

SAKINA BOOKS

OXFORD

Text copyright © Ruqaiyyah Maqsood 2000
All rights reserved
Colour photographs © Muhsin Kilby
ISBN   0 9538056 6 2 cloth
ISBN   0 9538056 7 0 paperback

Published by:
Sakina Books
3 Galpin Close
Oxford OX4 1PR

The cover shows a detail from 'Christ driving the Traders from the Temple' by El Greco,
reproduced by kind permission of The National Gallery, London.

Designed by Abd al-Lateef Whiteman

Printed in Great Britain by Alden Press, Oxford.

In the name of God, Most Compassionate and Merciful

Some related books by Ruqaiyyah Waris Maqsood

(As Rosalyn Kendrick)

Does God have a body? (SCM, 1977)
In the Steps of Jesus (Hulton, 1979, 1983)
Jesus of Nazareth: the Way of the Kingdom (Arnold, 1979)
Jesus of Nazareth: the Way of the Cross (Arnold, 1979)
The Trouble with God (Henry Walter, 1983)
Setting The Foundations (Hulton, 1983, 1984)

(As Ruqaiyyah Waris Maqsood)

The Separated Ones: Jesus, the Pharisees, and Islam (SCM, 1991)
Islam (Hodder and Stoughton, 1994)
Examining Religions: Islam (Heinemann, 1989, 1995)
Thinking About God (American Trust Publications, 1995)
Petra: A Traveller's Guide (Garnet, 1994, 1996, 2000)
Living Islam (Goodword, 1998)
Muslim Prayer Encyclopedia (Goodword, 1998)
After Death, Life (Goodword, 1998)

CONTENTS

You shall love the Lord your God
with all your heart, soul, mind
and strength; and you shall love
your neighbour as yourself.
This is the whole of the Law;
the rest is commentary.

Rabbi Hillel

Introduction

SOME EIGHTY GENERATIONS of Christians have gone to the grave believing with reasonable confidence that Jesus was the son of God. Twenty-five percent of the world's population, we are told, still entertain no doubt on the subject. Many talk about Jesus with great familiarity and certainty, as if they actually knew him personally, or had witnessed the events of his life. Some people know their New Testament so well, and have analysed it so minutely, that they have been able to erect wonderful descriptive edifices and theories on rather modest foundations. If any Christians begin to experience doubt the utmost disquiet ensues, because love of Jesus has always been seen by them as the highest of all possible callings, and service to him the noblest way of life. The claim with which they have been familiar is that the self-sacrifice of God in the form of Jesus Christ is the only way to salvation. Jesus alone is 'the Way, the Truth and the Life' (Jn 14:16). No matter how pious a believer of some other faith might be, their faith must ultimately be a tragic error; for according to that same verse Jesus said quite clearly that 'No man comes to the Father but by me.'

For centuries, instead of querying the background, authorship and circumstances of that verse,[1] Christian preachers have used it to justify a sense of proud superiority, especially when confronted by those who claim to believe in the same God while holding different views of the person of Jesus: the Jews and Muslims. Jews and Muslims might well be noble and pious people, but no matter how devout, their faith must be in vain, for it is not good lives but faith in the Risen Saviour that calls down the gift of grace from God upon the humble believer. Modern educational programmes presenting other world faiths are only justifiable to such Christians insofar as they provide information on what different people believe and why. The notion that the other world faiths are different paths to the One True God has long been popular amongst students in higher education, but to the committed Christian all other attempts to find salvation miss the point about Jesus.

Jews are perverse, because although as followers of an antique religion they could hardly be blamed for not believing in Jesus in the centuries before his actual birth, his contemporaries should have had the sense to study the prophecies in their own scriptures, and recognise Jesus properly and all become Christians, instead of allowing him to be executed for blasphemy or treason. Jews were therefore not only wilfully ignorant, but 'Christ-killers'. Some narrow-minded and benighted folk have even considered it to be entirely just that Jews of later centuries – who could not possibly be held responsible for the crucifixion events – should nevertheless suffer persecution and loathing down the ages because according to one Gospel (that of Matthew), the crowd at the trial of Jesus invoked a great curse upon themselves: 'His blood be on us and on our children!' (Mt 27:25)

As regards Islam, a religion 'younger' than Christianity, it need not be taken seriously because, in the view of these Christians, Muhammad – a desert Arab with an amalgam of half-baked ideas picked up from various heretical forms of Christianity – simply took everyone back to the unpleasant ways of how it was before Jesus came to enlighten the world and set it on the path of salvation.

Such injustice and ignorance about other faiths is, quite frankly, shocking. Scholarly Jews and Muslims *have* seriously considered the Christian claims, but far from finding them superior, have found them wanting. Indeed, they conclude that Christians, who are ostensibly worshipping the same God as themselves, actually entertain blasphemous and inadequate notions about Him.

It is a common experience when faced with life's riddles and calamities for people to feel disappointed and perplexed, or to consider God to be unjust, when they receive no sudden and miraculous solutions to their suffering and grief. It is also common for Christians who are convinced by the 'truths' of modern science to abandon faith altogether, because they no longer accept its mythological and miraculous setting. Others study theological dogma and give up faith because they are honest. They cannot muster enough perverse piety to accept that they *must* believe what they cannot believe, because it defies their reason and logic.

When Christians lose their faith, the experience can be devastating. Living a life without God or the focus a religious belief-system brings is an appalling thing; to do so with the memory of faith makes it more painful still. This author has heard many ex-Christians describe how sad and downhearted they have become when they find that they can no longer believe in God. What the author finds so depressing is that they have never considered 'moving the goalposts', or 'looking over the fence' at the green grass on the other side – and in the case of Islam, it really is greener.

Having been brought up to believe that Christianity is the only faith that possesses the truth, they may either sustain or reject their belief, but they rarely pause to consider whether its premises are the only ones worth considering.

As a Muslim who was once a Christian, I know for a fact that Christians are frequently among the most compassionate and noble of people. Many of them I consider to be admirable Muslims, although they are not aware of it. On occasion I become so irritated with Muslims whose lives, attitudes and beliefs are not as noble as they ought to be that I consider that some of the *best* Muslims are not found in the mosques but in the Christian Churches. But I believe Christians have been convinced of a grievous error.

I believe that Muhammad, the Prophet of Islam, was called by God to receive a divine message for this very reason. The Muslim point of view is that if Christians had remained true to the original message taught by the Prophet Jesus, there would have been no need for God to call the Final Prophet. Every doctrine that Muhammad taught, Jesus taught – but the theology that most Christian people now accept and believe is not that which Jesus himself advocated. It was because the pure faith was so massively undermined by the mistaken theology foisted upon his teachings that Muhammad – upon him be the best of blessings and peace – became necessary. He came to give the world a path back to the Truth.

Through early Christianity two threads of tradition about Jesus can be discerned. One tells of a God who became human, and was sacrificed and rose again for the salvation of humanity. The other, originating in the earliest strata of the Synoptic Gospels (i.e. Matthew, Mark and Luke)[2] and notably in the source known as Q[3], tells not of a Man-God but of a *man* regarded by his followers as a prophet, hero, and martyr.[4]

In the first centuries of Christian history, attempts were made to bring about church unity by fusing the two. By the time of the Council of Nicaea in 325, the Athanasian Creed, affirming that 'our Lord Jesus Christ, son of God, is both God and Man,' was officially imposed as the statement of orthodoxy that all Christians must accept.

But as we will see in this book, the problems were nowhere near resolved.

Modern theologians are now asking whether Jesus was a human Messiah, a descendant of David. Or was he God Incarnate? Was he a real individual in whom historians can believe, or just another mythological manifestation of the many dying-and-rising god cults popular in that time? The arguments have been raging for decades. It is now time for Westerners to consider a third element: the Muslim interpretation. Was Jesus in fact what the Muslims claim he was – not just a political Messiah but a great prophet; not another cultic Son-of-God-Saviour but the chosen Messenger of God of his time? By asking this question, and by answering it, Islam allows believers in God to accept honestly the conclusions of modern scholarship about Jesus' humanity and his Jewishness, but without losing their faith in God.

Why did the second generation of Christians so disparage St James of Jerusalem and his followers, and obliterate information about him to the extent that few Christians today have even heard his name? Why do we know almost nothing about Jesus' family? Why do the Gospels give the impression that Jesus' family did not believe in him, although it is a fact of history that his brothers and other relatives were the leaders of the original Church? Why do Roman Catholics insist that Peter was the first head of the Church, when the sources clearly state that it was James? Why does so much purportedly eye-witness material in the Gospels turn out not to be historical at all? Why do we hardly ever detect in the gospels the harsh presence of the Roman occupation or the thrusting Zealot resistance movement? Why are the much-admired Essenes, and the Qumran writers of the Dead Sea Scrolls – who were so important at that time – never mentioned? And outside the New Testament, why are there almost no references to Jesus or the early Christian movement in the contemporary works of pagan historians?

Why do Muslims believe that God did not allow Jesus to die on the cross, but that he was rescued and lived on until the time of his Ascension? Why, in modern times, has the evidence unearthed about the beliefs of the first followers of Jesus so alarmed the established churches? Do the churches have anything to fear from the new evidence, and if so, what?

This book attempts to pull together many of the controversies discussed today by New Testament scholars, including the latest discussions concerning the Dead Sea Scrolls and the Qumran community, the Zealot movement, the role of James, the documentary sources of the Gospels such as Q, very early Christian literature rejected by the later Trinitarian Church, and references to Jesus in the Qur'an.

Detectives usually commence their investigations with a careful consideration of the accessible facts, not of people's impassioned theories and points of
view. These facts frequently present a puzzle, but they are vital; even more vital
than near-original witnesses, who could be vague, misled, inaccurate, or even
lying, mentally disturbed or malevolently biased.

One task of this book is to lay out before the reader a few oddities that happen
to be facts, of which the following are just a sample. The reader may make of
them what he (or she) will.

Fact one. The passages that historians would most like to read in the manuscripts of Tacitus, Josephus and other contemporary sources, have gone
missing, although the rest of the texts have survived.

Fact two. There is no mention of the place Nazareth anywhere in the Old
Testament, and no mention of the Essenes and/or the pious community of
Qumran anywhere in the New Testament.

Fact three. James the brother of Jesus was the first head of the Christian
Church in Jerusalem, not Peter or Paul; yet there is virtually no indication of his
history, and the Gospel references to the brothers of Jesus are hostile.

Fact four. The Jewish-Christian practices of at least three daily prayers,
male circumcision, ritual washing for purity, fasting, careful attention to clean
and unclean foods, setting aside a proportion of income as charity, and pilgrimage to a central Temple, came to be declared heretical by the 'orthodox'
Christians. However, these practices never died out. Most of them are as strong
as ever: in Islam.

The ancient struggle of the long line of Jewish witnesses to the One True God
against the many cults which presented a Trinitarian system (which usually
included a dying-and-rising son-of-god) reached a new pitch as Hellenistic culture percolated through the East. When Roman ruthlessness was added to this
atmosphere, any foolhardy souls who stepped out of line were simply wiped
out. Those who were determined to survive had to compromise politically and
find all manner of astute accommodations. Paul, for example, was well aware
that the victors write the history, and that in order to 'win', he had to be 'all
things to all men' (I Corinthians 9:24-27). Those who dug their heels in, 'beat
the air' and refused to compromise any detail of the 'true faith', ended their
days as martyrs.

But was what they believed in wiped out as well? How could that be possible?

Truth stands out clear from error.[5] Pure monotheism/unitarianism and trinitarianism cannot both be right. No doubt, with the conversion of the Roman Emperor in the fourth century, and his official campaign to repress those who refused to conform to the Trinitarian party line, the old struggle seemed finished. But was it? Is it? What did divine providence have in store for the Jewish-Christians who, persecuted and expelled as heretics, dispersed into sectarian groupings in the Syrian and Iraqi deserts, Arabia and Egypt, Ethiopia and elsewhere?

This study is an attempt to look again at the origins of the Christian Church, in the light of insights that have recently been coaxed from the obscure corners of scholarly journals to become knowledge available to any believer – namely, the conclusions of Gospel form-criticism and a study of early Christian, Jewish and Muslim source-material. The book also seeks to discuss theories such as those of Kamal Salibi, and Kertsen and Gruber, which are certainly less scholarly in form and intent, but which have provoked controversy and which may have hit upon insights of relevance to the case which we present. Pulling together these discussions, the objective is to ask in all seriousness and humility whether the churches have, in fact, got it all wrong.

In the age of Galileo and Copernicus, traditionalist Christians were led into an untenable and ultimately unpopular position by denying what new scientific observations were disclosing. Today, many theologians are coming to terms with the fact the Bible is a multi-layered text, the intentions of whose authors need to be carefully understood, and that 'literalist' interpretations of what is essentially poetic and symbolic language in many biblical passages show a profound lack of awareness of the style and agenda of the biblical writers.[6]

When understood literally, some biblical passages imply that God may only be adequately known and responded to through Jesus, so that the rest of the world lies outside the charmed circle of salvation. The vast majority of the human race is therefore damned. Is it credible, some troubled consciences began to ask, that the loving God of all humanity should have decreed that only those born within one particular thread of human history would be saved? Is there no way of affirming many, even all, of the founders of the great world religions, as perfect guides to God?

Many Christian theologians and church hierarchies are acutely aware of the need for a universal religious vision and a global ethic, one that is conscious of the unity of all humanity before God. At the same time, many are disturbed by the uncomfortable feeling that Islam is a more serious rival than it has been for hundreds of years, and that it has a grandiose plan to take over the world. Most Westerners are highly sensitive to any suggestion of 'takeover' or submission to anything 'foreign'. The media highlighting of Islamic fanaticism and extremism, of the lunatic fringe of the religion, and those misguided persons calling themselves Muslims who have positions of authority but have consciously renounced its traditions, all combine to make the churches nervous, suspicious and fearful.

The author humbly submits that it is essential for theologians and thinkers of all the three theistic faiths – Judaism, Christianity and Islam – to accept as the premise for all subsequent discussion that they are one family, that what has been revealed has come from the one and the same God, the Only True God, by the mediation of prophets and Messengers who lived in roughly the same patch of sand in the Middle East. Faced with the shared threats of secularism and materialism, they should not be enemies or rivals, but one community of faith. Their rituals and practices differ, and they have different visions of their own role in history; but although we can and must seek to understand where God's favour lies, the decisive unveiling must wait for the Last Day, in the humble knowledge that what matters to Him beyond all else is the attitude of the *heart*, the *intention*.

It is my suggestion that the longed-for global vision has already been revealed, and that it is the same vision which inspired the whole stream of prophets, not only those named in the Bible, but the unknown thousands of every time and place, who have been called by the One True God, of whom Jesus was among the noblest and greatest, and of whom Muhammad was the Seal. It is partly for this reason that those who, like myself, have made the voyage to Islam from Christianity do not feel the least sense of having 'abandoned' Jesus; we do not feel disloyal to him in any respect. We love and honour him no less than before; in fact, we believe that we love and honour him more. Likewise, in coming to Islam we certainly do not feel that we have abandoned the quest for truth, but that we have progressed along it. We may feel we have found a different path to God, but we are secure in our confidence that it is the right path; and we feel it is that same path that Jesus taught. Converts to Islam often feel a sense of 'coming home'. Puzzles which troubled our minds suddenly fall into place, and our love for Jesus is now confirmed, where once it had been disturbed, by the findings of modern scholarship.

The old view of Christ began to crumble from within in the nineteenth century, even though it had prevailed for fifteen hundred years. The last really able defence of a fully 'orthodox' Christ in the UK was H.P. Liddon's *The Divinity of our Lord and Saviour, Jesus Christ,* published in 1865. In the next generation, as scholarship advanced, Bishop Charles Gore was able to assert that the old formulae did not explain the incarnation or analyse its content, but merely defined certain limits to orthodox systematic thought and banned certain deviations from it. They were not genuine premises for dogmatic construction, but only boundaries within which it had to keep.[7]

With great pain, it was admitted in the universities that what Christians had been taught to call 'orthodoxy' was really only one form of Christianity which had managed to triumph over another. The discovery that the ecclesiastical Christ was not to be found in a critical reading of the records of Jesus led to a profound scepticism with far-reaching consequences for Western life and thought.

The task of the Muslim scholar is to help Christians move away from the dogmatic faith promoted by western bishops in the fourth century CE, towards a more critical and historical faith. Genuine seekers after truth need not fear that the search will take them further from Jesus; on the contrary, it will bring them far closer to him. The man Jesus is easier to relate to, easier to understand, and easier to love, than the complicated man-god proclaimed at Chalcedon. The quest may even enable us to *recover* truths which have long been lost. The true doctrine of Christ can only strengthen and purify, and not compromise, our understanding of divine transcendence.

In short, we must face the question of whether in order to be a true Christian, it is necessary to be a Muslim.

Chapter One

A MISCARRIAGE OF JUSTICE

ROM THE MOMENT that the colourful King Tarquin the Superb was dislodged from the throne of Rome by the ancestor of Caesar's republican assassin Brutus, to the time of Jesus of Nazareth, the Romans would have nothing to do with the concept of 'royalty'. Rome was a republic run by elected men, and any citizen who plotted to seize power and restore the principle of a 'royal family' could expect the extreme penalty. As a check against possible tyranny, the chief office of the Senate was shared by at least two elected consuls who had equal authority and were able to veto each other. Some forty years before the birth of Jesus, Julius Caesar was assassinated, precisely because his enemies suspected that he craved the royal purple.

Even when Octavian, the grandson of Caesar's sister Julia, did contrive to make himself sole ruler and was declared 'Augustus', he did not attempt to claim the royal title. This hardly meant that he had no delusions of grandeur: his coins announced that he was *divi filius*, a son of God. In his case, the 'god' was the dead but newly-deified Caesar. By the time he died in 14CE, he had been deified officially by the Senate and recognised as a god throughout the far-flung reaches of the Empire, with temples and a *cultus* of his own. Keeping it in the family, Tiberius, the next Emperor, was also therefore the son of a god, although he, like Augustus, could only claim his divinity by adoption.

The notion of a man being called 'son of God' had a long pedigree in Jewish tradition too. The ancient kings of the line of David were 'adopted' as sons of God when anointed to office. The words of Psalm 2:7 ('You are My son, today I have begotten you') were employed at the coronation ceremony; and in I Samuel 7:14, God says of the king, 'I will be his father, and he shall be My son.' However, in contrast to the Roman usage, this never implied the king's divinity, or real 'begotten' sonship.[1] It denoted an entirely created and obedient degree of being (the phrase 'sons of God' was also used of the angels). [2]

In short, to lay claim to divine sonship was something neither new nor unacceptable at the time of Jesus. Around the Mediterranean, the gods were many and their qualities various. It was a brave philosopher, or a fool, who dared to state categorically that the gods did not exist, or could not engender offspring when and where they pleased. So if a group of Levantine religious enthusiasts claimed that a pious young carpenter-turned-missionary was a son of their god, it might amuse the cynical, but would hardly be regarded as a capital offence.

But to claim to be a *king* without the permission of Rome was a very different kind of proclamation. That was an arrogant and highly dangerous usurpation of the royal prerogative. It was, in short, treason.

Why was Jesus and arrested and condemned to death? The Gospels combine to give the impression that it had nothing to do with his politics, but was triggered mainly by the jealousy and bitterness of members of a contending Jewish religious sect known as the Pharisees. It is claimed that their hostility towards the popular young teacher spurred the wicked Temple priesthood at Jerusalem into action and brought about his downfall.

However a growing number of scholars have regarded this point of view with suspicion. Perhaps Jesus, as a charismatic leader with genuine descent from the legendary King David, *had* claimed to be the 'King of the Jews' (the charge which the Gospels admit was written on his placard at his execution); maybe it was the Romans who were responsible for his death in actual fact, and not just as a 'rubber stamp' for malicious Jews.

Of course, the Romans had some very powerful allies in the priestly hierarchy, particularly the wealthy houses of Annas, Boethus of Alexandria, Phiabi and Qamhit, who bid for their office from the government on an annual basis. [3]

Nevertheless, and despite their power, the High Priests were to a certain extent in an awkward position. They were generally very unpopular, both with the common people and also with a large number of religious enthusiasts and extremists who regarded them, with much justification, as corrupt lackeys, the running-dogs of imperialism. The Pharisees were no more fond of their cruelty, avarice and nepotism, as the broadsides of the time delicately recall:

> Down with the Boethusians! Down with their bludgeons! Down with the Annanites! Down with their viperous hissings! Down with the Kantherites! Down with their libels! Down with the family of Ishmael ben Phiabi! Down with their blows with the fist! They themselves are High Priests, their sons are Treasurers, their sons-in-law are captains of the Temple, and their servants strike the people with staves! [4]

The men in question owed their exalted positions to the protection of the Herodian dynasty[5] and of far-off Rome, rather than to legitimate descent or the desires of the hapless populace. Therefore they might well have been grateful for any public relations exercise that would have shown them as good and loyal Jews, and not just as Roman stooges. It would hardly have improved the touchy relationship between High Priest and people if the supreme figure in Judaism were forced by his Roman lords to mastermind an arrest and then hand over one of their pious and popular young teacher-heroes for crucifixion.

Mark's gospel indicates that the priests knew perfectly well what would have happened if Jesus had been arrested openly: there would have been a 'tumult of the people' (Mk 14:2). Luke's understanding is similar: 'The scribes and the chief priests sought to lay hands on him, but they feared the people' (Lk 20:19). Those who have witnessed uproarious crowds clamouring for their incarcerated heroes in this century, whether in Iran, Europe, Russia, South Africa, or Cuba, can be in little doubt that the most popular move the Sanhedrin[6] could have made would have been to acquit Jesus of any sedition, and to release him into the bosom of the crowd!

Neither is it credible to suppose that the Jews were anti-Messianic. It is a matter of historical fact that in their various uprisings against Rome, the Jews lost everything, 'not because they opposed the Messiah, as early Church fathers or the New Testament writers in their tendentious presentation of Christ's death and its meaning would have us believe, but, on the contrary, because they were so uncompromisingly Messianic'![7]

What if Jesus had been arrested, but the Sanhedrin had decided *not* to execute him? Could they have spared him? In fact, it was quite possible had they so wished. They could have prevented his death by either of two Roman legal means. If Jesus had pleaded not guilty to the charges brought against him, and witnesses could not be found to confirm his guilt, then he should have been set free by the Roman amnesty of *absolutio*, the straightforward acquittal of a man not condemned. The second option, that of the suspended sentence, was offered only rarely; but even if Jesus had been found guilty of a capital offence he could have been pardoned if he admitted that he had been misguided, and promised on oath never again to indulge in treasonable activity. This amnesty was known as the *indulgentia*.

However many details in the Gospels suggest that far from attempting to be merciful to Jesus, the Jewish authorities were so determined to have him done away with at all costs that the priests resorted to illegal practices. For example, Jesus was apparently taken to the house of the High Priest where he found that the Sanhedrin had been convened for a night sitting. This itself was illegal. There, he was charged with blasphemy and convicted upon his own confession. Yet in order to prevent bias against a prisoner, and to rule out accusations of corruption, any secret judgement behind closed doors was forbidden. No Sanhedrin session was allowed to try criminal offences outside the Temple precincts, and certainly not in a private house where an influential individual's animosity might intimidate a jury and sway the verdict.[8]

Moreover, in fairness to a prisoner whose life was at stake, the Sanhedrin was not allowed to try criminal cases at all during the hours of darkness, when the members of the court would be tired, or impatient. All such trials had to be commenced and completed during the daytime and the verdict had to be delivered the next day, after a night's rest and reflection.[9] No defendant should be tried on a criminal charge on festival days or on the eve of a festival, when the minds of the jurors would be preoccupied with the forthcoming celebrations.[10] Neither could he be convicted on the strength of his own confession, for then, as now, innocent but disturbed people confessed to all manner of things.[11] A person might only be convicted of a capital offence upon the testimony of two lawfully qualified witnesses,[12] and in the case of blasphemy, these witnesses had not only to agree in verbal detail, but also had to have given a clear warning to the person accused of the seriousness of his blasphemy and the penalty he would incur if he did not desist.[13] If he did desist, the charge was to be dropped. Furthermore, if witnesses were proved fraudulent, they should be condemned themselves, and should suffer the penalty to which the accused was liable.[14]

In the case of Jesus, this did not happen; nor, according to the approved gospels, was any attempt made to find witnesses or arguments for his defence. However the 'apocryphal' literature suggests that a stalwart defence *was* put up by at least three people: Nicodemus, a Pharisee who had become a secret convert; Joseph of Arimathea, a senior relative of Jesus, in one source given the title of prince; and Stephen, who was to become the first Christian martyr.[15]

So irregular are the circumstances that it must have been a *very* biased court, highly prejudiced against Jesus, that took the initiative in the prosecution, and deliberately sought out witnesses who would give hostile testimony. The High Priest, as chief judge, had no right to offer his opinion on the verdict before it was given.[16] Moreover, a fully unanimous verdict of guilt was usually thought suspect, and was declared null and void.[17] If a second sitting of the Sanhedrin then became necessary, it had to be postponed for a whole day;[18] and in any case it was illegal to pass *any* sentence of death anywhere except in the Chamber of Hewn Stones.[19] Therefore, by Pharisaic standards, this Sanhedrin session, which ought to have had a quorum of at least twenty-three members,[20] was simply not eligible to pass judgement.[21]

If the witnesses brought against Jesus were 'false', how was it that they did *not* agree? False witnesses usually have their stories off pat. How incredibly awkward and inept of them to have let the High Priest Caiaphas down by not having a better-coordinated version. No, it makes far more sense to accept that the witnesses were by no means pre-arranged, but were quite genuinely giving their versions of events as they understood them; and this was simply not accurate enough legally to condemn Jesus.

Therefore, if we assume that the Gospel narratives are complementary and that the regulations contained in the Mishnah were in force during the period in question here, they lay bare the grossest examples of illegality. Do scholars accept this as a sign of the perverse wickedness of the Jewish authorities, or do they offer an explanation which might exonerate them? As it happens, they offer not one, but two.

Firstly, they argue that these were not the laws in force at the time; they represent an ideal Pharisaic position, and the Sanhedrin that condemned Jesus was mainly composed of Sadducees, that is, members of the ruling priestly hierarchy. Pharisees were not priests but laymen, highly religious individuals who had chosen to subject every detail of their lives to submission to God's Revealed Law. Many had become eminent scholars. Rabbinic literature suggests that they were generally much loved for their charity, wisdom and humanity. As scrupulous men, however, they are said to have been less interested than the Pharisees in searching for ways to acquit the foolish.

This objection will not do, however; for such was the influence of the Pharisees at the time of Jesus that the Great Sanhedrin *was* in fact ruled by Pharisaic Law, the Pharisaic members refusing to take any part in it otherwise, with the people refusing to accept the authority of the Sanhedrin unless their beloved Pharisaic leaders, such as Rabbis Hillel, Shammai and Gamaliel, were included. In any case, the assumption that all Sadducees were corrupt, cruel, greedy, unenlightened men is sweeping and unjustifiable. Furthermore, modern research on the subject of Sadducees has come up with some interesting revelations, as we shall see.[22]

The second way out is to state that since all the laws detailed above are from the Mishnah they are irrelevant, since Mishnaic law was not codified until many years after Jesus' death, and therefore its precepts apply only to later times. However this argument is scarcely more acceptable, since the regulations codified in the Mishnah did not suddenly arise out of the blue: they were drawn from the existing law of the time of Jesus.[23]

There is a third alternative: one which some Christians might be very loath even to consider. It is this. The Gospel narratives are not accurate historical records at all, but either a hotchpotch of inaccurate hearsay assembled years after the events portrayed, or deliberate falsifications and manipulations of ancient source-material, one aim of which was to promote enmity against those Christians who remained true to Judaism and did not accept Trinitarian theology.

Why is this suggestion worth taking seriously? The argument is straightforward. The original followers of Jesus, the friends and relatives who knew Jesus most intimately, remained faithful to the worship of the One True God, and insisted that all Christians should keep the Law which God had revealed through the prophets. They did not regard Jesus as a divine being, but as a chosen Messenger of God, the latest in a long line of noble prophets and messengers.

However, there were other Christians who came to believe that Jesus was much more than human, and as Christianity spread outside Palestine into areas where the religious-minded tended to be members of various élitist mystery cults, the conviction grew that Jesus was an incarnate Son of God, and an atoning saviour. By the time the four gospels in the present New Testament were written there was a strong desire to show that Jewish beliefs about God were inadequate, reinforced by the wish to break free from Judaism's demanding rules, especially circumcision, ritual purity laws, and the dietary code. Since the Jewish Christians resisted this rupture, and opposed the 'new' faith with the same vehemence that all the prophets of old had resisted priestly ritualism and the Baal cult, so Judaism had to be shown up as 'the enemy' if the new Christianity was to succeed.

If any reader is offended by the thought that those ancient authors were guilty of deliberate manipulation of the evidence (if, that is, we are courteous, and stop short of actually accusing them of malicious plotting to suppress the truth),[24] then they may console themselves with the thought that Jews (and later Muslims) have been made to suffer just such accusations for centuries.

Rather than bury pious heads in the sand, let us take a good, hard look at the material, and see what conclusions we can reach.

Chapter Two

PROBLEMS, PROBLEMS

ALL MANNER OF problems arise when dealing with the narratives of the trials of Jesus. For example, John's gospel[1] specifically states that Pilate had little desire to be involved in his execution, and told the Jews to deal with it themselves, only to be bluntly reminded by the Jews that it was 'not lawful for them to put any man to death' (Jn 18:31). This version then goes on to indicate a theological motive for their wanting Jesus to be killed by crucifixion, as opposed to any other form of execution, for reasons that will be suggested later. On the other hand, Mark's gospel, which most scholars accept as the earliest of the four gospels in the New Testament, offers no comment whatsoever on the right of the Jews to execute people, or the supposed ignorance of Pilate in the matter. Was John's comment, therefore, totally unhistorical?

The claim is often made that however surprising it might seem, it *must* be accurate, for the Jews simply did not have the right to inflict the death sentence, and Rome had to give its permission for all executions, and carry them out. Yet, as recent scholarship has shown, the Jewish sources indicate otherwise. For example, Rabbi Eleazar ben Zadok recorded how he, as a child, had watched a priest's daughter, Imarta bath Tali, being put to death by burning for adultery,[2] an incident which probably took place in the reign of Agrippa I (41-44CE). Other evidence suggests that the Jews could carry out executions: 'the property of those put to death by the state falls to the king; the property of those put to death by the Law Court belongs to their heirs.'[3] This surely indicates not only that the Sanhedrin did have the right to execute in the New Testament period, but also that *it was advantageous for the family of the condemned person if it did so.*

Furthermore, the Mishnah stated that the procedure for trials of 'rebellious elders' had to be before three separate courts: one at the entrance to the Temple Mount, one in the Temple entrance, and one before the Sanhedrin in the Hall of

Hewn Stones, a physical impossibility after 70CE, when the Temple was destroyed. Three passages mention Ben Zakkai's procedure for testing the trustworthiness of witnesses in capital cases, a wasted procedure if there were no such capital cases to consider.[4]

The Jewish historian Josephus also bears witness that executions were carried out by Jewish courts: 'Our Law forbids that a person should be executed, even if he is a criminal, *unless he has first been condemned by the Sanhedrin.*'[5] He also comments that as the siege of Jerusalem reached its final stages, Titus, who was 'appalled by the ravages of the war', protested that he had offered to give the Jews back their self-rule if only they would lay down their arms.[6] Surely this statement implies that the Jews did have the right of self-determination at some time prior to the revolt?[7]

Josephus also reports that when Titus was trying to persuade the defenders of Jerusalem to surrender, he asked: 'And did we not permit you to put to death any who passed (the balustrade of the Temple) even if he were a Roman?'[8] Positive evidence of this exists, cut in solid stone. Pagans were specifically warned that to trespass in the Temple courtyards reserved for Jews alone carried the death penalty. A slab of limestone bearing this very inscription was discovered by Clermont-Ganneau in 1871, and is now in the Cinili Kiosk Museum in Istanbul.

'Municipal libertas', the right to carry out capital punishment without a fiat from the procurator, may not have been normal in the Empire, but it *was* sometimes granted as a reward for loyalty to Rome.[9] Turbulent Judaea might be the very last place in which one might expect to find extraordinary concessions, but in fact King Herod the Great had enjoyed enormous influence in Rome, and had been granted many other exceptional privileges. Maybe, therefore, such a concession had been granted, as the Jewish evidence seems to suggest.

As far as we know, both Stephen and James were executed without a Roman trial, but their cases could be irrelevant because they were not legal executions. Stephen was apparently stoned by a mob, although we should be careful before drawing conclusions here: it may have been a 'rebellious elder' stoning; and the execution of St James did bring down retribution on Ananus, the High Priest of that time, for he had carried it out in the interregnum following the sudden death of one governor before a new one was appointed.[10]

The point is that it seems from this evidence that there was no reason why the Sanhedrin should *not* have carried out the sentence on Jesus. If Jesus really had been found guilty of blasphemy, the penalty would have been death by stoning, and the Jews could have carried out the sentence themselves had they so wished.

Yet the fact that Jesus was crucified and not stoned surely suggests that it *was* a Roman court of law. If Jesus had been sentenced to death by a Jewish court, it would presumably have been in accordance with the law of Deuteronomy 13:1-11:

> When a prophet or dreamer appears among you [...] and calls on you to follow other gods [...] that prophet or dreamer shall be put to death, for he has preached rebellion against the Lord your God; he has tried to lead you astray. If (even) your brother [...] or your dearest friend should entice you secretly to go and worship other gods [...] you shall have no pity on him [...] you shall stone him to death because he has tried to lead you astray.

Deut 21:22 specified that 'when a man is convicted of a capital crime and put to death, you shall hang him on a gibbet.' Mishnah Sanh 6.4 later agreed that 'all who have been stoned must be hanged.' Acts 5:30 and 10:39 agree that Jesus was put to death and hanged on a gibbet. In Galatians 3:13 Paul actually quotes from Deut 21:23: 'Cursed be everyone who hangs on a gibbet.' The actual death penalty for an 'enticer' was the stoning; the 'hanging' was gibbeting afterwards.

Events as portrayed in the Fourth Gospel were actually the closest to the Jewish tradition.[11] Jesus' examination before Annas was entirely non-theological in character. There was nothing about threats to destroy the Temple, Messianic claims, or blasphemy. Annas simply interrogated the prisoner about the nature of his teaching and the extent of his following. In view of Deut 4:19, 13:7 and 23:17, he was entirely within his rights to do so. The Fourth Gospel also agreed with the Jewish tradition, incidentally, in affirming that the execution of Jesus took place on the eve of the Passover (Jn 14:14), which conflicts with the Synoptic tradition.[12]

Now, if it could be proved that Jesus was not crucified but stoned and then gibbeted, the Romans would surely be completely exonerated of any role in Christ's death. If the 'anti-Jewish-Christian' writers had any sense at all, that would have been the story they agreed on telling. However the tradition is overwhelming to the effect that Jesus really was crucified: a death sentence alien to the Jews, but widely practised by the Romans.[13] In the Acts of the Apostles, two references (Acts 2:36 and 4:10) present occasions when Peter spoke to Jewish audiences saying: 'Jesus, whom *you* crucified.' These references have surely to be understood in the light of Acts 2:23 where Peter states: 'You killed him by fastening him to a cross, through the agency of heathen men.' In other words, what he meant was that Jesus was crucified by the Romans, who were carrying out the *intent* of the Jewish authorities.

The early Christians who were themselves Jews had no quarrel with this. They agreed that Jesus was killed by the Romans acting along with specific Jewish collaborators. They did not assume for one moment that the Jews *as a whole* would find themselves blamed for the affair. They certainly did not attempt to exonerate the collaborators, but took it for granted that everyone would know the difference between such righteous Pharisees as Nicodemus and Gamaliel, and the arrogant houses of Annas and Boethus.

As we pass from Mark to John there appears a clear tendency to exonerate Pilate and place the blame on the Jews. The earlier the tradition, the less the Jews appear responsible, and the more the Romans seem to be blamed for the crucifixion.[14] The fact that the author of the Fourth Gospel, whose sympathies lay with the Romans rather than the Jews, felt obliged even to mention a part played by the troops of the Emperor must surely mean he had in his possession an unavoidable tradition bearing out such Roman participation.[15]

Who were these 'troops of the Emperor'? They were not just a few soldiers sent out for a small job, but a considerable force, and they were obviously expecting serious trouble. The word used was *speira* (Jn 18:3,12), the Greek equivalent of the Latin *cohors*: a force with the theoretical strength of 760 infantry and 240 cavalry. As it happens, legionary troops were not stationed in Judaea at that time, but in Caesarea. However, we know there was an auxiliary cohort in Jerusalem. They had an officer with them, a 'chiliarch' or military tribune.[16]

Can we glean anything from the part played by Judas Iscariot, named as the betrayer of Jesus? His name 'Ish-Sicariot' or 'man of the Sicarii' suggests that he could have been a Zealot.[17] Zealots were a Jewish Liberation Front, and the Sicarii were the 'dagger men' particularly enlisted to assassinate Romans. If that was the case, surely it would have been very unlikely that he would have betrayed Jesus to a Roman *speira*?

Furthermore, if the Romans had arrested Jesus, why on earth should they have allowed him to be taken to Annas, the old firebrand High Priest whom the Romans had deposed for his outspoken nationalism in 15CE, or to Caiaphas his son-in-law, the contemporary High Priest,[18] instead of bundling him straight into a cell? And why was Peter not arrested too, if the Romans had gone out to put down troublemakers? Peter was involved in armed resistance. How was he allowed to get away? Why did Jesus declare to these Roman troops: 'Day after day I was among you in the Temple, teaching'? (Mk 14:49) Are we to assume that these unwelcome pagans had been thronging the Temple courtyards, eager for his words? On the contrary, the Synoptic Gospels give the strong impression that the party responsible for the arrest of Jesus was the Jewish Sanhedrin, and Luke's version even mentions the *strategos* or 'captain of the Temple' (Lk 22:52).

In view of the resemblance of the Passion traditions in Luke and John, it seems likely that the chiliarch of Jn 18:12 and the *strategos* of Lk 22:52 are identical. This would surely allow the conclusion that the arrest party might after all have been the Temple Guard under the leadership of the Sanhedrin's officer known as the Sagan, a unit which was permitted to carry weapons.[19]

The Synoptic Gospels are unanimous in stating that when Jesus was arrested 'by the chief priests and scribes' he was taken to the house of Caiaphas for questioning, apparently with a measure of secrecy, in the middle of the night (Mk 14:53; Mt 26:57; Lk 22:54). The Fourth Gospel, of course, differs by stating that Jesus was taken to Annas, and not Caiaphas (Jn 18:13). However it has been suggested that since Caiaphas was married to Annas' daughter, both priests may have occupied apartments in the same building, although this cannot be proved. Either way, Jesus was in the hands of a High Priest and not in a Roman barrack-house.

The Sanhedrin proper then met at daybreak, but the charge made against Jesus that he had threatened to destroy the Temple would not stick. The charge then shifted to one of blasphemy, and Jesus was found guilty.[20]

Now the fact that Jesus was not immediately condemned to execution by stoning but was handed over to Pilate suggests that the proceedings at the High Priest's house may not have been a formal trial at all, but something quite different. According to all four Gospels, as soon as Jesus appeared before Pilate, the first question put to him (and the only one that Pilate was really interested in) was 'Are you the King of the Jews?' The Gospels then attempt to exonerate Pilate from any responsibility for the crucifixion, and give the impression that it was forced upon him by the Jewish leaders and people.

The accusation that Jesus claimed to be 'King of the Jews' (a placard stating this was, we are told, nailed to his cross) is usually passed over by Christian commentators as a mere ironical or cynical gesture. Yet there is circumstantial evidence that Jesus had indeed made this claim.[21]

Surely, if Pilate had truly decided that Jesus was innocent of the political charges and was simply a religious fanatic, he would never have condemned him to death once he had decided not to. Why should he have done so? What did he have to fear from priestly threats and hot air? He was a friend and protege of Sejanus, the iron minister of the Emperor Tiberius, who was the real ruler of the Empire during Tiberius' decline. Sejanus had set Pilate up in office. Much would depend on whether the trial of Jesus took place before or after the end of Sejanus' tyranny. If it took place *after* Sejanus had fallen, then Pilate might well have had reason to fear the accusation about not being 'Caesar's friend'.[22] However, we have no cast-iron evidence for the date of Jesus' trial, and if it took place *before* the fall of Sejanus, then Pilate would have had nothing at all to fear from the Jews. All letters to the Emperor passed though Sejanus' hands, and he only allowed Tiberius to see what he wanted him to see; and Sejanus positively *hated* the Jews and delighted in seeing them discomfited.[23]

The supposed conversations with the crowds really stretch credulity.[24] Would a Roman Governor have kept jumping from his seat of judgement at odd intervals to pop into the courtyard to talk with an excitable mob? If he had simply wanted information he would surely have sent for it, or summoned any person he wished. The idea of his rushing to and fro out of courtesy to the Jews, preventing them from defiling themselves by entering the praetorium (Jn 18:28), would mean that he was being extremely considerate and courteous in response to their impertinence. This was not the sort of behaviour known to be characteristic of Pilate, whose previous record of tactless and callous handling of Jewish affairs had made him extremely unpopular in the province. But this is only one of many details that do not ring true.

A further problem arises from the narratives which indicate that Pilate tried to get Jesus off the hook by offering the crowd the choice of saving either his life or that of the prisoner Barabbas who had been arrested for insurrection and murder (Mk 15:7; Jn 18:39-40). Why on earth should Pilate have risked releasing Barabbas, or even offered him as a choice to the crowd? There was no reason for him to do this, especially if it was intended as a device to save Jesus.[25]

The earliest of the 'canonical' gospels gives the text as follows:

> Now at the feast he [Pilate] used to release for them one prisoner whom they asked, And among the rebels [zealots] in prison, who had committed murder in the insurrection, there was a man called Barabbas. And the crowd came up and began to ask Pilate to do as he was wont to do for them. And he answered them, 'Do you want me to release for you the King of the Jews?' For he perceived that it was out of envy that the chief priests had delivered him up. But the people stirred up the crowd to have him release for them Barabbas instead. (Mk 15:6-11).

Christians, remembering the passion of Jesus with deep emotion, are so involved with their saviour at this point that few have given much thought to this mysterious person who is suddenly inserted into the drama. Yet the whole affair of Barabbas is shot through with mysteries. Here is a Roman Governor, answerable to the Emperor, calmly inviting the crowd to pick over the list of condemned men incarcerated on death row, to choose one of them, and to take him away. Even a traitor, a rebel leader, perhaps captured after a laborious chase and much bloodshed – no matter! The crowd wants him, off he goes. Take him away. Set him free immediately!

As for this supposed Passover custom of releasing a prisoner, there is very little in the way of evidence that can be produced to substantiate this practice. When one examines the gospel accounts, it is interesting to observe how the wording varies. In Mk 15: 6-8, 'Pilate used to release one whom they asked of him.' Mt 27:15-21 reports that the Governor 'was wont to release to them one whom they chose'; and in Jn 18:39 Pilate declares 'You have a custom that I should release a man at the Passover.' In fact, *there is no record of any such custom in any Jewish document.*

The only extant reference that could possibly refer to such a custom is the provision in the Mishnah, Pesahim 8.6, that the sacrifice of a Passover lamb was sanctioned 'for one whose release from prison had been promised'. This probably meant no more than that a family which was expecting the release of someone in the normal way in time to eat the feast might take provision for him.[26]

Why should a Roman governor, at the whim of a crowd and without consultation with Caesar, release a prisoner who had been condemned for leading people into rebellion against Rome? It makes no sense. Who was this man Barabbas?

One suggestion, known as the 'Karabas theory', is that a garbled version of a later historical event was mixed up with an earlier text. The populace of Alexandria in Egypt used to dress up a local idiot as a king with robe, gown and sceptre, give him the name or title 'Karabas', and then beat him up, or even put him to death. According to Philo of Alexandria, the Greek mob performed this ritual in a particularly insulting manner on the occasion when the Jewish king Agrippa passed through their city. Since the soldiers mocked and tormented Jesus in a similar fashion, we may ask whether this old Egyptian tradition of the Karabas-king and the insult to Agrippa has somehow been blended into ancient Christian tradition.[27]

A completely different theory holds that Barabbas was neither a ritual figure nor a run-of-the-mill rebellious thug, but a real, well-known and important person, indeed, a local celebrity. Matthew's gospel calls him a 'notable' prisoner, using a word that signified 'distinguished' rather than 'notorious'. The very fact that he had been kept in jail at all is interesting, because it was not the usual Roman policy to squander funds on keeping prisoners. Bribery, fines, enslavement, mutilation, or summary execution were the normal order of the day. Perhaps Barabbas was being kept for his bargaining value?

Some scholars have suggested that the Barabbas released by Pilate was a son of Gamaliel, who might have been mistakenly arrested by the troops who didn't really know who they were looking for (Mk 14:44; Jn 18:5-6), because his name also happened to be Jesus. There is evidence of such a person: in 64CE Agrippa deposed the High Priest Jesus son of Damnaeus and gave the office to Jesus son of Gamalas or Gamaliel.

Some versions of the text spell his surname with two 'r's, as Barrabbas, which suggests that he was the son of a particular Rabbi. In fact, one of these texts, the *Codex Koridethi*, gives the name as Bar Rabban, leaving a gap between the two words. Now, it just so happens that the Rabban was the honorific title of the deputy of the presiding officer of the Sanhedrin, who was also known as the Ab Beth Din, or Father of the Court of Justice. This office was traditionally held by members of the Pharisaic movement, and at the time of Jesus' trials the incumbent was indeed none other than the eminent Gamaliel, the first holder of this office to have been given the title *Rabban*.

So: if Barabbas was really Gamaliel's son, the priests and the crowds would have had every reason to cry that they did not want Jesus, but Barabbas.

Another theory comes from Haim Cohn,[28] who is an interesting representative of Jewish writers who have suggested that the Gospels give a very false picture. Ignoring the Barabbas question, he presents the theory that the High Priest was not trying to destroy Jesus at all, as has so often been assumed, but was instead trying to *save* him when he took him into custody. Cohn reasons that Jesus had been arrested by the Romans, but that they were accompanied by the Temple *seganim*, who somehow managed to gain custody of the prisoner for one night. The curious gathering of notables at the house of Annas was not, therefore, a trial. The old priest had sent out urgent messages to select Sanhedrin members, informing them of what had happened, and stressing to them that if anything was to be done to save Jesus from the Romans, it had to be done at once. It could not wait: it was a matter of life or death, and they must come at once. And they all came.

Cohn then argues that the priests were able to establish quite simply that the witnesses were false and not to be feared; however if Jesus had to face political charges in Roman law (which was less merciful than Jewish law) his own admission of guilt would be enough to condemn him. Jesus foolishly insisted on refusing to deny his claim. He had somehow to be dissuaded from this fatal stubbornness, and coached in how to reply to the questions Pilate might put to him. He had to co-operate with the Sanhedrin if he was to be saved.

Jesus' blunt reply to the question 'Are you the Christ?' caused the High Priest to give up in despair, and rend his garments, not as a sign of horror at his blasphemy (it was not blasphemy), but as a sign of grief and frustration. If Jesus actually *had* blasphemed, then all those present would have been obliged to rend their garments.[29] The reply 'I am' or *Ani hu* as given in Mark's Gospel was not counted as capital blasphemy. Jesus had not pronounced the Ineffable Name, but he *had* admitted to something that in Roman eyes was treason: that he was a Messianic claimant. Annas knew that this would make Jesus' disastrous fate inevitable. In effect, rather than be untrue to himself, Jesus was deliberately rejecting the High Priest's offer of a way out, a way that would have saved him. The outcry 'he must die' was therefore not a condemnation, but a statement of despair for what would certainly follow.

Weighing against this interesting suggestion is the somewhat embarrassing mention in Mk 14:65 (followed by Mt 26:67) that some of these Jewish priests then gave vent to their 'despair' by spitting in Christ's face and buffeting him![30]

However, Cohn dramatically concludes that

> hundreds of generations of Jews, throughout the Christian world, have been indiscriminately mulcted for a crime which neither they nor their ancestors committed. Worse still, they have for centuries been made to suffer all manner of torment, persecution and degradation for the alleged part of their forefathers in the trial and crucifixion of Jesus, when, in solemn truth, their forefathers took no part in them, but did all that they possibly and humanly could to save Jesus, who they dearly loved and cherished as one of their own, from his tragic end at the hand of the Roman oppressor. If there can be found one grain of consolation for this perversion of justice, it is in the words of Jesus himself – 'Blessed are those persecuted for the sake of righteousness, for theirs is the Kingdom of Heaven'.[31]

Chapter Three

WHERE HAVE ALL THE ROMANS GONE?

C HRISTIANS PREPARED TO concede that Jews are decent
enough people might well wonder why they took such offence
at Jesus, and were so corrupt as to do to death such an obviously wonderful and godly person. They might regard Jesus' goodness as so
patently obvious that those Jews must have been wicked and blind indeed to
reject, condemn and crucify him.

They might even redouble their efforts to convince and convert today's Jews,
and run into fresh resistance. What rarely occurs to such zealous Christians is to
take seriously what is very obvious to religious scholars who are *not* Christian:
namely, that the Gospels do not contain an accurate record at all, but are built
up of layers coloured by an increasing anti-Semitic bias.

Jewish scholars often point out that most Christians conveniently forget that
Jesus was not a Christian: he was a Jew. He did not preach a new faith, but taught
people to do the will of God: not a new God, but the same God that his people
knew. In his opinion, as also in that of all Jews, that will of God was to be found in
the Law and in the other books of scripture.

He never went to church, and never underwent any of the sacraments
(excepting, perhaps, his own baptism in the Jordan), neither did he claim the
credal beliefs foisted upon him in the later history of the Church. He kept the
Jewish Law in its entirety. His followers did not suddenly cease to be Jews. They
continued meeting at the Temple, and they attended diligently. 'Day by day,
attending the Temple together and breaking bread in their homes, they partook
of food with glad and generous hearts, praising God.'[1]

They did not break the dietary regulations of the Torah, and continued the
practice of circumcision.[2] Some even took the strict Nazirite vows.[3] In other

words: the Christians who had been nurtured by the closest relationship with Jesus did not see that their acceptance of Jesus as the Messiah signified that they had to give up Judaism, and they certainly had not been directed by Jesus to do so! On the contrary, the original Christians were so distinguished for their orthodox zeal that many priests of the lower orders and Pharisees were attracted into their ranks, a fact that often goes unnoticed.[4]

The synagogue authorities considered them to be an aberrant *Jewish* sect, classifying them as *minim*, meaning schismatics. They continued to allow them to worship alongside them in the synagogues until c80CE, when they were cast out.

Again, the conflicts, and editorial compromises with the truth, seem to begin as the new faith spread into non-Jewish society:

> Cannot one discern the palpable shift of responsibility from Pilate to the Jews, through the patent devices by which Pilate is portrayed as reluctantly giving in to Jewish malevolence? Can the fact that the cross was a Roman punishment and not a Jewish one be so glossed over as to exclude the Romans entirely, as Christian literature does, and not absolve the Jews at all? What shall we make of the circumstances that the Gospel accounts clarify to us [Jews] why the Romans would will the death of Jesus, but leave someone like me uninformed, even mystified, as to why Jews would have willed it? *The Gospels show me no persuasive basis on which Jews as Jews would have levelled an accusation against a fellow-Jew* [...] I can see in the Gospels what the Jews would have rejected, and what they could have, as Jews, disliked. I cannot see in the Gospels themselves, as I can see in Paul's epistles with his scorn of Moses' Law, what Jews as Jews would have resented so bitterly. I can understand the Roman motives; but *from the Gospels I detect no convincing Jewish motive.* I believe that the shift of responsibility is patent, is motivated, and that we Jews have been made to pay for what the Romans did. [my italics][5]

To redress the balance, let's have a look at some archaic Jewish material. Jewish sources do not, as it happens, resound with impassioned cries in defence of Jesus. The Mishnah (completed between 90-220 CE) never refers to Jesus or Christianity, but the Gemara (a supplementary collection created during 220-500) does contain references to both. The Talmud, which is the combination of Mishnah and Gemara, contains only one brief account of the condemnation and death of Jesus, in the Tractate Sanhedrin of the Babylonian Talmud. It states simply that someone called Jesus was hanged on the eve of the Passover. The herald went before him for forty days saying: 'he is going forth to be stoned because he practised sorcery and enticed and led Israel astray. Let anyone knowing anything in his defence come and plead for him.' But nothing was found in his defence, so he was hanged on the eve of the Passover.[6]

The problem is that this passage, which calls Jesus *ha-Nozri* or 'the Nazarene', refers to a certain Jesus or Jehoshua ben Pandera (or Ben-Stada) who seems to have lived much earlier than the Gospel Jesus, in the reign of Alexander Jannaeus (103-78 BCE). Some have tried to see in this a reference to the virgin birth of Jesus by speculating that Pantera or Pandera is a corruption of the Greek *parthenos*, meaning 'virgin'. However, scurrilous stories about Jesus in the later Tannaitic period claimed that Jesus was the illegitimate son of a Roman soldier variously called Pandera, Pantera or Panthera. The Christian writer Origen claimed he knew of this from the second-century philosopher Celsus,[7] showing that the rumour was circulating before 150 CE.[8]

Interestingly, a tombstone has recently been discovered at Bingerbrück in Germany, identifying the grave of a Roman archer who had served in Sidon and whose cohort was posted to the Rhine in 9CE. The soldier's name was Tiberius Julius Abdes Pantera of the first cohort of archers, and he died aged 62 after 40 year's service. Was this the real father of Jesus?[9] Another possibility is that 'Ben Panther' simply meant an illegitimate child. To this day 'son of lioness' (*ibn al-labwa*) is an Arabic insult, still sometimes heard in Egypt. The Talmudic 'name' Ben Pantera is probably just such an insult.

Whether or not the Jewish writers thought Jesus ben Pandera to be the same man as the Christian Jesus, a specific defence is made against allegations that he had been rushed through his trials with unseemly haste, or that no defence witnesses had been called. It may have stemmed from circles well aware of the growing anti-Jewish polemic in some Christian communities, and it is interesting to note in this account that this Jesus was said to have been stoned and gibbeted, rather than crucified. Here we can see plainly that the Jews did not deny their involvement in *this* man's trial, or even minimise their part in it. On the contrary, their defence lay in a statement of the reasons for, and the justice of, their involvement.

How can one explain the growing Christian hostility to the Jews? Was it theological, or was there a political ingredient to it as well? It should not be forgotten that the most important event in the history of the Jews in the first century CE was undoubtedly their revolt against Rome, which resulted in the destruction of the Temple and the obliteration of the sacrificial system. By the time the Gospel of Mark was written (64-70 CE?), Christians in Rome who were *not* Jews were embarrassed by the hostility towards Rome of extremist

Christians who *were* Jews. The Jewish resistance movement may not at that stage have reached its climax in open revolt; nevertheless it is quite reasonable to suppose that Christians who were Roman citizens did not wish to give the impression that they were in any way part of a rebellion. Public support for a man executed for sedition could easily be interpreted as antagonism to Rome. Christians were not popular in Rome, but were the subject of ill-informed and malicious gossip and rumour. They were accused of drowning babies, committing incest, and practising cannibalism.[10] In 64CE the Emperor Nero easily foisted onto them the blame for starting the great fire in the capital.

Even more dangerous in its potential consequences, it was believed that Christians were subversive elements attempting to abolish slavery and overthrow the state. Did they not seduce away respectable matrons on the middle of the night to clandestine meetings amongst the corpses in the catacombs[11] where they were taught to believe that Christian slaves were equal to, if not superior to, Roman citizens? Why, a senator's wife might find herself in subjection to a member of her own household, if he was one of the Christian hierarchy! Christians were thought to be a pernicious influence in society, and came to be feared as seditious troublemakers who intended to overthrow the status quo.

No doubt any Christian who emphasised that Roman injustice was to blame for the death of Jesus would be putting himself and his family in a very hazardous situation. In any case, as far as second-generation gentile Christians were concerned, the real cause of Jesus' death was not Jewish politics but the Sin of Mankind; the business of identifying who had technically killed him was of small importance beside the fact that he died for our sins and rose again to bring our eternal salvation. Details of the trials may thus have been deliberately fudged; instead of being vilified as his executioner, Pontius Pilate gradually became thought of rather as a witness to Jesus' innocence, virtually exonerated of all blame. His only fault lay in his weakness in not standing up to the villainous pressure of the Jewish priesthood.

In the Gospels that were written after 70CE, it was 'the Jews' who represented stony-hearted and blind inhumanity, a notion made crystal-clear in the Fourth Gospel where 'the Jews' and the world of evil (i.e. everything outside the Kingdom of God) are virtually synonymous.[12] 'The Jews' had plotted from the start to destroy Jesus. They were behind it all. It was they who had forced Pilate to crucify him.

As the anti-Jewish tradition developed, Pilate progressively became ever more innocent, until finally the Ethiopian Church canonised him as a Christian saint![13] Justin Martyr (c100-165) was able to cite a book supposedly written by Pilate as bearing witness to the miracles of Jesus.[14] Tertullian (160-220) believed that even before the death of Jesus, Pilate had been a Christian in his heart, and had sent his report of the affair to Tiberius in such a way that the superstitious Emperor also became convinced of Jesus' divinity, and sought to persuade the Senate of it![15] Origen (185-254) insisted that Caiaphas bore the sole responsibility. The second century *Gospel of Peter* even portrayed the distraught Pilate as begging the body of Jesus from the villain Herod, the 'Jewish king' who had been in charge of the crucifixion (this Herod was neither Jewish nor a king!).[16]

The Gospels undoubtedly thrust the moral blame on the Jews and not the Romans. If one were to glance casually through the Gospels with its pastoral preaching scenes, fishing expeditions and family parties, one would be hard put to gather the impression that Palestine was an occupied country, where the hated Roman troops or their spies were to be found in all places where there was the slightest suspicion of crowd activity or trouble. Where have all the Romans gone? Thousands had been slaughtered by them, and whole towns reduced to rubble. They were a byword for cruelty. Fear of them was everywhere; and yet the Gospels remain strangely silent. Apart from the trial sequences they are only mentioned a couple of times, when they are given a very 'good press'. A Roman centurion is praised for paying for a synagogue in Capernaum (Lk 7:5); and another recognises Jesus as 'a son of God' at the crucifixion (Mt 27:54),[17] taking the variant reading which gives 'a' rather than 'the'. In Acts 10, Peter is a guest in the house of Cornelius, a noble Roman officer stationed at Caesarea. The fact that the Roman cohort there was infamous for its savage behaviour against zealous Jews is completely absent. Cornelius' patronisation of individuals like Peter would hardly have been a good career move in Caesarea!

Jesus and his cousin John are presented as gracious and forgiving towards Roman soldiers. Some soldiers meekly accept being told by John the Baptist not to rob people with violence but to be content with their wages (Lk 3:14). Traditionally soldiers had always relied on pillage and booty for their income, but Augustus had recently introduced the novel reform of paying them wages in order to prevent looting. This humanitarian notion was not welcomed by many soldiers, who did better out of the old ways, especially since wages were frequently slow in coming.

A man could be picked at random and compelled to carry a soldier's substantial baggage for one mile. Jesus was said to have encouraged the hard-done-by populace to carry their burdens for a further distance than they were forced to do (Mk 5:41).

Yet reading between the lines, the Gospels do reveal that these were very distressing times for the Jews. A man who could not pay his lord the exorbitant dues demanded was liable to be sold with his wife and children to defray the debts (Mt 18:25). A poor widow, whose little livelihood had been taken away, might have to deal with an unjust judge who feared neither God nor man, and have no means of redress other than her importunity (Lk 18:1-5). Burglary and brigandage were common crimes (Mt 6:19; 24:43; Lk 10:30). State tax-collectors extorted excessive revenues (Lk 19:8). Rich noblemen, hated for their harshness, went off to enjoy themselves on trips abroad, leaving their underlings to amass money for them in the best way they could in their absence (Lk 19:12-17). Self-satisfied capitalists retired on their gains (Lk 12:16-21), or feasted sumptuously in their villas, caring nothing for the beggars covered in sores lying at their gates (Lk 16:19-31). Dazed by their privations, the common people followed benefactors around like dogs (Mt 9:35-38, 14:13). False prophets traded on their misery (Mt 7:15-16). On signs of open disaffection the Romans thought nothing of cutting down innocent people in cold blood, even when they were engaged in worship (Lk 13:1-2). Reformers and patriotic preachers were arrested, and, more often than not, executed (Mt 10:16-39). Their sympathisers ran grave risks in giving such persons shelter (Mt 10:40-42). Spies and informers abounded, and mingled with the crowds lurking to monitor any antagonism which might be brewing against the authorities (Mt 13:9-13), and sometimes even brazenly risked revealing themselves by asking pointed questions involving political issues (Mt 15:15-21). In fact, the authorities were in continual fear of popular uprisings (Mt 26:5).

Surely all the answers concerning Roman involvement in Jesus' crucifixion could be simply proved by referring to the legal documentary archives? No capital cases throughout the Empire were ever tried without documentary records. Once they had been read in court and approved by the judges, it was forbidden to alter them, and officials were compelled by law to deposit one copy in the archive of the governor or the supreme authority of the region. Justin and Tertullian took it for granted that the records of Jesus' trials were still in existence in the State Archives where anyone could refer to them.

However, the 'Acts of Pilate' referred to by the Church Fathers Justin and

Tertullian have been dismissed as forgeries by Christian scholars because in 311, when the Emperor Maximin Daia wished to discomfort the Christians he specifically ordered them to be copied and distributed in large numbers. These Acts claimed to be based on the newly opened Roman chancellery records regarding the administration of Pontius Pilate. Eusebius, of course, fulminated effusively against them in his *Ecclesiastical History*, especially as Emperor Maximin insisted that they be read in every school,[18] specifically *because* they contained material offensive to the Christians. These Acts were supposed to be dated from the years 19-21, covering the fourth consulate of Tiberius. However according to Josephus, Pilate didn't even enter Judaea until the year 26. Naturally, after the conversion of the Emperor Constantine a few years later, the Church used the first opportunity it had to destroy them.

But if the documents were forgeries, why didn't the Christians produce the *genuine* Acts of Pilate, with the same enthusiasm with which they produced other Acts for their martyrs? Was it because no such Acts really existed? Or was it because the Acts Maximin published really were the genuine ones, and really did contain material highly offensive to the Christians, such as a proof that the capital sentence against Jesus was justified from a Roman, or even a Jewish, point of view?

When we look at Luke's narrative we see that the charges against Jesus were plainly political: perverting the nation, refusing to pay tribute, and claiming to be a king (Lk 23:22). These were Zealot matters. On the face of it, they seem to indicate that Jesus either was, or was considered to be, a Zealot, and that the real reason for his arrest, trial and crucifixion was political after all, the Romans regarding him as a prominent member of the movement. Yet this is another matter of which the average Christian has no knowledge whatsoever. Only those who have studied Josephus and the history of that turbulent century are familiar with the Zealot Movement and its resistance to Rome. Why is it not even mentioned in the Gospels, as if it did not matter at all, or did not exist? And why should Jesus have been executed as a Zealot if he really had been so welcoming and accommodating to the Romans and their tax-collectors?

Chapter Four

ZEALOTS AND THE ROYAL FAMILY

T HE ZEALOTS, or *Qannaim*, were a religious resistance party. Academics have placed their origin at various stages of the recurrent historical persecution of the righteous, but usually locate it during the Maccabean period. In the year 6 CE the new Roman procurator Coponius was sent from Rome following the deposition of Herod the Great's son Archelaus,[1] and ordered a population census in order to organise fair taxation. A certain Judas the Galilean, or the 'Gaulanite', who came from the town of Gamala east of the Sea of Galilee, and a Pharisee named Zadok (the Righteous) led a spirited resistance to this, maintaining, firstly, that to hold *any* census infringed an ancient cult law (2 Samuel 24) and was against the will of God, and secondly, that in any case tribute should *not be paid at all* by people of God to a Gentile monarch, for to do so would be a form of blasphemy. These men were religious to the point of fanaticism, and seem also to have supported the notion of the restoration of the sacral kingship, the priest-kings of the Hasmonaean[2] line.

The Zealots organised a movement that attacked Romans and those Jews, not least the family of Herod, who collaborated, who had sold their souls to them by becoming their tax-collectors. Consequently they were often referred to as *lestai*, a word meaning brigand or pirate, robber or plunderer.[3]

In fact these Zealot outlaws were not robbers or desperadoes, but highly ideologised revolutionaries. When they launched their attacks, they were after not loot, but political advantage, in the same spirit that Islamic extremists attack foreign banks in their territories that run on the forbidden principle of taking interest.[4] Their key concept and rallying-cry was the Absolute Unity of God, and a total allegiance to Him: what Muslims call *tawhid*.

The Judas of Gamala who opposed the census in 6 CE was almost certainly either Judas ben Hezekiah (who had led an uprising in the north some years previously, on the death of Herod the Great) or, more probably, his son. Hezekiah had been killed by Herod at the start of the latter's meteoric rise to power, when he was given the post of governor of Galilee. Josephus reports that the ambitious Herod resolved to rid the country of the 'troublesome pests, bandits and brigands who infested Galilee'. He chased Hezekiah into the hills above Cana – later a Zealot settlement – and after a bloody battle won the day. Hezekiah and his band were captured, and beheaded on the spot.

Now, if Hezekiah's bandits were really no more than 'troublesome pests', one might have supposed that the country-folk would have been delighted by their destruction. But on the contrary, there was a national outcry, and Herod the governor found himself on trial for murder. Only the dramatic intervention of his Roman friends saved *him* from the axe.

This was a time and place where life was held cheap; yet the Hasmonaean High Priest Hyrcanus risked a showdown with Herod and an open break with Rome on Hezekiah's behalf. Surely Hyrcanus' perilous reaction and the nation-wide outcry strongly suggest that Hezekiah must have been more than just a brigand leader of a few petty criminals? Is it not possible that he may have been a Hasmonaean himself, a contender for the vacant throne of Israel, and therefore a direct rival who might wreck Herod's grandiose plans for himself?

Josephus records that from that time onward Herod hunted down and destroyed any Hasmonaean who might have threatened his hopes: the ageing priest John Hyrcanus, Hyrcanus' nephew Antigonus, Herod's own Hasmonaean wife Mariamne, her mother Alexandra, her father Alexander, her brother Aristobulus, and Herod's own two sons by Mariamne. His troops also eliminated the more distant heirs, 'not so much because they claimed the throne,' as Josephus remarks, 'but because they were entitled to it.'[5]

In view of the strong loyalty of the people towards the family line of Hezekiah, it seems very likely that his descendants were among these distant heirs. Just before Herod died a reprisal took place in the form of an attack on Sepphoris by Hezekiah's son Judas. Herod's troops stormed into Sepphoris and captured Judas; then, accusing the whole city of collusion with the Zealots, the Roman General Varus destroyed and burned it, razing it to its foundations. No fewer than two thousand prisoners were crucified, this being the first time that crucifixion was made the official punishment for Zealot rebels and those whose royalist aspirations they supported.[6] At around the same time there erupted the strange business recorded in Matthew's Gospel of Herod's attacks on two more families with possible royal connections: those of John the Baptist and Jesus.

Despite the terrible penalty paid for their failure, the family of Hezekiah continued to act with energy in the following years. As we have seen, Judas of Gamala (the possible son of Judas ben Hezekiah) rebelled against the census in 6CE. His sons James and Simon both suffered precisely the same fate for exactly the same reason. In 66 CE his son or grandson Menahem led the Zealot movement against the Romans. A break intervened when a man with no known family connection, John of Gischala, took over the leadership in 67; but by the time the revolt was finally crushed with the fall of the Masada fortress, the leader was Eleazar, another grandson of the same Judas.[7]

So: was Jesus a Zealot? Are there any clues? Take the first meeting of the disciple Nathanael with Jesus reported in Jn 1:43-51. Nathanael (who is usually identified with the Apostle Bartholomew)[8] was brought to Jesus by Philip of Bethsaida, who had just left the ranks of John the Baptist's disciples to follow him. When Jesus told Nathanael that he was 'a true Israelite, in whom is no guile', a reference back to the Patriarch Israel (Jacob), Nathanael asked Jesus how he knew him, indicating that they had not met previously. Jesus replied that he had seen him under the fig tree. This was enough to startle Nathanael, and draw from him the response: 'Rabbi, you are the son of God! You are the *King of Israel!*'[9]

Who knows what Nathanael had been thinking or doing under the fig tree? Perhaps he had been considering something to do with the setting up of a national Messiah-king? In any case, Jesus said he would be impressed by greater things than this show of psychic awareness (or very efficient information-gathering), and again made a reference to the patriarch Jacob/Israel and his famous vision at Bethel of angels ascending and descending a ladder between earth and heaven. Jesus stated that heaven would be open again, and that the linking ladder would be the Son of Man.

Christians naturally spot Nathanael's description of Jesus as 'Son of God', but generally ignore the 'King of Israel'.[10]

Are there any other clues? Yes, indeed. The miracle of the feeding of the five thousand is the only miracle related in all four canonical Gospels, and in John's version there is one important detail mentioned which the others omit: 'When the people saw the sign which he had done, they said – "This is indeed the prophet who is to come into the world!" And perceiving that they were about to come and take him by force *to make him king,* Jesus withdrew again to the hills by himself.' (Jn 6:14-15) The time for him to make a public declaration had not yet come, despite the wishes of the people.

A better-known reference is the one of Jesus' birth, when Herod the Great was alerted to the birth of 'the King of the Jews' by the magi (Mt 2:2). We are told that he took the threat so seriously that he took the precaution of slaughtering all the male infants in Bethlehem. Many scholars do not trust this passage at all, for it only occurs in Matthew's Gospel, but there could be other reasons for the omission or obscuring of details, as we shall see.[11]

When Jesus was around thirty years old he was 'baptised', and a voice from heaven recited the words from Psalm 2:7: 'You are My son, this day have I begotten you.' The latter phrase was edited out and remains only as a footnote to Lk 3:22, because it suggested a 'heresy' to the 'orthodox' Trinitarians, namely, that Jesus was born as a normal human being, and was only 'adopted' by God on the day of his baptism. In fact, Psalm 2 was not a proof-text of divine sonship, as so many Christians assume, but was the psalm used in the coronation ceremonies of Hasmonaean kings. The full text, known by heart by any devout Jew, was specifically political, and certainly did not indicate any earthly incarnation of a pre-existent divine entity. The speaker is the new king:

> Why do the nations conspire, and the people plot in vain? The kings of the earth set themselves, and the rulers take counsel together against the Lord and His anointed one, saying: 'Let us burst their bonds asunder, and cast their cords from us.' He who sits in the heavens laughs; the Lord has them in derision. And He will speak of them in His wrath, and terrify them in His fury, saying: 'I have set My king on Zion, My holy hill.' I will tell of the decree of the Lord. He said to me: 'You are My son, today I have begotten you. Ask of Me, and I will make the nations your heritage, and the ends of the earth your possession. You shall break them with a rod of iron, and dash them in pieces like a potter's vessel.' So therefore, O kings, be wise; be warned, O rulers of the earth. Serve the Lord with reverence, with trembling kiss His feet, lest He be angry, and you perish in the way; for His wrath is quickly kindled. Blessed are those who take refuge in Him.

It is a specific political warning.

Was Jesus ever anointed as a king? It is recorded in Mk 14:3 that he did undergo some sort of anointing in Bethany, shortly before his public mission in Jerusalem. Was it really done with pure nard – an aromatic from the Himalayas sealed in cases of marble from Alabastron in Egypt, that would have cost over 300 denarii, or a year's wages (Mk 14:3); or might it really have been the special sacred oil described in Exodus 20:22-25, that was specifically for anointing holy things and, in particular, king-messiahs? The manufacture and even possession of this oil were severely restricted. It was a capital offence for anyone to compound the mixture, or use it for unauthorised purposes.

It was the day after this anointing that Jesus made his triumphal entry into Jerusalem cheered by the crowds, followed by his raid on the Temple. This may have been the insurrection mentioned in Mk 15:7 in which prisoners were taken, including a 'notable prisoner' named Barabbas. It must have been a major attack, with vast numbers supporting Jesus, and not just a brawl hardly worth mentioning, otherwise Jesus would surely never have got away, given the failure of the attack. Why didn't the soldiers pursue and catch him? If the hillsides surrounding Jerusalem were at that time seething with Zealot supporters of a Messianic claimant, it would be easier to explain how he managed to stay at liberty for several more days. Several other puzzles that we will look at later would likewise become much easier to understand.

Mark's Gospel records that a deputation of Pharisees and Herodians approached Jesus, flattered him, and put this question to him: 'Teacher, we know that you are true, and are not influenced by human opinion; you are not swayed by the prestige and influence of men, but truly teach the way of God. Is it lawful to give tribute to Caesar, or not?' (Mk 12:13)

How many times these Herodians (whose masters were kept in power by the backing of Rome and who were in charge of collecting the hated taxes) must have heard the defiant Zealot cry: 'No God but One! No King but God! No tribute but the Temple tribute!'

It has long been assumed that the Pharisees were the party of extremists, separated from the masses by their extreme ritual purity,[12] and contemptuous of Rome. What on earth were they doing 'hand in hand' with the Herodians? Recent scholarship suggests that, on the contrary, the Pharisees sought political accommodation with the Herods and the Romans, whereas the populace as a whole were 'infected to an incredible degree' by zealotism.[13] In his later work *The Jewish War*, Josephus states plainly that 'the thing which most moved the people to revolt against Rome was an ambiguous prophecy from their scriptures that one from their own country would rule the world.'[14] Apparently the Pharisaic Rabbis associated this famous Messianic 'star Prophecy' with Vespasian, the destroyer of Jerusalem! Josephus reports that it was 'the principal Pharisees, the Chief Priests, the men of power [Herodians], and all those desirous for peace' who *invited* the Roman army into Jerusalem 'to put down the uprising.'[15] Those who were sick of servility 'went to the wilderness' as rebels. They attacked Romans, the Herodians, the Herodian Temple hierarchy and Pharisees alike.

The Romans, of course, tolerated both the accommodationist Rabbinic (Pharisaic) Judaism, and later, the accommodating 'pagan' Christianity. They certainly did not tolerate militant, aggressive and apocalyptic Jewish patriots who were totally unyielding in piety and purity, who were 'straight, not straying to right or left.'

Most Christians assume that Jesus' reply to the tribute question was pacifist, and that he reluctantly endorsed the requirement. He realised that they were insincere and trying to trap him. He asked to be shown a coin, and inquired whose head and inscription were upon it. Then came his answer: 'Give to Caesar the things which are Caesar's, but give to God the things which are God's.' (Mk 12:17).

But what did this reply really mean? Yes, or no? It is interesting, incidentally, that Jesus did not have about his person any of the coins with the objectionable head of the Imperial *Divi Filius* on it. Look at his reply again, carefully. What were the 'things of God'? To any Zealot, *the Holy Land and all its resources* were the 'things of God', and certainly not Caesar's. If Jesus' reply was in line with Zealot thought, for 'those who had eyes to see' his answer really meant that he was emphatically *against* the tribute.

Did his answer satisfy the questioners? Did they go away convinced of Jesus' political innocence? Surely if there had been the slightest suspicion that he was insulting Rome, or hinting that Jewish money (the 'things of God') should not be paid to Caesar, then Roman judgement would have been swift and severe? And indeed it was: in a matter of days after giving this reply, Jesus was executed.

According to Luke, one of the specific charges against Jesus was 'forbidding [the nation] to give tribute to Caesar' (Lk 23:2); and this is rather surprising, since the Gospel tries to give the opposite impression (Lk 20:22-25). It is most likely that the charge represents Jesus' real point of view, for the Dead Sea Scrolls and Josephus make it clear that this was the authentic position of Messianic movements in Palestine and their *bona fide* representatives. It also explains why the authorities were interested in Jesus being a *Galilean*; 'Galilean' being considered almost synonymous with 'Zealot'.

Can we find any other evidence that Jesus might have been a Zealot? One of the most valuable characteristics treasured by students of Mark's Gospel is its apparently unconscious use of little eyewitness details, or the use of recognisable Aramaic words and thought-forms, thereby putting us in close touch with the teacher. One such detail was that one of Jesus' disciples was known as Simon the Cananean (Mk 3:19), suggesting he came from Canaan. The word *Qananaios* (or Cananean) was probably as meaningless to any Greek-speaking reader as it is to today's western reader. *Qananaios* probably meant Zealot.[16]

So what is particularly revealing in this? The point is that elsewhere Mark *always* gives translations of the Aramaic words he uses in his text (see 5:41; 7:11,34); but in this instance, he does not. Was the fact that one of the Twelve was a resistance fighter too dangerous to be explained, so that the word was therefore deliberately left untranslated?

Another untranslated Zealot hint comes in Mt 16:17, where Jesus calls his impulsive disciple Peter by the name 'Simon Bar-Jona'. This was not necessarily a surname meaning 'son of John', it could have been a nickname. The Aramaic word *Baryona* means 'son of a dove', but it also means 'unrestrained', and it had particular Zealot implications. It could also be translated 'son of the wilderness'.[17] *Baryonim* was a slang term for those who rose up in open hostility to Rome.[18]

When Jesus entered Jerusalem on Palm Sunday, he did not slip in quietly: he had made quite elaborate preparations. A 'colt upon which no man had ever sat' was fastened ready outside a certain house, and a password arranged so that when Jesus sent two disciples ahead of him to take it, the owners knew what was going on, and let it go.[19] Jesus presumably did this quite deliberately: not because he was suddenly tired and needed to ride, but specifically to fulfil the Messianic prophecy in Zechariah 9:9f:

> Rejoice greatly, O daughter of Zion! Shout aloud, O daughter of Jerusalem! Lo, your king comes to you; triumphant and victorious is he; humble and riding upon an ass, on a colt the foal of an ass. I will cut off the chariot from Ephraim and the warhorse from Jerusalem; and the battle bow shall be cut off, and he shall command peace to the nations; his dominion shall be from sea to sea, and from the river to the ends of the earth. As for you also, because of the blood of My covenant with you, I will set your captives free from the waterless pit. Return to your stronghold, O prisoners of hope; today I declare that I will restore to you double, for I have bent Judah as My bow, I have made Ephraim its arrow. I will brandish your sons, O Zion, over your sons, O Greece, and wield you like a warrior's sword. Then the Lord will appear over them, and His arrow go forth like lightning; the Lord God will sound the triumpet and march forth in the whirlwinds of the south. The Lord of Hosts will protect them, and they shall devour and tread down the slingstones; and they shall be turbulent like wine, and full like a bowl, drenched like the corners of the altar. On that day the Lord their God will

save them, for they are the flock of His people; like the jewels of a crown they shall shine on His land.Yea, how good and how fair it shall be!

Any devout Jew who knew this passage would realise instantly what Jesus' entry into Jerusalem upon an ass's colt signified. The crowds did not greet this role-playing innocently shouting 'Hooray!', which is what most Christians take to be the meaning of 'Hosanna'. This was not a cheer, but the Aramaic word *Oshana* meaning 'Free us!' or 'Deliver us!': a seditious expression. Put this together with the crowd hailing Jesus as 'Son of David', and the situation was clearly doubly dangerous. According to Lk 19:40, some of Jesus' Pharisaic supporters tried to have this chanting suppressed, but Jesus condoned it, averring that if the people were silent, then the very stones would cry out.

That there had recently been a separate unsuccessful insurrection is stated in Mk 15:7.[20] One wonders how many more references to Zealot activity might have been edited out. Hierocles, an anti-Christian writer of around 300 CE is quoted by Lactantius as saying that Jesus had been the leader of a band of some 900 revolutionaries. Where did he get this idea from? Another curiosity: the Roman historian Tacitus comments that Judaea was 'quiet' in the reign of Tiberius, which hardly coincides with the dramatic tableau painted by Josephus. Could the Christian copyists and editors have been busy on Tacitus' work too, if Tacitus had connected Zealot disturbances with Jesus? It is surely suspicious that although in its original form Tacitus' history of the Roman Empire covered the entire period from CE 14-68, the years 29-31, 37-47 and 66-68 are now missing, these being the precise pages we would like so much to see!

Josephus is the only first-century historian who deals specifically with the period and places covered by the New Testament. He is famous for two surviving works: the *Jewish Antiquities*, written in Greek, which modestly covers the period from the creation of the world to the year CE 66; and the *Jewish War*, written first in Aramaic and then translated into Greek, which deals with Jewish history from 170 BCE – CE 73. The *Jewish War* mentions nothing at all about the origins of Christianity, a fact which is highly suspicious, and the *Antiquities* merely have an interpolated section which was written in later by a Christian.[21] (Origen's copy of this book in the third century did not have this section; it first occurs in a quotation by Eusebius in the fourth century.)

This does not mean, of course, that Josephus gave no account of the life of Jesus and his fate, or that the rise of Christianity was simply so insignificant amid the general tumult of first century Middle Eastern affairs that no-one in authority thought it worth mentioning. What it *does* suggest is that when Josephus wrote about Jesus, he may not have described him as a claimant to divinity, but simply described his political Zealot connections and activities. Since during the fourth and fifth centuries the Church authorities ruthlessly hunted down and burnt any writings hostile to the Trinitarian faith, it is entirely possible that any truthful account Josephus gave was censored out at that time.

Robert Eisler is one scholar who has turned up some Josephus evidence which is very interesting. Apparently, a group of monotheistic 'Ebionite' Christians translated the Greek version of the *Jewish War* into Old Russian in the thirteenth century, and this text contains some very significant differences from the extant Greek version. It preserves some passages about John the Baptist and Jesus which are absent from the standard Greek version. Some may be medieval interpolations, but Eisler contends on linguistic grounds that the Old Russian translation was made from a text older that the one now extant, in fact from a text based on the original Aramaic draft.[22]

The version states that the first adult appearance of the Baptist was after the death of Herod in 4 BCE, and not in the fifteenth year of Tiberius (i.e. CE 28-29) as the Gospels would have it. The Baptist was not named, but was referred to as a 'wild [or wilderness] man', a political agitator preaching national independence. He reappeared in CE 34 and denounced Herod Antipas' marriage to his niece Herodias, after which he was put to death.[23]

Eisler concedes in his conclusion that the Jesus references are largely forgeries, but notes that if one took the trouble to strip the texts of anything incompatible with Jewish authorship he would be left with the 'authentic Josephus'. In this case, Jesus definitely appears as a wonder-worker with Messianic hopes, denounced by priests and executed by Pontius Pilate.

If Mark's Gospel was written after the fall of Jerusalem in 70 CE, his motives for softening the part played by Zealots make even more sense. Zealot activity was 'news' in Rome. It threatened possible repercussions for Gentile Christians, especially converts of the Church of Rome, for although they were not Jews they had deferred to Jerusalem as the Mother-Church. As Roman antagonism towards Jews increased, the Gentile Christians must have become increasingly alarmed by their connections with Jerusalem, and probably lived in dread of any suspicion that might connect them with Zealot-Messianists, who believed that their Messiah would overthrow the Roman Empire. If Christians gave allegiance to any *imperium* other than Caesar's, they would be instantly branded as enemies of the State. Jews who had been born and bred in

Rome and had no Zealot sympathies whatsoever were also alarmed and embarrassed by the arrival of these nationalists, who now imperilled their own comfortable security.

The Emperor Claudius, who earlier succeeded Caligula, was certainly alert to the threat of Zealot-Christians, and wrote to the Jews of Alexandria warning them not to entertain itinerant preachers from Syria and Upper Egypt, if they did not wish to be treated as abetters of 'a pest which threatens the whole world.'[24] More drastically, he ordered the expulsion from Rome of Jews 'who were continually making disturbances at the instigation of Chrestus.'[25] Many synagogues had already been closed.[26]

When Paul and Silas preached in Salonica they were taken to be Zealot agitators, and were duly denounced to the politarch. 'These subverters of the civilised world (i.e. the Roman Empire) have now reached here [...] and they are actively opposed to the imperial decrees, saying that there is *another king*, one Jesus.'[27] Paul was later indicted before the procurator Felix at Caesarea as a 'plague-carrier, a fomenter of revolt among all the Jews of the Empire, a ringleader of the Nazarene sect'.[28]

This was ironic, because these years saw the gradual triumph of Paul's teachings over those of the original Jewish-Christians. His popularity had been in something of a decline during the years 55-66, because missionaries from the Mother-Church of Jerusalem had publicly repudiated his claim to be a legitimate Apostle, and had tried to bring his converts into line with what they insisted was the original and pure faith of Jesus. It had been made clear to Paul's communities that the original followers of Jesus, including Jesus' actual relatives, repudiated much of Paul's message as 'innovation'.

Paul had been challenged in Jerusalem to prove his orthodoxy, since he seemed to be attempting to change the understanding taught by those disciples who had been personally trained by Jesus. Following an uproar, he was arrested in the Temple, taken to Rome after he revealed that he had Roman citizenship, and was eventually beheaded, a seriously depressing sequence of events for Pauline converts.

When Jerusalem fell in 70 CE, Paul's supporters doubtless recalled his attacks on Judaism and the Law, and saw the sack of Jerusalem as confirmation at last of his statements that God's Old Covenant with Israel was obsolete.

The 'tearing of the Temple veil' when Jesus 'died' would have been of interest to Roman Christians who had just seen a later veil from that very Temple paraded before them in Titus the Conqueror's triumphal procession. They knew what it was and what its function had been: it was the priestly symbol par excellence of the ritual barrier between God and man. The word 'veil' suggests it was a flimsy thing, but in fact it was a massive curtain, the thickness of a man's fist.[29] Rending it in two suggested symbolically that Paul was correct: Jesus really had been the Son of God, and Judaism really had been overthrown. Rome had simply been used to fulfil God's purpose.

After 70 CE Christianity in the West virtually became a new movement, and Western Christian writings after that date are all the products of that transformation. Zealot political ambitions could have no relevance to the new theology. What was far more important was the new representation of Christianity as a Mithras-type saviour cult, with the difference that their hero was not a myth, but had lived as a real man. Any awkward elements in the historical record of Jesus that conflicted in any doctrinal way with the new image of him as Divine Son were discarded as nothing more than the ignorant and inferior beliefs of people who had not truly understood.[30]

Christianity had little use now either for a Hasmonaean king, or a young rabbi who preached to crowds in all the synagogues of Galilee, and hotly debated the true spirit of the law to over-meticulous scribes. The 'new' Jesus was presented as a loyal subject of Rome who, although a Jew by birth, had no essential connection with the Jewish religion. It was a gentile, a centurion at the cross, who was the first to perceive the esoteric truth, that Jesus was the Son of God.[31] To this truth, the Jews (even Jesus' closest friends and family) had been blind. On this steadily-evolving view, Christ was certainly not a local anti-Roman revolutionary, but a man-god who presented no threat to Rome.

The literature of those early centuries must have been full of evidence of the fierce and continuous antagonism between those Christians who were horrified by any attempt to deny the Oneness of God, and those who re-imaged Jesus with a Baalistic Trinitarian theology.[32] It is not surprising that the bulk of this material seems to have been deliberately suppressed.

Moreover, Jesus' teaching was twisted so that it looked as if it was the malice of 'the Jews' which had led to the crucifixion. Take the parable of the Wicked Husbandmen, for example (Mk 12:9). The authentic, Jewish meaning of this tale was that the corrupt priests who had always persecuted the prophets or true messengers of God would be replaced by righteous believers who submitted to God. The 'new' slant was that it was 'the Jews' as a whole who were the wicked husbandmen who had always persecuted God's servants; so that now the vineyard would be taken from them and given to other, more enlightened keepers: the Gentile Trinitarians. Under this rubric of 'the Jews' came the whole spectrum of Jewry lumped together: all the old rival factions of priests, Pharisees, Sadducees and scribes, whose principles and varying positions were no longer relevant or even interesting. The 'wicked husbandmen' who had persecuted all the prophets and then done away with Jesus were no longer specific politically-minded priests who collaborated with the Romans, but all 'the Jews'. Real anti-Semitism had arrived. [33]

So: looking back through the thickets of re-editing: was Jesus a Zealot?[34] He was certainly a troublemaker for the Romanised priests, and was put on trial for being so uncompromising and 'zealous for God' that he was prepared to run the risk of a showdown with them. Did Caiaphas twist his opposition to aspects of the Temple's life and present it as an attack on Rome? John's Gospel reports Caiaphas as saying: 'It is expedient that one man should die for the people, and that the whole nation should not perish.'[35]

Of one thing we can be sure: he was not thinking of the salvation of believing humanity though the sacrifice of the Son of God, but of how to stop a Zealot uprising and save his own corrupt neck!

Chapter Five

THE RELATIVES OF JESUS

JOHN THE BAPTIST was the famous cousin of Jesus, the son of the ageing priest Zechariah and Elisabeth. When Elisabeth fell pregnant (in very singular circumstances), instead of celebrating, she inexplicably 'hid herself' (Lk 1:24), and when the child was born everyone was fearful and apprehensive as to what his fate might be (Lk 1:65-66). According to traditions not in the official Gospels, as soon as Herod found out about the birth of John, he slaughtered Zechariah in the Temple; however the infant John had already been hidden 'in the wilderness' where he remained until he became an adult, possibly under the protection of the Qumran community.

The mystery deepens. Why was none of this recorded in the official Gospels? Why should Herod have done away with Zechariah? Was there any special reason for this? The occasion on which he burned incense in the Temple while great multitudes waited outside with bated breath may indicate that he might actually have been functioning not just as a priest, but as *high priest* (Lk 1:8-23). At first sight, this seems nonsensical, for he was obviously not the official High Priest. However, it is now known that the Essenes of Qumran actively opposed the Jerusalem priesthood and regarded it as invalid. One of their chief aims was to purify the Temple ritual and restore the rightful priesthood, and it is possible that they ran 'alternative' candidates from the earliest days of their sect.[1]

Zechariah's nephew James, the brother of Jesus, was also said (by Hegesippus and others) to have officiated as High Priest, when it was also obvious that he was not the official incumbent. The possibility that James was serving as *alternative* High Priest at the same time as he acted as leader of the Jerusalem Church is almost never remarked upon, and yet this possibility is of the utmost importance.

Jesus' brothers James, Joses, Judas and Simon are named in Mk 6:3-4, where it is also revealed that he had at least two sisters. The text does no more than say: 'Are not his sisters here with us?' which means that there was more than one. However, whether there were two or three, or even a dozen, we will probably never know. They 'took offence' at him, and Jesus commented that 'a prophet is not without honour, except in his own country, and among his own kin, and in his own house.'[2]

On another occasion his mother, brothers and sisters came and stood outside the place where he was, and called him to come out to them, but Jesus said: 'Here are my mother and my brothers. Whoever does the will of God is my brother, and sister and mother.'[3]

In the Fourth Gospel, Jesus' brothers wanted him to go to Jerusalem for the Feast of the Tabernacles, but Jesus hesitated to go about openly in Judaea, because 'the Jews' sought to kill him. The brothers challenged him: 'No man works in secret if he seeks to be known openly. If you do these things, show yourself to the world. *For even his brothers did not believe in him.*'[4]

However, far from being doubtful about Jesus, James, the eldest of Jesus' brothers, actually held the key position in the 'church' from the resurrection of Jesus until his own martyrdom in 62 CE, when he was succeeded by his relative Simeon son of Cleophas. The devotion with which James was cherished was vouched for not only by his loyal followers, or by the fact that he was held in honour even by his enemies, but most importantly by the fact that he had the authority to guide, if not command, even Peter.

Who was Cleophas, and Simon or Simeon his son? The Gospels give only two clues: someone called Mary Clopas watched the crucifixion, and an otherwise unknown person, Cleophas, was granted one of the earliest resurrection sightings of Jesus as he walked home to Emmaus with another, unnamed, person. Luke does not tell us why, or who these two disciples were. In fact, they were very probably Jesus' uncle and aunt.

Cleophas is the same name as 'Chalphai', which can be rendered in Greek as Alphaeus, Cleophas, Clopas or even Cleopatrus. Alphaeus was believed to have been a brother of that Joseph of Nazareth who married the Virgin Mary. If it is true that Joseph was much older than his bride, he may certainly have passed away shortly after their visit to Jerusalem when Jesus was twelve years old (Lk 2:41-52). By Jewish tradition, when Mary became a widow, Joseph's brother would have been the most likely person to have taken her into his household, which leads us to one possible explanation of who James, Joses, Jude, Simon and their sisters, really were.[5] They could have been the children of Cleophas/Alphaeus, and therefore really *stepbrothers* to Jesus. This theory also preserves the Catholic claim that Mary remained a perpetual virgin, and did not have other children herself; it would also explain why in the traditions James always seems to have been *older* than Jesus, and not younger.

Mary the wife of Clopas (who by this reasoning would not have been an otherwise unknown stranger, but Jesus' aunt) stood at the foot of the cross and watched the death and the burial of Jesus (Jn 19:25). She was also called 'the other Mary' (Mt 28:1), 'Mary the mother of James and Joses' (Mt 27:55), and Jesus' mother's sister (Jn 19:25). Many commentators have argued that two sisters could not both be called Mary, but this is nonsense. Such a practice was very common at that time.[6] In any case, if the Virgin Mary lived with Joseph's brother Alphaeus/Cleophas, she would not have been the other Mary's actual sister, but her sister-in-law; moreover, it was commonplace (and still is in many polygamous Muslim marriages) when a man had more than one wife for them to be referred to as 'sisters', or 'sister-wives'.

One son of Alphaeus, named Levi, who worked as a tax-collector, was called to follow Jesus (Mk 1:14). Some scholars identify this person with Matthew the tax-collector (Mt 9:9 and 10:3), but others with James the son of Alphaeus. Against this latter identification we must set the fact that James bar Alphaeus is usually known as 'James the Less', as opposed to the Greater James, who was the brother of John bar Zebedee. Also, Jesus' famous brother James is usually known as James the Just.

However, it is not impossible that James the Just and James the Less were one and the same person. If this was so, it is interesting that the Gospel writer *demoted* James by implication in giving him the title 'the Less'. It is also interesting that Mark preserved the name Levi, which suggests a connection with the priesthood. It is an unlikely name for an ordinary tax-collector working for the Romans or the Herods, but it might refer to a person collecting the Temple tax, or involved with the money-changing for the Temple. If Levi/James bar Alphaeus was the same person as Jesus' brother James, it means that he was not only *not* hostile to Jesus but on the contrary was called to be an apostle right at the start of Jesus' ministry, a fact that the gospel writer (or a later editorial hand) has obscured. If Mark really wrote the Gospel in his name, he ought to have known, his uncle Barnabas being a Levite himself, and Mark was presumably destined to be a Levite too had he not joined the Christians and become a missionary.

The principal sources for our knowledge of Jesus' brother James are Eusebius of Caesarea (c160-240) and Epiphanius of Salamis (c367-404), both natives of Palestine. Epiphanius quoted from an earlier lost work, *The Ascents of James*, which narrated the discourses James gave on the steps of the Temple. It may be that this text was a variant of the arguments with the Temple authorities recorded in the first part of Acts. The narratives concerning James in Acts and the *Ascents* overlap, but have interesting differences. There is also material about James in Jerome's *In Praise of Illustrious Men* (c347-420). The greater part of these sources is based on two earlier works from the second century, both now lost, by Hegesippus of Palestine (c90-180), and Clement of Alexandria (c150-215). Eusebius is quite frank about his dependence on them, and quotes large sections verbatim.

Furthermore, Peter had several companions who knew about James: John Mark was his companion at one stage, ending up as a martyr in Alexandria, having written his gospel; and another Clement (c30-99) who became one of the earliest bishops of Rome.[7] The works associated with this Clement are known as the Pseudoclementines, although they are no more spectacularly 'pseudo' than any other literature of this period. These works included the *Recognitions* and the *Homilies*, and were largely about James.

James also plays a prominent role in the Gospel of Thomas, unearthed at Nag Hammadi in Egypt, where two Apocalypses of James were also found. He is also central to an early gospel known as the *Protevangelium* of James.

According to Hegesippus, James was not only a Nazirite, he was also a priest, perhaps even a High Priest.

> This man was holy from his mother's womb, drank no wine or strong drink, nor ate anything in which was life (blood); no razor came upon his head; he anointed himself not with oil, and used no bath. To him alone it was permitted to enter the holy place; for he wore nothing woollen, but linen garments. And alone he entered the sanctuary, and was found on his knees asking for forgiveness on behalf of the people, so that his knees became hard like a camel's, for he was continually bending the knee in worship to God, and asking forgiveness for the people. In fact, on account of his exceeding great justice he was called 'the Just' and 'Oblias', which is in Greek 'bulwark of the people' and 'justice'.[8]

The phrase 'used no bath' means rather that he did not go to the public baths to be seen naked and be rubbed down with oil. It does not indicate that he did not wash; on the contrary, the sectarians with whom he has been associated used to bathe day and night in cold water. The sceptical Eusebius called such bathers 'Hemerobaptists' or 'Daily Bathers'.⁹

This bathing or baptism was not what most Christians understand today by baptism, but was a ritual immersion for the sake of purity, on the same principle as the Muslim *ghusl* or *wudu'*. An abnormally high number of immersion pools were provided at Qumran, a place where water was notoriously scarce and certainly did not flow regularly.

Jerome writes of James: 'He alone had the privilege of entering the Holy of Holies, since indeed he did not wear woollen garments, only linen, and he went alone into the Temple and prayed on behalf of the people, so much so that his knees were reputed to have acquired the hardness of camels' knees.' This makes plain what Hegesippus meant by the 'holy place'. Epiphanius records: 'But we find further that he also exercised the priesthood according to the ancient priesthood.¹⁰ For this reason he was permitted to enter the Holy of Holies once a year, as scripture says the Law ordered the High Priests.' He rephrases this in his second version of these things as follows: 'To James alone it was permitted to enter the Holy of Holies once a year because he was a Nazirite and connected to the priesthood […] James was a distinguished member of the priesthood […] James also wore a diadem [the *Nezer* or sacerdotal plate] on his head.' In this version he reiterates this: 'Many before me have reported this of him – Eusebius, Clement and others. He was, also, allowed to wear the mitre on his head as the aforementioned trustworthy persons have testified in the same historical writings.' He mentions the mitre rather than linen, but according to the Old Testament the High Priest's mitre was in any case made out of linen (Exodus 28:39).

The reference to his knees being calloused 'like those of a camel' amuses those who are not aware of prayer-callouses. It is easily explicable to a Muslim, accustomed to seeing marks on the knees, feet and ankles of those who practice long night devotions over and above the normal requirements. One doesn't develop such callouses by praying for a whole day just once, but as the result of very frequent daily prayer practice.

James was killed by his rival, Ananus, but a few years later. in 66 CE, the Zealots took control of the Temple, and their first act was to depose the hated official High Priest and install the current rival High Priest, one Phanni (or Phanuel) ben Samuel, a stonemason with an impeccable Levitical pedigree, as the rightful Priest of the true blood.¹¹

The fact that there was a rival High Priesthood of this kind is so important that one can only assume its existence has been deliberately obscured. Robert Eisenman suggests that in Luke's Gospel Zechariah's line was originally given as Habijah ('Yahweh has hidden') and not Abijah, and the editors 'corrected' it to Abijah to obscure this fact. The family of Habijah was one of four priestly families returning from the Exile in Babylon who could not produce their proof of pedigree, and were therefore excluded from serving in the Temple, much to their distress.[12] Eisenman's suggestion is that this was a deliberate clue for 'those who had eyes to see': they were not really descendants of Habijah, but from the clan Joiarib, which was the first of the post-exilic priestly families. This needed to be 'hidden', because this was the line of the Hasmonaean priest-kings, and in the time of Herod, this status would have put them in danger of their lives. The editors must have known that Zechariah was not a real descendant of Habijah, and so altered it to Abijah without realising the significance of the clue that the name Habijah supplies.

On the other hand, Abijah ('my Father is Jehovah') was a descendant of Aaron, and when King David divided the priesthood into twenty-four divisions, each to serve at the sanctuary for a one-week period every six months, the House of Abijah was chosen by lot to head the eighth division.[13] One Abijah returned to Jerusalem with Zerubbabel after the Exile (Nehemiah 12:1-7). A generation later, in the time of the High Priest Jeshua, his family was represented by a man called Zichri (or Zechariah: 'Jehovah has remembered'), demonstrating that Zechariah was indeed a family name in this line.[14]

At least half a dozen church fathers record that Zechariah was slain between the Temple and the Bronze Altar by Herod himself. Zechariah was included among the martyrs of the Christian church, and a relic reputed to have been his head was exhibited in the Lateran Basilica in Rome. Why did Herod kill him? Is it beyond the bounds of possibility that this was because Zechariah could also have been a claimant for the role of 'one born to be King of the Jews'? The magi in search of a Messiah were not just looking for any rebel leader, but for someone who had been born to the rôle, a descendant of David. An interesting oddity that might now be seen to fit the jigsaw is that the Mandaean sect of semi-Christians just north of Palestine always claimed that John the Baptist was the real Messiah, being the elder of the two children John and Jesus, and that Jesus was an usurper.[15]

Outside Jerusalem are thousands of pre-Islamic tombs, all apparently insignificant except three: those said to be of Absalom, a son of David who rebelled against his father and was killed in fighting against him, Zechariah the father of John the Baptist, and James the brother of Jesus. Archaeologists dispute these claims as wishful thinking, and say rather that they are the tomb complex of a priestly family known as the Bene Hezir – based on an inscription found there. This, however, is fascinatingly odd. Why should this family have built such magnificent mausoleums? The Bene Hezir were not hugely important: according to 1 Chronicles they were only the seventeenth of the twenty priestly families who could prove their genealogies on the return from the Exile. What is so significant is that the word *hezir* also referred to the gold circlet worn by the High Priests, and also by Israelite kings when they went into battle. There was only one family that had combined the role of both priest and king: the Hasmonaeans. Surely, therefore, it makes far more sense to propose that these massive tombs were not those of an obscure priestly family, but of the 'Bene Hezir' or 'Sons of the Crown', the Hasmonaeans.[16] Moreover, this suggests that the families of Zechariah and Jesus could really both be reckoned among the claimants.

Jesus' Jewish 'trained men', the apostles, were disparagingly portrayed as a dull, uncomprehending bunch, and the noble family of Jesus, the line of David, disappeared almost without trace from the record. Christians were given to understand that Jesus' relatives did not believe in him, and his 'real' brothers and sisters were the elect faithful who understood his true significance, despite the fact that Jesus' brother James had been the leader of the Jerusalem Church for years, and after his martyrdom his nephew Simeon was immediately elected as his successor. Simeon was referred to as 'among the witnesses who bore testimony to what had both been heard and seen of the Lord' (Hegesippus). There is not a word of this in the orthodox gospels, or the Acts of the Apostles, unless it was Cleophas' son Simeon who was the unnamed disciple who saw Jesus on the road to Emmaus,[17] and not Cleophas' wife Mary as suggested earlier. In fact, the government of the Nazarenes remained chiefly in the hands of Jesus' family until the following century.

Among the 'heirs' (*Desposynoi*) we hear in particular of James and Sokker (possibly Judas Sokker) the grandsons of Jesus' brother Judas.[18]

The few surviving references to the relatives of Jesus in the 'official' New Testament either denigrate them, or are straightforwardly hostile, and all Hebraic documents which did not present the Jesus of the Trinitarian theology were either 'lost' or suppressed. The 'Gospel According to the Hebrews', which several sources claimed to have been written by Simeon, was one important casualty, as was the document now known as 'Q'. In the Hebrew

Gospel, Jesus' brother James plays a much more important part than the present four Gospels reveal. There must have been a kind of agreement amongst the 'orthodox' Church hierarchy of editors to eliminate the rôle he played, and even to allow the supposition that he was 'against' Jesus, or that he disbelieved in him. In the Nazarene Gospel, on the contrary, he is honoured with an appearance of the Risen Jesus to himself alone, an appearance which was acknowledged by Paul in pre-Gospel days. [19]

According to Eusebius, Hegesippus stated frankly that the descendants of Jesus' brother Judas 'came forward and presided over every church, as witnesses and members of the Lord's family', a point entirely missing in Acts! Hegesippus commented, moreover, that 'until then, the Church remained as pure and uncorrupted as a virgin [...] but when the sacred band of Apostles and the generation of those who had been privileged to hear with their own ears the Divine wisdom reached the ends of their lives and passed on, then impious error took shape through the lying and the deceit of false teachers, who, seeing that none of the Apostles were left, shamefacedly preached, against the proclamation of the Truth, their false knowledge' (lit. 'pseudo-gnosis'). [20]

Chapter Six

KEEPERS AND DOERS

THE LAW OF GOD required all who accepted the Covenant to be 'holy' (Leviticus 19:2). The ritual state of purity is not something familiar to most Christians of the west, who concentrate on being good and prayerful people, and do not practise it. To them, it seems odd to emphasise living a separated or submitted life. Hygienic people will wash their hands before eating and after relieving themselves, and women will no doubt have a bath after childbirth and menstruation. Most people would probably wash their hands after touching something dead, but today this is virtually restricted to meat being prepared for cooking. The practices of ritual washing before prayers, separating clean from unclean foods, and the practice of serious fasting have long gone among most Christians. Moreover it is hard to understand principles which look like fussiness or even racism in such matters as mixing in Gentile society, or eating with Gentiles.

At the time of Jesus, it was not just the priests at the Temple who practised ritual purity; ordinary citizens who belonged to the Pharisaic and Essene groups practised this pure life-style in all aspects of their everyday lives, and not just in matters connected with Temple ritual. It is highly unlikely that priests, Pharisees or Essenes would have been attracted by the lifestyle of Jesus and his followers, unless they also practised purity laws.

A saying of Jesus in Matthew's Gospel backs up this notion: 'Except your righteousness exceed that of the scribes and Pharisees, you can never enter the Kingdom of Heaven!' (Mt 5:20). The gospels suggest that Jesus disagreed with, and broke, some of the laws that Pharisees had applied to everyday life, as in the case of plucking corn on the sabbath (Mk 2:23-28). In fact, this is an example of an incorrect criticism, since the Pharisees had ruled that the plucking and eating of a few ears of corn was perfectly permissible if done to assuage the hunger of a passer-by, so long as it was plucked by hand and not done in large quantities by some farm implement.[1]

As regards healing on the sabbath, this was not forbidden at all by Pharisees: the gospels are quite wrong here. Mixing medicines and making cloth for bandages were forbidden, but treatment was allowed for the simplest things on the grounds that you would not know if it would develop into some life-threatening condition, and help was *always* allowed in life/death situations. In fact, Jesus used a Pharisaic argument to prove that people could work on the sabbath in certain circumstances, as with, for example, the rule of circumcision on the eighth day overruling the prohibition on labour (Jn 2:22-24). Jesus argued that God Himself (who neither slumbers nor sleeps, as attested by sura 2:255) does not cease working on the sabbath (Jn 5:1-18).

There are *no records at all* of Jesus breaking the ablution or dietary laws. The case of Jesus apparently breaking the lesser rule of washing before eating (Mk 7:1-23; Mt 15:1-20) is very interesting, for it favours the Muslim position rather than the assumed Pharisaic position. Jesus' disciples, but not Jesus himself (v.5), were accused of eating with defiled hands. This example is worth quoting in full, and is given here in Matthew's version:

> Then Pharisees and scribes came to Jerusalem and said, 'Why do your disciples transgress the tradition of the elders? For they do not wash their hands when they eat.' He answered them, 'And why do you transgress the commandments of God for the sake of your tradition? [...] For the sake of your tradition, you have made void the word of God. Well did Isaiah prophesy of you, when he said 'this people honours Me with their lips, but their heart is far from Me; in vain do they worship Me, teaching as doctrines the precepts of men'. And he called the people to him and said to them: 'Hear and understand; it is not what goes into the mouth that defiles a man, but what comes out of the mouth, this defiles a man.' Then the disciples came and said to him: 'Do you know that the Pharisees were offended when they heard this saying?' He answered: 'Every plant which my Father has not planted will be rooted up. Leave them alone; they are blind guides. And if a blind man leads a blind man, both will fall into a pit.' But Peter said to him: 'Explain the parable to us.' And he said: 'Are you still without understanding? Do you not see that whatever goes into the mouth passes into the stomach, and so is evacuated? But what comes out of the mouth proceeds from the heart, and this defiles a person. For out of the heart come evil thoughts, murder, adultery, fornication, theft, false witness, slander. These are what defile a person; but to eat with unwashed hands does not defile a person.'

In Islam, the process of eating food does not break *wudu*. Although people (especially those who eat with their hands) would wash them before eating, this is a *sunna* of normal hygiene, and not a law pertaining to worship.[2] Simply eating with unwashed hands would not make a Muslim ritually unclean (although actually eating forbidden food would; but this was not the point at issue in this passage).

Muslims, of course, understand very well the concepts of ritual cleanliness before prayer and separating clean from unclean foods, which form part of a rich symbolic language. Hence Muslims find nothing odd in the early Christian practices.

The *salat* prayer requires a special state of purity,[3] involving the washing of hands, arms, face and feet. Clean water must also have been used to remove defilement from waste matter and urine. Most Muslims like to perform *wudu* for each of the five prayers, without finding it much of a hardship. It is an aid to concentration, as well as symbolically very important. Furthermore, Muslims perform *wudu* in *running* water. Baths, as opposed to showers, are regarded with distaste, since immersing a whole dirty body in still water distributes traces of dirt and faecal matter all over that body.

As regards food, the purity rules are familiar from the Old Testament and from the Council of Jerusalem ruling issued by James. Muslims are forbidden to eat pork, meat cut from animals that are still living, or have died 'of themselves' (carrion), or have been strangled, clubbed or gored to death, or have not been killed by a sharp implement, or have not had their life-blood drained from them, or have been sacrificed in the name of any deity other than the One True God.[4] In today's world, that includes any produce directly manufactured from forbidden (*haram*) animals or animals killed in a *haram* way, including products such as gelatine and lard. Most Muslims satisfy this requirement when living in a non-Muslim environment by having their own meat-suppliers, and not eating meals in non-Muslim households or environments unless they are vegetarian (or fish-based) and have been cooked in vegetable oil.[5]

Fasting is another rigorous discipline in Islam. Many Muslims fast for one day every week, or on one or two special dates during the year, in addition to the mandatory fast during the month of Ramadan. The Muslim calendar follows the lunar cycle, so the month cannot be equated with any specific Gregorian month, but begins approximately eleven days earlier each year.

During Ramadan, nothing must pass the lips from first light (long before sunrise) to sunset: whether food, drink, or tobacco fumes. The purity laws also forbid sexual intercourse during those hours (all these restricted things becoming lawful again during the hours of darkness). Apart from the physical discipline, the state of mind of the fasting person is of paramount importance: it is a time of detachment, peace, reverence, and compassion. To act harshly, rudely, violently or dishonestly violates the law of Ramadan no less than eating or drinking. A hadith insists that 'whoever does not abandon lies and false witnessing; God has no need that he should abandon his food and his drink.'

All Muslims accept that these practices are required by God and should be done, even if there are plenty of lax Muslims to point fingers at. Muslims who are 'keepers and doers' react to those who try to justify dropping these practices in exactly the same way as the Jewish-Christians reacted to the lax Gentile ways which were coming into the Church.

None of the Jewish followers of Jesus believed that they were being asked to become converts to a new religion. They recognised Jesus as a Messenger of God; not a new God, but the One revealed by all the Prophets since history began. Jesus might have been a reformer, a purifier, but he was not considered to be the founder of a new faith.[6] Evidence outside the New Testament backs this up. As we have seen, Suetonius talks of the banishment of *Jews* from Rome because of their propaganda on behalf of Chrestus (probably to be identified with Christ), implying that the Romans did not distinguish between Christians and Jews. From the Roman point of view they were the same, particularly those carrying the 'incendiary bacillus of Jewish Messianic and Apocalyptic propaganda'.[7] Tacitus also thought this,[8] and so did Pliny.[9]

Jewish Christians did not assume that the sufferings Jesus experienced indicated the failure of his mission, or that he had gone against what God required. All had been foretold in the scriptures. Jesus, the true Messiah and servant of God, had made an earnest attempt to bring spiritual reform, and his maltreatment at Roman hands for refusing to accept Roman sovereignty was regarded as an honourable sacrifice for Israel. This belief was especially true for the Zealots of Galilee.[10]

The first Christians did not use the name 'Christian'.[11] They were usually referred to as the 'Followers of the Way'. The notion of being a 'Christian' commenced in Antioch, a Greek city famous for coining a nickname for anything. Devout Jews would actually have disapproved of taking a sectarian title in the name of a human individual, because it might suggest that the followers were worshipping that human leader rather than the One True God. Muslims can react in exactly the same way when they are labelled 'Mahometans'. They do not worship Muhammad, but God.

The Jesus-partisans were known as 'Nazarenes', and Jesus became generally known as 'of Nazareth'. However, the word Nazarene probably had no geographical connection whatsoever with Nazareth. Religious movements in the ancient world were not generally named after places.[12]

Matthew 2:23 states, and most Christians today accept, that when the parents of Jesus returned from Egypt after the death of Herod, the reason they wanted to live in Nazareth was specifically to fulfil a prophecy that foretold 'he shall be called a Nazarene'. This is most interesting, for this supposedly well-known prophecy mentioning Nazareth *does not exist* in the Old Testament as we now have it. Now, the Greek text of Matthew actually has the word *Nazoraios* and not Nazarene, and this word bears a very different meaning. Mark always refers to 'the Nazarene', as does Luke 4:34; but elsewhere and in Acts (2:22; 3:6; 4:10 etc) he uses *Nazoraion*. In Hebrew, the word 'Nazorean' spelled with a 'tz' means 'Keeper'. Spelled another way, a Nazirite with a 'z', it means 'consecrated' or 'separated'.

It therefore seems very likely that the idea that Jesus was called 'Nazarene' because he came from a place called 'Nazareth' is quite wrong; instead, and more impressively, he was a 'consecrated' or 'separated' one. This is reinforced by the tradition that his brother James was a life-long Nazirite.

As it happens, the place Nazareth is nowhere mentioned in the Old Testament, or in the writings of Josephus, or in the Talmud. The present word can only be traced back with any certainty to the fourth century, despite some intriguing cave-dwellings preserved by the Christians in present-day Nazareth which are claimed to include the homes of Joseph the Carpenter and the place where Mary lived before her marriage to him. There is certainly no evidence that Nazareth was a *city* at the time of Jesus, as Matthew and Luke claim, and it is amazing indeed that it does not figure at all in the historical events that overwhelmed Sepphoris, a mere six miles away!

At the time when the early Church fathers were writing, the term Nazarene had nothing to do with Nazareth, but specifically denoted the Jewish Christians, those who recognised Jesus as Messiah but remained faithful to the Jewish Law. Jews did not always call these followers of Jesus 'Nazarenes' but used the words '*Nazaraioi*' and 'Nazoreans'. In the Talmud they are called *Notzrim*. These words have links with either the Hebrew *Netzer* or *Zara*, the former meaning 'Branch', presumably an allusion to the

'Branch of David', while *Zara* means 'seed'. Both are conspicuously Messianic titles.[13]

Combined with the other strong possibility, that the root-word is *Nazar*, which means 'to keep' or 'to observe', the implication is that these Jewish Christians were to be distinguished from the pagan Gentile converts because they remained 'keepers' or 'doers' of the Law.

In Hebrew 'Keepers of the Covenant' is *Nozrei ha-Brit*. The term 'Doers' of the Torah or *Osei-ha-Torah* is key terminology in the Dead Sea Habakkuk Pesher. Moreover, it is highly possible that the Qumran 'Priests who *keep* the Covenant', or the 'Keepers of the Covenant' par excellence, had a strong connection with the Rechabite movement, the Rechabites being those seekers after righteousness and purity who took to the wilderness (here called 'the land of Damascus') and eschewed all corrupt society.[14]

The fullest presentation of these Rechabites is supplied in Jeremiah 35 where Jonadab son of Rechab gives instructions to Rechab's descendants, in the 800s BCE. The Rechabites were probably the first groups to be known as 'Keepers'. Their behaviour was sharply contrasted to that of other Israelites in Jeremiah's time. Jonadab's 'zeal for the Lord' was specifically mentioned (2 Kings 10:16); he was the prototypical Zealot. The descriptions of Jesus' brother James in the early sources fit in perfectly: 'He was holy from his mother's womb; he drank no wine or strong drink, nor did he eat meat; no razor touched his head; he did not anoint himself with oil', and he lived to be 96, typical of the long life of the austere and ascetic Rechabites. His relative, Simeon bar Cleophas, whom Epiphanius actually identified as the Rechabite priest who tried to stop his execution, was said to have died at the age of 120.

In the Damascus Document, the 'Keepers' are the 'Sons of Zadok', those who will be saved, and who will save others; they are those who will 'stand on the Last Day', also called the 'Standing Ones'. The 'Sons of Zadok' described by the Prophet Ezekiel (Ezek 44:17-31) wore only linen, did not shave their heads (because they were life-long and not temporary Nazirites), did not drink wine nor eat flesh with blood. They taught the difference between holy and profane (*halal* and *haram*), clean and unclean (Ezek 44:23).

In the fourth century CE Epiphanius did not distinguish between the Essenes and a group he calls the 'Jessaeans', who according to him were followers of David's father Jesse. Elsewhere he calls them Ossaeans. We might wonder if these should really be the followers of Jesus. Epiphanius wrote that 'All Christians were once called Nazoreans.[15] For a short time they were also given the name Jessaeans (that is 'Essenes'), before the disciples in Antioch began to be called Christians'.[16] Hippolytus favoured the term 'Nazarenes', in a form which seems to be a combination of *Netzer* and Essene.

The Dead Sea Scrolls prefer terms such as 'the Poor' ('Ebionite'), the Meek, the Little Ones, the Simple of Judah, those *doing* the Torah, 'the Way', 'the Sons of Zadok', 'the Perfect', 'the Sons of Light', the 'Holy Ones' and such combinations as the 'Zealots for the Day of Vengeance' or the 'Poor Ones of Piety', or the 'Zealots of Righteousness'.

Obviously the Qumran 'Sons of Zadok' have absolutely nothing in common with the Sadducees of the New Testament and Josephus, who comprised the establishment priesthood of the Herodian period. It seems that one can no longer refer to *a* religious party of the time of Jesus called the Sadducees.

There were very definitely two varieties: the former dominated in all things by the Pharisees, who were simply the upper class priests who accommodated the Romans, and hence the very opposite of the Qumran 'Sons of Zadok'. The purist *Zaddikim*, on the other hand, were consistently resistance-minded, xenophobic, non-accommodating and 'zealous for the Law'. The 'purist' Sadducees of the Maccabean period, they became the 'Messianic' Sadducees of the Herodian period, and developed as 'Zealots', 'Essenes', '*Sicarii*', 'Palestinian Christians' or the 'Jerusalem Church', followers of James the Just. They would never compromise with a foreign power, or accept foreign gifts as sacrifices in the Temple (which were considered polluting or idolatrous), and could not condone Herodian access to the sacred site or Herodian priestly appointees.

It was these latter Righteous Ones, the Keepers of the Law, with whom the Jewish-Christian Church made common cause.

Chapter Seven

WHY DID PAUL REJECT THE TORAH?

EVEN IF THE first 'Christians' remained Jews, it is obvious that Christians today are no longer Jews. It is also obvious that the Jews rejected Christianity, and have remained true to their own principles to this day. When one reads Paul's letters written before 64 CE one can see that the moves to break away from Judaism began early. The Luke-Acts stream of tradition, usually dated some ten years or so after the fall of Jerusalem, deliberately set out to show how 'true' (i.e. Pauline) Christianity commenced within the bounds of Judaism, after which the new wine began to stretch the old wine-skins until bursting point was reached, and the old faith was superseded and decisively abrogated by the new.

The influence of Paul in this campaign was paramount. Firstly, he maintained that Judaism was inadequate. Secondly, he taught an amazingly different theology: that Jesus was much more than the long-awaited Messiah. He was no less than a divine incarnation, and his terrible 'death' was not a political martyrdom but a cosmic sacrifice intended to free all who believed in him from subjection to the powers of evil. The human life of Jesus, his political persuasions and religious teachings, were almost irrelevant: Paul hardly mentions anything of them.

His Jesus was the 'image of the invisible God, the first-born of all creation; in him were all things created in heaven and on earth, visible and invisible. […] He is before all things and in him all things hold together. […] He is the beginning, the first-born from the dead […] for in him all the fullness of God was pleased to dwell, and through him to reconcile to himself all things, whether on earth or in heaven, making peace by the blood of his cross.' (Colossians 1:15-20)[1]

Pauline salvation theory must have struck faithful Jews as blasphemy, an extraordinary capitulation to Baalism. They grasped straightaway the implication that his teaching made a nonsense of all previous revelation from God as expressed through the Torah. The Jews appear, after all, to have been the one race of people in the world who claimed to have been specifically taught that God was One, and was without form or substance, and did not bear the likeness of anything in the created universe. He was not the personification of fertility, or the cycles of nature. He certainly did not father sons like the Baal gods.

Paul claimed to have been a Pharisee the whole of the first part of his life, and had been particularly zealous, even though scholarly Pharisaic characteristics, as discernable in the teachings of Jesus, do not show in any of his recorded teaching. In Philippians 3:5 Paul announced himself thus: 'circumcised on the eighth day, of the people of Israel, of the tribe of Benjamin, a Hebrew born of Hebrews; as to the Law, a Pharisee; as to zeal, a persecutor of the Church; as to righteousness under the Law, blameless.' He claimed that the brilliant Hillelite Rabbi Gamaliel was his teacher (Acts 22:3), although he had clearly not absorbed Gamaliel's tolerance. Paul violently opposed the growing 'Christian' movement with a vehemence never sanctioned by Gamaliel (see Acts 5:34-40), right up to the moment of his dramatic conversion.

Then, having experienced this blinding and traumatic event, Paul reacted as violently against the Law of his youth as he had previously campaigned against the Christians. In regarding the Risen Christ as his 'personal saviour', he concluded that the Torah could no longer be thought an adequate vehicle for salvation. In fact, he stated it had never been.

Let us consider what this implied to a Jew, or would imply to a Muslim. The Torah (or *Tawrat*) was the expressed Will of God, utterly sacred, never to be adulterated by addition or subtraction from it.[2] If one loved God, one accepted and kept His commands, whether one understood the reason for every particular law or not.[3] It was not for a human mind to judge definitively which parts were most or least important, for no human had the full picture, or thought as God thought. Obedience was what counted. What Paul claimed was that the Law was not a blessing but a stumbling-block, and was the actual *cause* of the downfall of the Jews.

The full impact of this may be grasped if one substitutes for the perhaps unfamiliar word 'Torah', or the unemotive word 'Law', the phrase expressing what it really means: 'God's Revealed Will'. Consider how this sounds: 'Israel, following after God's Revealed Will of righteousness, did not [successfully] arrive at His Revealed Will. Why not? Because they did not seek it by faith, but only by the action of their lives.' (Romans 9:31-32)

In other words, Paul accused the Jews of engendering the wrong sort of religion, a legalism that produced an unhealthy anxiety leading to intimate concern for self, rather than concern for God and for others. No-one could deny that some people have a tendency to be too literal, seeing the letter rather than the spirit of any law-system, and such people might well become blind to those aspects of the relationship with God which really matter: love, honesty and compassion. It was a human characteristic true of certain Pharisees and Christians, and the same problem can of course recur in Islam: an obsession with the literal obedience to minutiae which can take over a person's life, and turn him or her into an intolerant, 'superior', rejecting 'blind guide', instead of an influence attracting people to God. Islamic thinkers such as al-Ghazali constantly warn against that possibility. Indeed any collection of interpretations of any laws can become so cumbersome that it is impossible for an ordinary person to know them all, let alone keep them. A wonderful opportunity thus arises for insecure individuals to criticise, denigrate, and make other people feel small; in short, instead of 'submission to God' being a joyful way of life, it can produce a crushing guilt or inferiority complex in the masses who cannot hope to compete with the extremists. But this interpretation is hardly what Christianity or Islam is all about, any more than it was what Judaism was or is all about.

The accusation is that 'legalism' reduces true service of God: humility, compassion and a 'clean and upright heart', to a knowledge of trifling regulations and one's ability or desire to keep them. It suggests that all legalistic systems are *bound* to be unsatisfactory in the end, since they involve an impossible search for a complete whole which covers all possible eventualities, and they lead to the danger of believing that striving to obey any given set of rules is sufficient to be right with God. Oddly enough, it also allegedly fosters the notion that there is a limit to one's duty, at which point, presumably, obligation ceases.

It is hardly what was expected of true Jews, Christians or Muslims: 'Be not like servants who serve on condition of receiving reward, but rather like servants who serve under no condition of receiving anything.' (*Pirke Aboth* 1.3)

'When you have done all that is commanded you, say 'We are unworthy servants; we have only done what was our duty.' (Luke 17:1-10)

'Feed, for the love of God, the needy, the orphan and the captive, (saying): "We feed you for the sake of God alone; no reward do we desire of you, nor thanks".' (Sura 76:8-9)

It was, and is, sometimes forgotten that God is the Most Generous (*akram al-akramin*). 'If God punished us according to what we deserve, He would leave on earth not one living thing.' (Sura 34:45; 16:61). Even those Pharisees who *were* over-zealously legalistic taught that if a person's good and bad deeds exactly balanced, then God would always take away one demerit and tip the scale in the person's favour. A variant point of view stated that 'God will incline the scale in the favour of one who performs one commandment.'[4]

The most important aspect of a person's life is the *niyya* or directing of the heart. Paul did not reject that aspect: 'He is not a real Jew who is one outwardly, nor is the true circumcision something eternal and physical. He is a Jew who is one inwardly, and real circumcision is a matter of the heart, spiritual and not literal' (Rom 2:17-21, 18-19). This is precisely the point. Any Jew or Muslim should wholeheartedly agree with that statement; but they would not also draw the conclusion that this meant one should decide *not* to circumcise boy babies, or eat forbidden food, or the other conclusions that Paul went on to draw. One of Jesus' reported sayings was that not one jot or tittle of the Jewish Law was to be broken, and that whoever tried to tell people otherwise would be least in the Kingdom of Heaven! (Mt 5:17-20)[5]

Paul's reinterpretation of the role of Jesus convinced him that God's Revealed Will, the Law, instead of being the outward means by which a person could combat the passions, cultivate inward obedience and hence gain grace and access to God, had become a burden and a prison, and that if Christians clung to it (perhaps as a precaution, not really trusting in the 'saving power' of Jesus) they were still 'slaves' and not of the true faith, or free. They must reject the whole edifice.[6]

If we still retain the phrase 'God's Revealed Will' instead of 'Law' to feel the true force of the meaning, Paul taught that 'no human being will be justified in God's sight by works of God's Revealed Will, since through God's Revealed Will they came to knowledge of sin' ('Rom 3:20). No Jew could ever have uttered that sentence and remained a Jew! And one can imagine what a Muslim would make of it if a Muslim reformer said the same things replacing the word 'Law' with Qur'an! Try a sentence out. It may be hard for a modern Christian to understand the impact and offense caused to Jews by what Paul stated, but it is obvious enough to a Jew or a Muslim.

What did Paul offer in place of God's Revealed Will? He offered an insight already accepted by every true believer: that God's grace *can never be earned*. It can only be given as a gift which humanity must either accept or reject.[7] But to this gift Paul now added a condition, presumably believing that he had the authority to speak on behalf of God. He claimed that the receipt of God's grace was dependant entirely on realising and believing that Jesus was part of the Godhead, and not an emissary *from* God: a prophet or messenger. Only those who accepted the saviour element were 'the elect' (IThess 1:4; I Cor 1:24,26; Rom 9:11f, 11:7).

'Before faith came, we were imprisoned by the Torah, kept under restraint until Christ came, that we might be made justified by faith. But now that faith has come, we are no longer under a custodian, for in Christ Jesus you are all the children of God, through faith [...] If you are Christ's, then you *are* Abraham's offspring, heirs according to promise' (Gal 3:23-29). This sounds acceptable to Christians, because they have been brought up to think in those terms. It does not sound acceptable to a faithful Jew!

When we read the letter to the Galatians, we can only be surprised at the vehemence with which Paul rejected not just the ritual practice of God's Revealed Will, but the whole principle of it. No Jew, or Jewish-minded Christian, could possibly have read that epistle without anger and dismay; and from the point of view of general church policy it was hardly conducive to peaceful relations between Gentile and Jewish converts!

So what was the point of God giving Jews the Torah? The point, said Paul, was that it had the curious function of making sure that all earnest believers were consigned to sin, *so that* they could all be saved later by God's grace in Christ. He saw this as the Divine Plan.[8] Needless to say, for this point of view there were no parallels at all in Rabbinic Judaism. On the contrary, Rabbi Acha, for instance, taught that 'the Laws were given only that man should live through them, not that man should die through them.'[9]

The Rabbis considered that a person was 'saved' so long as the *intention* was to remain within the Covenant, and one truly repented of transgressions. Paul, on the other hand, considered that every person had been 'damned' until the new situation was created which offered salvation. 'To the Rabbis, man's problem was his transgression of the commandments, which could be put right by repentance and forgiveness; for Paul, man's problem was the very fact that he was 'in the flesh', in bondage to the Law, sold under sin, enslaved by the fundamental spirits of the universe, and, in short, dead. The cure was liberation from slavery and death by union with Christ, who had conquered death and sin.'[10]

Just as other Triad saviour-cults common in the region at that time taught of their own incarnate God-sons, Jesus' submission to death was supposed to break the power of sin over humanity in a mystical way, and his blood became humanity's atoning salvation. Those who were 'baptised into Christ' were baptised into his death, buried with him, and raised with him also, to newness of life (Rom 6:3-11). Christians were then discharged from the Law, dead to that which had held them captive, so that they might serve not under the old written code, but in the new life of the spirit.

One can grasp straight away how vital it is in this philosophy that Jesus really did suffer actual physical death: it is the ground of the whole system. Jews and Muslims, in considering this, feel that Trinitarian Christians harbour a misunderstanding of God's true nature, of His love and compassion. If God is Supreme, He can do as He wills. He does not *need* a sacrifice in order to forgive anyone.

> O son of Adam! So long as you call upon Me and ask of Me I shall forgive you for what you have done [...] were you to come to Me with sins as great as the earth itself, and were you then to turn to Me, ascribing no partner to Me, I would forgive you in equal measure. (Hadith in Tirmidhi, Ahmad)

The split-second of turning from Christianity to Islam is the realisation of the truth of the parable of the Prodigal Son. It is to admit that Jesus' death was *not* an atoning sacrifice, that his virgin birth and his ascension did *not* make him divine, and that belief in this theory as the only means of salvation is actually a blasphemous denial of the loving nature of God. It appears, instead, as a suspect desire to form an 'elect' group of people.

Paul anticipated perfectly well the inevitable reaction of sadness, outrage and indignation which would fall upon his head as he preached his new doctrine among the synagogues of the Diaspora. Trinitarian Christians were the new 'spiritual men', and the Jews were condemned as being unspiritual simply because they could not see or accept this. By the time Paul wrote to the Philippians his vehemence against Jews had branded them as 'the dogs, the evil workers, those who mutilate the flesh.' (Phil 3:2)

Paul seems to have become completely antagonistic towards circumcision, although for the previous two and a half centuries since the Maccabean Revolt in 167 BCE, Maccabean and Zealot martyrs had laid down their lives rather than abjure it. [11]

There really is a problem to be solved here that is more than a mere esoteric academic wrangle. If one accepts the accusation that Jews or Muslims believe salvation can *only* be achieved 'legalistically' by performing works of righteousness, then obviously it is easy to understand the conflict between Paul, on the one hand, and Judaism, Jewish Christianity, and Islam on the other. This antithesis has always been presupposed in the larger part of Protestant theology until recently.[12] Jewish and Muslim scholars have naturally been offended as well as saddened by the assumption. Solomon Schechter expressed his feelings in very blunt terms: 'Either the theology of the Rabbis must be wrong, its conception of God debasing, its leading motives materialistic and coarse, its teaching lacking in enthusiasm and spirituality – or the Apostle to the Gentiles is quite unintelligible.'[13] As a Jew, Schechter naturally took the latter view.

Judaism, as a historically developed religion, can certainly be criticised from various points of view. Jewish reformers and thinkers have themselves done this, as did the Prophet of Islam. But Paul's argument was irrelevant, his abuse unmerited, and his conception of that which he was attacking was strangely inaccurate.

Paul offered the Jews an atonement for which they felt no need, based on a theory whose premises they denied, involving a stereotype of their own religion which they repudiated. They saw the moral corruption of the Gentile world as clearly as Paul did, but could see no reason why they should adopt his theory with respect to it: for they considered it to be nothing more than a speculation of his own. The proffered 'deliverance' was as unreal to them as the alleged universal bondage under sin.

It is a sobering realisation that the Christian churches received a dangerously distorted view of Judaism at the hands of a Diaspora Jew who had become alienated from the faith ideas of his fathers, a view which ignored the idea of the Covenant as a sanctifying ordinance, and which presented Judaism as no more than ethical self-justification and ritual exhibition.

Still more astounding is the fact that Trinitarian theology throughout Christian history has assumed that Paul was unacceptable to the Jews because the Jews were completely insensitive to his ideas! Its authors never asked whether it might not be due to the fact that Paul simply misrepresented Jewish theology. This, of course, leads to yet another knot of problems. How could it have been possible for a Pharisee of Paul's zeal to have misinterpreted Jewish theology so categorically? This query can only lead us, in our franker moments, to challenge his integrity and motivation.

Paul's train of thought sprang from his conviction that God *had* presented humanity with a saviour. In His wisdom, He had withheld full salvation for countless millennia. If God had done this, then although it had not previously been recognised, it *must* have meant that all other previous and possible methods of salvation were lethally inadequate.

'If righteousness could have come through the Torah, then Christ died for nothing.' (Gal 2:21) This was his whole point, and this solitary sentence sums up the reason for the continuing vehemence of Christian resistance to Jewish and Muslim theology. Obviously Paul could not allow that Christ had died in vain, or, as Muslims would maintain, that he may not have suffered crucifixion at all.

Paul admits it himself, quite bluntly. 'If there is no resurrection of the dead, then Christ has not been raised; if Christ has not been raised, then our preaching is in vain and your faith is in vain. We are even found to be misinterpreting God, because we testified of God that he raised Christ, whom he did not raise if it is true that the dead are not raised. [...] If Christ had not been raised then your faith is futile, and you are still in your sins' (Corinthians 15:13-17).

To a Muslim, a 'resurrection' of Jesus would not prove his divinity, or that he was God Incarnate. The raising of the dead to life as a concept was a good deal more believable in the time of Jesus than it seems to be today: Jesus himself raised three people: Jairus' daughter, who had just died (Mk 5:35-43, Lk 8:49-56); the son of a widow at Nain, who was being carried in procession to his grave at the time (Lk 11:11-17); and Lazarus, who had been dead for four days (Jn 11:1-44). When John the Baptist's messengers were sent to see if Jesus confirmed his messiahship, they were told to report back to John that they had themselves seen with their own eyes the dead being raised up (Mt 11:5). Neither was it anything new: in Old Testament times 'women received their dead by resurrection' (Heb 11:35), the best known case being that of Elijah, who prayed for a widow's son and restored him to life (I Kings 17:17-24).

The 'resurrection' of Jesus would not, therefore, make him unique: special, yes, but not divine. The first Christians assumed he had been *raised by God,* and not that he *was* God. For example, Stephen is said to have proclaimed: 'People of Israel, hear these words! Jesus of Nazareth, a *man* attested to you by God with mighty words and wonders which God did through him in your midst, as you yourselves know – this Jesus, delivered up according to the definite foreknowledge and plan of God, you crucified and killed by the hands of lawless men. But God raised him up, having loosed the pangs of death, because it was not possible for him to be held by it. (Acts 2:22-24)

He then goes on to quote Psalm 16:8-11: 'I keep the Lord God always before me; because He is at my right hand, I shall not be moved. Therefore my heart is glad, and my soul rejoices; my body also dwells secure, for You do not give me up to Sheol, or let your godly one see the Pit. You show me the path of life; in Your presence there is fulness of joy, in Your right hand are pleasures for evermore.'

The author of Acts uses this passage to suggest that the Psalmist, being a prophet, had foreseen the resurrection of Jesus. However, this text does not imply the divinity of the resurrected person. If someone you knew died and then was resurrected, you might well revise your ideas on science or the finality of death, but you probably would not conclude that unbeknown to you, your acquaintance had been divine, born as a 'son' of God, and destined to 'save all those who believed in his resurrection'.[14]

Muslims feel that the argument over whether or not the resurrection of Jesus' body took place has no bearing on whether or not there is life after death, or on our fate after death. Neither does it influence whether or not *we* are 'still in our sins'. Nor does it affect the concept of the survival of our *souls* after the deaths of our bodies. It is patently not true that if Christ was not raised, the faith of other people would be futile.

Paul's whole line of argument rested solely upon accepting his premises. Thus he took the shattering step that divided the Christian from the Jew, triggered centuries of bitter anti-Semitism, and opened the door to 'empartnering God': to *shirk*.[15]

Chapter Eight

THE GOAT FOR AZAZEL

SUCH WAS THE message preached by Paul, and the Jewish-Christians would have none of it. They simply did not accept the premises of his argument. They could see that Paul's whole theory was based on two ideas they rejected: firstly, that the message Jesus taught was very different from God's Will as expressed in the Torah, so that they should 'accept Jesus' rather than the Torah, and secondly that they should accept a misinterpretation of the Jewish religion.

Mercy bestowed freely as a gift of God's grace had always been an essential part of Judaism, which stressed that God, in His infinite love and compassion, would always receive even the most objectionable sinners, so long as they repented. God is not a 'legalist'. 'If a man is wicked all his life and repents at the end, he will be saved.'[1] The harbouring of a good intention would be enough for God to welcome any penitent back into the Covenant Bond.

In fact, Jesus said that because of God's compassion there would be *more joy* in heaven over one sinner that repented than over ninety-nine just people who did not need to repent. (Lk 15:7,10) Jesus' most famous of parables, the Prodigal Son (Lk 15:11-32) concerns the return of the wretched youth to his father, after realising his sin and truly repenting of his situation. 'While he was yet *at a distance*, his father saw him coming and had compassion, and ran and embraced him and kissed him.' The boy tries to apologise, but the father is already rejoicing. 'This my son was dead; he is alive again!'

Unfortunately, even as Jesus told the story, he was aware of well-meaning and pious people in his own audience who could not imitate the open arms of God for the returning sinner. The bad boy had a 'good' elder brother, who refused to accept him and share the father's joy.

Jesus and the Pharisees both taught that not only was God *always* ready to forgive the penitent, but that sins against God were actually more easily forgiven than sins against one's fellow men, since those required proper restitution in human terms, and that was much harder to achieve. This is also taught in Islam. God will only accept the repentance of a person who has offended another person *once he has appeased the human brother.* [2]

As Jesus said, in connection with Temple offerings: 'If you are before the altar of God and there you remember that you have offended someone, leave your gift and go! First be reconciled to your brother, then you may come and make your gift to God.' (Mt 5:24)

If the sin that needed penitence was between the sinner and God alone, God was ever waiting with open arms to receive the lost sheep or the prodigal son. The beautiful mediaeval poem of Jehuda HaLevi expressed God's love thus:

> Longing, I sought Thy presence,
> Lord, with my whole heart did I call and pray;
> And going out towards Thee,
> I found Thee coming to me on the way.

In Islam there are many moving *hadith qudsi* [3] where God expresses the same generous love and will to forgive.

> I am with him when he makes mention of Me. If he draws near to Me a hand's span, I draw near to him an arm's length. (Hadith Qudsi)

> A man said of another: 'By God, God will never forgive him!' But Almighty God said: 'Who is this who swears by Me that I will never forgive a man? Truly I have forgiven him already.' (Hadith Qudsi)

In other words, the idea that humanity suffered from the inescapable taint of Original Sin and the need for an atoning saviour was simply not a part of Judaism, and has never been a part of Islam. In fact, both faiths regard the idea that one person could 'buy off' the sins of another as unjust, if not absurd. [4]

The Qur'an is quite specific on the matter.

> One burdened soul shall not bear the burdens of another. And even if the heavy-laden soul cry out for its burden to be carried, not one part of it shall be carried, not even by the next of kin. (35:18)

> Guard yourselves against the Day when one soul shall not avail another, nor shall compensation be accepted from another, nor shall intercession profit, nor shall anyone be helped. (2:123, see also 82:19, 41:46, 45:15)

The point is that all who are *muslim* in the true sense of the word (sub-mitted to God) cannot consider for one moment that God can possibly be made *more* merciful by taking the life of some innocent creature. That is a notion Jews and Muslims find blasphemous. The way to be redeemed is to repent, and then cease to do evil, and to do well.

As a scribe said to Jesus on the Day of Questions in Holy Week: 'To love the Lord your God with all your heart, soul, mind and strength is worth more than all offerings and sacrifices.'[5] When Jesus saw that he answered wisely, he agreed and commended him as being 'not far from the Kingdom of Heaven.'

The ritual of sacrifice had become the prerogative of priests. In the earli-est times, any individual might feel the urge to make a ritual slaughter and share the meat in a communal meal, and it was thought proper for this to take place. It particularly applied to heads of households, although other individuals might from time to time perform sacrifices for themselves. The usual reasons were thank-offerings, when the person had entreated God to do something or other and the result had taken place, or sin-offerings, when the person had done something wrong and felt the need to make expiation before a punishment descended.

In ancient times, people usually sacrificed animals, and occasionally other people. Archaeologists have unearthed infants sacrificed to 'bless' the foun-dations of houses and city walls. The notion that the firstborn that opened the womb was sacred to God was also widespread: sometimes the infant was killed; more frequently a redeeming price was paid in money, produce or animal blood.

It did not take long before the accompanying idea of *priesthood* arose: ser-vants of particular shrines whose sole business it was to know how to per-form the rituals correctly, and see to it that the sacrifices were valid. Priests who enjoyed power found it easy to create more and more conditions, rules, paraphernalia. The more influential the notion of priesthood, the more the idea of the personal moral responsibility of individuals receded.[6]

The irony was that the priests came to be regarded as the 'servants of God', the people in the know, the select few with the expertise; whereas authentic Judaism, as taught by all the Hebrew prophets who received direct messages from God, tried to show how the system of priesthood was flawed.

That the entire notion of vicarious sacrifice had already been rejected in the Jewish prophetic tradition is a point usually passed over in silence by

Trinitarian Christians. Yet it is of manifest significance to the arguments about the role of Jesus.

The prophets always denounced as a travesty of Divine Love the notion that God would be appeased by token animal sacrifice. We have, for example, the famous words God spoke through the prophet Hosea: 'I desire steadfast love and not sacrifice, the knowledge of God rather than burnt offerings.' (Hosea 6:6.)

Similarly, God revealed through the prophet Amos: 'I hate, I despise your feasts, I take no delight in your solemn assemblies. Even though you offer Me your burnt offerings and cereal offerings, I will not accept them; and the peace offerings of your fattened beasts, I will not look upon them. Take away from Me the noise of your songs; I will not listen to the melody of your harps. But let justice roll down like waters, and righteousness like an ever-flowing stream!' (Amos 5:18-24.)

A revelation through Isaiah declared: 'To what purpose is the multitude of your sacrifices to me? I have had enough of burnt-offerings of rams, and the fat of fed beasts; I do not delight in the blood of bullocks or lambs or he-goats. When you appear before Me, who requires of you this trampling of My courts? Bring no more vain offerings; incense is an abomination to Me. New moon and Sabbath and the calling of assemblies My soul hates; they have become a burden to Me, I am weary of bearing them. Even though you make many prayers, I will not listen; your hands are full of blood. Wash yourselves; make yourselves clean; remove the evil of your doings from before My eyes; cease to do evil, learn to do good; seek justice, correct oppression, defend the fatherless, plead for the widow!' (Isaiah 1:11-1.)

The same God, speaking through the prophet Muhammad, proclaimed: 'Neither the flesh of the animals of your sacrifice nor their blood reaches God; it is your righteousness that reaches Him.' (Sura 22:37.)

It simply will not do for Christians to shrug off these teachings as no longer relevant after the coming of Jesus. The Gospels themselves reveal that Jesus' opinion on the subject was entirely in harmony with the prophetic line: 'Go and learn what this means: "I desire mercy and not sacrifice". For I came not to call the righteous, but sinners to repentance.' (Mt 9:13, see also Mt 12:7.)

Now, Jews, Jesus and Muslims all did and do take part in sacrifices. We do not have a Gospel pen-portrait of Jesus actually wielding a sacrificial knife, but he did eat the Passover meal each year, and the roast lamb on the table was lamb that had been chosen and sacrificed for the household on the after-noon of Nisan 14, the afternoon before the full moon. The meat Jesus ate at his Last Supper was presumably just such a lamb.

But the true point of these sacrifices for Jews, Jesus and Muslims, is not the propitiation of higher powers; it is a symbol of thanksgiving by sharing meat with fellow-people. No-one can seriously suppose that meat or blood is acceptable to God! It was a pagan fancy to reduce the Ineffable One to the level of a malicious entity that could be appeased or bribed by blood sacrifices. But God *does* accept the sacrifice of our hearts, and the visible institution of a special meal is a symbol of such an offer. A *symbol*, not the cause.

This is the important principle for Trinitarians to grasp. The death of Jesus as a martyr for God's cause, or as a sacrifice because of the sins of ignorant humanity, may well be accepted as such a symbol, but not as the *cause* of God's forgiveness of us.

It is time for Christians to reconsider the original meaning of the Eucharist, or Last Supper Meal. It is now notable for its references to 'eat-ing the flesh' and 'drinking the blood' of Christ. It is inconceivable that a gathering of Jews could, completely unprepared, calmly drink wine that was identified with blood.[7] Drinking blood was strictly prohibited (Leviticus 17:10-14). Although Christians these days may automatically think of the atoning sacrifice of Christ's body and blood, this is not likely to have been the allegory the real Jesus intended.[8]

On the other hand, the consumption of blood *was* one of the key cere-monies of a welter of Hellenistic mystery cults that had as their goal the ulti-mate conquest of death. This seems to be precisely what Paul had in mind: he announced in his letters that the main aim for Christians should be to enter the tomb with Jesus, or to be crucified with Christ (see I Cor 15:54-57; Gal 2:20). It is a well-known fact that devotees of the Divine Son in the Triads (for example, Mithraism) did drink blood from sacrifices that repre-sented the body of their 'lord'; but such a notion was *absolutely forbidden* in a Palestinian Jewish milieu. It must be highly doubtful that Jesus could have promoted such matters as consuming blood, even if only symbolically, and still have been a popular leader with the people of Palestine.

What is far more likely is that Jesus celebrated himself and his followers entering into their Way by eating and drinking together, and that he used the symbolism of blood poured out in sacrifice (but certainly not drunk). It is perhaps significant that the L source of Luke indicates there were *two* cups. It seems that the two separate ideas became fused at an early stage, and the 'blood pouring' of sacrifice became predominant over the shared fellowship of those in the Kingdom of God, even though reportedly Jesus spoke of the 'cup of the Covenant'.

Robert Eisler[9] points out the detail that at the Passover meal a piece of unleavened bread called the *afikomen* was broken off the loaf and put aside, and then shared at the end. The word apparently meant 'he who comes', and was a reference to the expected Prophet or Messiah. Jesus' actions represented the creation of a new community, and were not primarily a comment on the atoning significance of his death, but on the significance of what God would do as a *result* of his death.

The bread was broken so that the 'body of Christ' might be represented not in the person of Jesus himself, but in the persons of those who believed in him and followed him. This is the concept known in Islam as *Umma*.

What Jesus did at the Last Supper was a prophetic action. It was surely not blood-drinking but the concept of 'brotherhood' or community, or fellowship that was really intended at that meal: the sharing of a common loaf, common meal and common cup. The followers of Jesus were to be a united body. The idea of a sacramental meal signifying a mystical sharing in Jesus' sacrifice through drinking his blood was a pagan idea that cannot have figured in the imagination of anyone present.

Trinitarian Christianity based its entire doctrine on the necessity for the crucifixion of Jesus. It is meaningless without it. Jesus lived only that he might meet death on the cross and be buried, and on the third day rise again from the dead. Afterwards he was taken bodily up to Heaven. This whole framework is necessary for the theological doctrines of blood sacrifice and vicarious atonement for sins. It is in direct opposition to the teaching of all the prophets, including Jesus and Muhammad, and the revelation of the Qur'an which completes and sets the seal on all previous prophecy.

From a purely monotheistic perspective, the life and death of Jesus cannot *cause* any change in God's already perfect mercy and compassion; no person's eternal future can be altered or 'saved' by believing in the efficacy of the sacrifice of another person. What must be altered is the sinner's attitude to life and way of life.

It was not impossible, of course, for a Jewish-Christian to believe that Jesus' martyrdom, his perceived death on the cross, was a sacrifice, but only

in a symbolic sense. The sin-offering of the lamb at the Temple was the traditional ritual symbol of redemption: the outward and visible sign of an
inward and spiritual change of heart, but it did not *cause* the change. God
was not being 'bought off' by the blood of lambs, nor were people's hearts
washed clean by the flow. On the contrary, in making the symbolic gesture
worshippers were *already aware* of the offer of God's benevolent love and
mercy, and the fact that they were unworthy to receive God's grace. Yet they
did accept it, and were proud to accept it, confident that God had forgiven
them, truly relieved them of their burden of sin and guilt, and had given
them the opportunity of a new beginning.

The Jewish-Christian could accept and understand the cross as an impressive example of atoning symbolism, but would never agree that Christ's
sacrifice *caused* the propitiation of God, or was in any way able to 'satisfy'
Divine justice.

Most Christians, of course, do not realise that the major festival in the
Jewish calendar for the symbolic wiping-away of sin is actually *not* the
Passover in the spring (which celebrates the Exodus from Egypt combined
with an early harvest festival), but the Day of Atonement in the autumn. The
Epistle to the Hebrews correctly picks this up, emphasising the sin-offering
of the goat to Azazel on the Day of Atonement rather than the redemption-
offering lamb on the Day of Passover. Christians would obviously prefer the
Passover lamb symbolism, commemorating the time of Exodus when a lamb
was slaughtered so that the firstborn child might live and the angel of death
'pass over' the household. In the Atonement symbolism, the Goat was
released into the desert *alive*.[10]

The Day of Atonement was the only day in the year when the High Priest was
allowed to enter the Holy of Holies in the Temple, the inner sanctum, to stand
before God, pronounce His name, and pray for the people. He took two goats,

> one for the Lord and the other for Azazel [...] and the goat on which the lot fell for
> Azazel shall be presented alive before the Lord to make atonement over it, that it may
> be sent away into the wilderness. [...] And Aaron shall lay both hands upon the head of
> the live goat, and confess over him all the iniquities of the people of Israel, all their sins;
> and he shall put them upon the head of the goat and send him away into the wilderness.
> [...] The goat shall bear all their iniquities upon him to a solitary land [...][11]

Hebrews 9:11-22 speaks of Christ as the 'High Priest of the good things to
come', entering the Holy Place not with the blood of goats but his own blood,

thus securing an eternal redemption. The old atonement sacrifices had been offered year after year (Heb 10:1); if it had been possible for them to have made perfect those who drew near, then surely they would have ceased to be offered by now! How true, all Jews and Muslims would agree.

However instead of concluding (as the prophets had done) that priestly jargon and ritual rhetoric were only symbolic and not efficacious as a kind of magic, the author of the epistle tries to show how the sacrifice of Jesus was different, because it was 'once and for all': 'When Christ had offered for all time a single sacrifice for sins [...] by a single offering he has perfected for all times those who are sacrificed'! [12]

But if Jesus had been some kind of divine avatar, then what are we to make of his agony in Gethsemane? To whom was he praying so desperately, in his agony of loneliness? To himself? And to whom did he submit? To himself? How are we to explain his suffering mentality, and his effort of will and discipline to submit?

> Many martyrs have gone to their deaths without undergoing such agony and without shrinking from what lay ahead of them. Are we to think that the Blessed Master was less heroic than they? [...] To accept the Pauline view of the Atonement is not only an insult to the Divine Love of God, but to Jesus himself, for it suggests that he shrank from accomplishing the world's salvation at the cost of a few hours of suffering, while knowing full well that he would come right in less than three days! [13]

The logic of this is inescapable. And there is a second inescapable point for Trinitarians to grapple with: the death of Jesus clearly did *not* accomplish the redemption of the world: a casual glance at the present state of it, two millennia on, makes that quite obvious. Perhaps the brute fact of his physical crucifixion, unpleasant death though it was, should not be interpreted in terms of Passover symbolism at all (the lamb that died so that you might live, as Trinitarians would like to have it), but in the symbolism of the Azazel goat, which is acceptable to both Jews and Muslims.

In that symbolism, Jesus' submission to God, even though it meant his death, was a healing process whereby he showed how all fear of evil elements and influences could be transmuted by confidence in the Divine Power, even death itself. He believed absolutely in God and life after death, he was a human being who was so complete a Muslim, so completely submitted and devoted to the will of God, that he was prepared to 'put his money where his mouth was'. His personal burden was therefore far more stupendous and meaningful than that of a divine being going through some sort of ritual sham. Although it was human nature to shrink from the ordeal, he was prepared to enter the horror of the wilderness of death and face it, if that was what God required of him, trusting in life after death.

People would not be 'saved' by him as if by magic: they would still have their own 'crosses to bear' but the sting of death would be removed. They were not 'redeemed', but led to face for themselves that crunch choice of whether they really believed in God and the afterlife, or not. How they believed would alter how they lived.

Whatever it was people shrank from, whatever they most loathed or abhorred, they could benefit from the *example* of Jesus; they could know that they were no longer alone in their loneliness and fear, for Jesus had trodden the path before them and illumined it. In the extreme darkness one could find the Light; and the person who followed that light would no longer walk in darkness but would have the light of life.

The At-One-ment between a person and God would then be in *living* the final result of the removal of this barrier: the confidence that one's soul is seen and known by God its Creator, that death is but a passing through a door, that one's weakness and human frailty is understood and forgiven so long as the heart is genuine in its desire to live in the best way, following the example of the Messengers. Now *that* makes sense.

Chapter Nine

COVENANT, CIRCUMCISION AND COOKERY

IT WAS PAUL'S experience of a vision and not the teaching of the Messiah Jesus that gave birth to the project of separating Christianity from Judaism.[1] The result of this encounter was that within a matter of months after his disappearance the faith Jesus taught began to be changed into something else.

Rather surprisingly, once Paul the foe of Christianity had been converted he did not go back to Jerusalem to meet, learn from, or even apologise to the Apostles, as one might have expected; instead, he went away to Arabia, then came back again to Damascus (Galatians 1:17). Only after three years did he return to Jerusalem, where he spent a mere fifteen days with Peter, and had an encounter with James. He did not meet any of the other Apostles, and he insists at this point, as if with some pride, that 'he is not lying in this matter'.[2]

Before very long Paul became the author of writings which are accepted today by Christians as part of their holy scriptures, in spite of the fact that they flatly contradict some of the teachings of Jesus.

This is nothing less than astonishing, because it suggests that if Paul was right, then the Master had been at fault, and that in selecting his disciples he had chosen the wrong individuals. If Paul's 'Gospel', received in a flash by a revelation, was all that was needed, a complete nonsense is made of the earthly life of Jesus, and of his careful and gentle training of his beloved friends. Christians who chose to follow Paul accepted as their mentor one who had not only never seen Jesus, but who actually rejected the teachings of those who had known him best. Our range of New Testament documents speak for themselves: Peter the Apostle, Barnabas (Paul's companion and his 'superior' on his first missionary journeys), and the direct family of Jesus led by James, all fade into obscurity behind the exciting career of Paul of Tarsus.

Luke's 'Book of Acts' gives a very smooth account of Paul's mission, with all the dramatic conflicts between himself and the Jerusalem elders toned down, with only very veiled hints to indicate the scale of the rift he was causing. But when we read Paul's letters we learn a very different story, for they reveal that the controversy with Jewish-Christians was in fact extremely heated.[3] Paul wrote on one occasion: 'If any man preaches to you a Gospel other than that you received from me, let him be cursed!' (Gal 1:9) It appears that he had James and Peter in mind.

In fact, throughout Acts the conflict between the Jewish Christians and Paul's new Gentile Christians is minimized, and the decree given in Acts 15 sees the end of it; yet Paul's letters show that the antagonism continued to rage for many years.

Paul was certainly not trained by the Jerusalem Apostles. After his very brief meeting with Peter and James, Paul went north to Syria and Cilicia, and worked on his own there for fourteen years, a fact not realised by many Christians (Gal 2:1). During this time the Christians of Judaea kept tabs on him, with growing anxiety. Investigators (called 'spies' by Paul) were sent from the Jerusalem headquarters to report on his activities.[4]

The controversies between Paul and the Jerusalem elders were not just a matter of differences of opinion, but were of enormous consequence. In the light of the way Trinitarian Christianity developed, they involved matters of the gravest significance for world history. Two of the most demanding requests made by God of all faithful Jews were the circumcision of males as the 'sign of the covenant', and ritual purity: both in physical purity and in careful regulation of what foods passed the lips. If Christianity was ever to break away from Judaism, it was necessary to break the power of these two laws.

Paul, in rejecting the necessity of keeping Torah, broke both of them. When the Jerusalem elders realised this, they knew they would have to confront Paul and 're-educate' him. So Paul, very worried lest his mission should be curtailed, which would have been embarrassing to say the least, finally 'received the revelation' that he should make the journey back to Jerusalem, with his Greek friend and convert Titus, in order to defend himself (Gal 2:2).

The Council that was convened proved to be the turning-point in the history of the New Church. Titus became the test case for all those who had been admitted to Christianity without first undergoing the rite of circumcision. Most Christians today have probably never given the matter much thought, but circumcision was one of the fundamental commandments of God to His people, the very sign of the believer. Jesus, of course, and all his disciples had been circumcised, and there is not a hint anywhere that he thought the practice unnecessary. Jewish and Muslim males are still circumcised, in accordance with this law, to this day.

> This is my covenant which you shall keep, you and your descendants after you throughout their generations [...] every male among you shall be circumcised. You shall be circumcised in the flesh of your foreskins, and it shall be a sign of the covenant between Me and you. He that is eight days old among you shall be circumcised; every male throughout your generations, whether born in your house, or bought with your money from any foreigner who is not of your offspring, shall be circumcised. So shall My covenant be in your flesh an everlasting covenant. Any uncircumcised male who is not circumcised in the flesh of his foreskin shall be cut off from his people; he has broken My covenant. (Genesis 17:9-14)

The commandment could hardly be clearer.

Although Abraham was an old man when he received the command, he circumcised himself that same day, and his sons, and all his household, and so it has been in Jewish and Muslim households to this day. To set aside the commandment to circumcise was a serious matter indeed: it meant that a follower of Jesus believed that Jesus really had taught that this was permissible, and that he really had overruled the fundamental duties of Torah.

It is the same story with the purification after defilement and before prayer, and the avoidance of inner pollution by eating pork and other unclean foods. This was regarded as a most serious matter, for the stuffs that were eaten converted into the actual flesh of the body of the eater. Literally, we are what we eat, and God had specifically ordered that no follower of His should eat pork and certain other foods. If Christians could only pause in their missionary zeal that sees their faith as categorically superior to everyone else's and consider the treatment of the commands of God from the point of view of Jew or Muslim, they might begin to realise, perhaps with a touch of embarrassment, why it is that they make so few converts from those faiths!

Although Jesus was circumcised himself, and pork never touched his lips, the end of Matthew's Gospel suggests that Jesus gave clear indications that they were to preach to all nations and baptise everyone indiscriminately (Mt 28:19). If that command really was his, it is amazing that the Apostles should have hesitated to eat at the tables of Gentiles, or to baptise Gentile converts. Yet Acts reveals that they did so hesitate, and were reluctant to admit into the fellowship of the Keepers any who were not willing to make the sacrifices it demanded. Surely they would never have taken this stance if Jesus had indicated that circumcision, a rather serious step for an adult male, was not necessary? Or that it was perfectly all right to eat the unrestricted Gentile diet?

According to Paul's letter to the Galatians, the Jerusalem Council meeting was informal, and everything worked out to his entire satisfaction. James,[5] Peter and John, the 'pillars of the Church', gave him permission to go back and preach freely to the Gentiles, and forget all about circumcision. The only request made of him was that he should 'remember the poor', which he was very eager to do.[6]

There was no question of Titus being circumcised. In fact, Paul declared triumphantly that to those 'false brothers secretly brought in, who slipped in to spy out our freedom which we have in Christ Jesus, that they might bring us into bondage – to them we did not yield submission even for a moment!' (Gal 2:4-5).

Paul also remarked in his letter that he was able to rebuke even one so exalted as Peter, because after the latter had taken the step of eating with the Gentiles at Antioch (as Paul did), he and Barnabas had then gone back to their original stance against this freedom when James' representatives arrived (Gal 2:12-13).

Yet the Acts version has nothing about Peter deciding to obey the 'men from James' rather than his 'heavenly voice'. It states rather that Peter had relaxed his food-laws specifically because he had heard a voice when he fell into a trance during a midday prayer. At first Peter was not at all happy at what the voice suggested, and actually protested that he had 'never eaten anything unclean' (Acts 10:9-16), but the voice reassured him, and Peter was then content to eat Gentile food; and, according to Acts, explained it all successfully to James' emissaries, who all 'glorified God' (Acts 11:18).

Paul's letters let slip the real battle. Paul, who did not regard himself as in any way inferior to Jesus' beloved friends (2 Corinthians 11:5, 12:11), states proudly that he did not hesitate to withstand Peter to his face. Since nearly everything in the New Testament is now written from Paul's standpoint, there is very little to show the scandal of this opposition to the Apostles. Paul is represented as a generous, Christ-like man, who was willing to admit Gentiles into the Christian fellowship, whereas Peter and James remained intractable, old-fashioned and stubborn.

The Acts account specifically states that Paul and Barnabas were *summoned* to the highly important Council meeting convened in Jerusalem because the men sent from James insisted that all converts *should* be circumcised before being admitted into the Church, and Paul had refused to go along with this.

In other words, James, as successor to Jesus, had laid down the specific condition that all Christians *should* be Jews. He was backed by the influential number of Pharisees among the believers (Acts 15:5). These Pharisees were no unimportant fringe group of extremists, but had far more influence than Paul, whom they presumably suspected of being at best a maverick and at worst a renegade, who claimed to have joined the movement but had never accepted spiritual training by those who had been trained by Jesus himself.[7]

Eventually, according to Acts, after Peter spoke in Paul's defence, and the success of Paul's ministry was recounted, James gave in and suggested the compromise situation which was finally accepted by the Assembly. The argument ran along the lines that the record of Paul's work was impressive, and no-one could deny the activity of the Holy Spirit. Therefore, in the compromise, circumcision was no longer demanded of Gentile converts, but an obedience to the laws of the old Noachide Covenant was. This Covenant involved three food laws and one moral one: abstinence from meat which had been sacrificed to idols, from blood, from what had been strangled, and from unchastity (Acts 15:20,29).

The obvious differences between the two accounts have led scholars to pose the question of whether or not Acts really is reliable as a historical document. Since Luke, universally accepted as the author of Acts, was not actually involved in the meetings at Jerusalem, whereas Paul was, one would naturally assume that Paul's own version in his letters would be more reliable as history. If so, Luke's version in Acts is grossly inaccurate. Yet, on other grounds, many scholars place a great deal of confidence in it. A choice must be made here: if the Acts version *is* reliable, it must mean that Paul was distorting the truth in his epistle. Not wishing to make Paul a deliberate liar, we are obliged to suggest that either Luke's version in Acts is a complete misinterpretation, or that the Jerusalem visit referred to in Galatians cannot have been the same occasion as that described in Acts 15.[8]

The vacillation of Paul and Barnabas mentioned in Gal 2:11-14 would fit better if it happened *before the Council took place*. 'When Cephas came to Antioch,' he said, 'I opposed him to his face, because he stood condemned. For before certain men came from James, he ate with the Gentiles; but when they came he drew back and separated himself, fearing the circumcision party. And with him the rest of the Jews acted insincerely, so that even Barnabas was carried away by their insincerity.' If Gal 2 and Acts 15 are the same event, it does seem very strange after his strong speech in Acts 15:7-10 that Peter should have acted as weakly as he did in Gal 2:12, backing down under pressure from James.

According to Acts 15, Peter had stated that 'God gave [the Gentiles] the Holy Spirit just as He made no distinction between us and them, but cleansed their hearts by faith. Now, why do you make a trial of God by putting a yoke upon the neck of the disciples which neither our fathers nor we have been able to bear?' Yet, in Gal 2, as soon as 'men from James' criticised Peter for eating with the Gentiles he backed down. This would seem very inconsistent. One must also wonder why the Decrees of Acts 15 were not even mentioned in Gal 2 to convince Peter. One would have thought that the quarrel that arose in Antioch between Peter and Paul over table-fellowship with the Gentiles would have been impossible after the resolution had been passed. Was it deliberately omitted, or does this indicate that the visit referred to in Galatians was one that took place prior to the Council?

The primeval laws mentioned at the Council had been intended as the basis for salvation for the rest of humanity outside Israel, applicable to all the sons of Noah and their descendants, and not just to the Shemites (later the Jews). These are stated in the Talmud[9], and entail the commandments not to worship idols, not to blaspheme against the Name of God, to establish courts of justice, not to kill, not to commit adultery, not to steal, and not to eat flesh cut from a living animal. A second list prohibited idolatry, adultery, murder, robbery, eating flesh cut from a living animal, the emasculation of animals, and mating animals of different species. If a man repented of idolatry and accepted these laws, he became *ger-Tosheb*, a resident alien or a 'stranger within the gates', and was entitled to as much care and protection under Jewish Law as a true Jew. Of course, if a person was willing to abandon his Gentile status altogether, he could become a proselyte. So in other words, it looks as if a face-saving solution was being offered to Paul at the Council: the Gentile Christians could become 'associate' Jews.

According to Acts, letters were then sent out to the churches to explain these rulings, while Barnabas and Paul returned to Antioch, apparently quite satisfied. One can only puzzle over the strange fact that when Paul then wrote to the Corinthians on the very subjects under debate, he did not refer to the Decree at all.

The Council's attitude, in which Hebrew Christians rather reluctantly decided to allow Gentile converts to enter the movement, although they still regarded them as no more than associate members, would not satisfy Paul's aims. Paul essentially demanded Israelite citizenship for all Gentile Christians on the terms of their faith in Jesus as the Son of God. Circumcision and the Law were to be replaced by baptism and the 'gifts of the Spirit'.

Shortly after this, Barnabas and Paul split up, supposedly over the issue of whether or not Barnabas' nephew John Mark[10] should accompany them. Barnabas and Mark went to Cyprus, and no further mention is made of them in the Book of Acts.

As far as Trinitarian Christians are concerned, this was, of course, Paul's great contribution and triumph. To use the language of Trinitarian enthusiasm, without the genius of his insight the Mother-Church might simply have remained just another sect of Judaism, and the massive edifice of Christendom might never have been. A Jew or Muslim might more cynically, and sadly, rephrase this: 'without the tragedy of Paul's sudden insight into "mystery religion" theology, the Mother-Church might have reformed Judaism into a new spirituality'. The founders could have built on the admiration common in the Roman world for the high standards of ethical monotheism, in order to establish it as the true, universal world-faith.

Muslims believe that this is indeed what Jesus' mission actually had been. Like the great prophets before him, he was a true and humble Messenger from the One Almighty God, but the error of incarnationism that swept in from converts not prepared to adjust the discipline of their daily lives overwhelmed the Church and adulterated its *islam*!

In making Christianity available to non-Jews, Paul's significance must never be underestimated. The New Testament would be much the poorer without some of those sublime passages in the epistles that many Christians treasure as much as they do the words of Christ. But surely in this present age, when scholarly literature about the religious atmosphere of the time is readily available, has the moment not come to consider seriously the painful but inescapable question of whether Paul's theology was what Jesus actually taught?

In the sixth century after Jesus a new prophet arose, one aspect of whose message was directly intended to make Christians think again about the direction in which they had been led. Vast numbers of Christians who were still hesitant about rejecting the laws of God as revealed to the earlier prophets gave up the puzzling Trinitarian theology and returned enthusiastically to the original path. The outpost of Western Europe still clung to the 'Constantinian Christianity' of the Nicene Creed, but North Africa and the

East, and the great believing cities of Alexandria, Antioch, and Jerusalem itself, reverted to Islam with a rapidity and enthusiasm that is hardly surprising.

Chapter Ten

PAUL OR JAMES?

Paul's doctrine of justification by faith in Jesus alone had multiple effects. It made Paul the implacable enemy of the Jewish people who refused to accept the premises of his argument. It brought him under the suspicion of many of the Christians of his day, and made him to a certain extent an outsider. And ultimately and most importantly it caused the severance of Christianity from Judaism and gave it its first real independent theological basis.

Paul's key innovation was that he gave the Gentile Church certain principles of belief that were capable of welding it into a unified whole and enabled it to amputate itself from its powerful parent. There were plenty of ears ready to hear in the Mediterranean world, where esoteric mystery religions satisfied deep-seated spiritual tendencies in local populations. But should Paul have taken this bold step? Again, we must ask ourselves whether the time has now arrived when the Church should be more frank abouts its sources and methods. It should address the problem of whether its teaching ought to be based on the theology Paul taught after Jesus' death rather than the message taught by Jesus in his lifetime.

Those who have grown up in an atmosphere of love and respect for Paul, the heroic and indefatigable missionary, may find this implied contrast between these two sorts of Christianity threatening. At worst, they regard the comparison as an invention of the liberal scholarship of the nineteenth century, seen as the Trojan horse of scepticism and outright secularity.

Central to our reflections should be the fact that a very large number of people did not love Jesus from a distance, as we do, but had walked with him and ate with him, worshipped with him, heard him laugh and watched him cry. One of the most important of those intimate companions became the leader of all the disciples, and the organiser of the first Christian headquarters at Jerusalem.

That person was not Peter or John, but James: not the Apostle James bar Zebedes but none other than Jesus' brother.[1]

Despite his obvious significance, a search through the Gospels reveals a very scant mention of him, confined to a few ambiguous and faintly hostile verses.[2] Paul's letters acknowledge the existence of James, but he is represented as an almost implacable obstacle to the 'true' Christian faith. We are surely obliged to seek reasons why this is the case.

Some scholars, notably Professor Robert Eisenman in his book on James, insist that puzzles of this type can only be addressed when all early Christian documents, including those not in the official canon, are rigorously examined. He suggests that the texts known as the Pseudoclementines actually present a parallel version of the Book of Acts, and could be much more accurate. Both works could have been written using the same sources, although the material was treated very differently. In the Pseudoclementines, James is the key figure and is greatly admired. His saintly and ascetic life is praised and cherished. Eisenman develops many interesting insights which suggest that the writer of Acts manipulated and altered the facts, and censored out the key references to James. The election of the new twelfth apostle, for example, may have been a very 'doctored' version of what should have been the election of James; and the stoning of Stephen may have been a 'cover' for the attack on James.[3]

Paul's reputation in the gentile Church, and the fact that his letters were preserved in the canon of scripture, have given the impression that from the time of his conversion he was the most influential figure in the Church, and, following from this, that his exposition of doctrine was the accepted norm in his day. A closer examination reveals that this was very far from being the case. As we have seen, the actual letters written by Paul, and Luke's account of the beginnings of Christian history, sometimes give startlingly different viewpoints or interpretations of events.[4]

Many Galatian and Corinthian Christians clung to quite a different theology from that dear to Paul, and they actively and vehemently challenged Paul's right to teach as he did. They also questioned his right to call himself an apostle. For his part, Paul accused *them* of 'teaching another Gospel' and 'preaching another Jesus' (Gal 1:6-8; 2 Cor 11:3-4).

Matthew's gospel, which may have been composed as late as 85 CE, might well have been written for such Jewish Christians who held fast to the Law and did not wish to break away from Judaism. Much of the teaching in it is Midrashic and Rabbinic in flavour, and can only be fully appreciated by scholars steeped in

Pharisaic tradition. Some have suggested that the author must have been a converted scribe. The fact that it stands in sharp contrast to Pauline doctrine is crystal clear.

'Do not think that I have come to abolish the Law and the prophets,' says Jesus in the Sermon on the Mount:

> I have not come to abolish them, but to fulfil them. For truly I say to you, till heaven and earth pass away, not the jot nor a tittle will pass from the Law until all is accomplished. *Whoever then relaxes one least of these commandments and teaches men so, shall be called least in the kingdom of Heaven;* but he who does them and teaches them shall be called great in the Kingdom of Heaven. For I tell you, unless your righteousness is even greater than that of scribes and Pharisees, you will not enter the Kingdom of Heaven. (Mt 5:17-20)

A statement such as this, written long after the death of Paul by a writer who believed such teaching to have been the intention of Jesus if not his actual words, must have been very embarrassing for Paul's followers. Luke preserves a similar saying of Jesus in his gospel version, but the stringent sentiments are predictably toned right down to a fairly innocuous single verse: 'It is easier for heaven and earth to pass away than for one dot of the Law to become void.' (Lk 6:17.) Very interesting!

Matthew also had much to say about false prophets: they 'come in sheep's clothing but inwardly are ravening wolves. You will know them by their fruits.' (Mt 7:15-16; see also 24:11f.)

Who were these 'relaxers of the commandments', the 'false prophets'? One cannot help concluding that they were the Christians who ignored Judaism. The Clementine Homilies 4:34-35 give us the following interesting quotation, which purported to have come from Peter:

> Observe the greatest caution, and believe no teacher, unless he brings from Jerusalem the testimonial of James, the Lord's brother, or of whomsoever may come after him. For no-one unless he has gone up thither, and there has been approved as a fit and faithful teacher for preaching the word of the Messiah [...] is by any means to be received. Let neither prophet not apostle be looked for by you at this time besides us [...] For there is *one true Prophet,* whose words we twelve Apostles preach!

Two things are significant: there were preachers doing the rounds who were not regarded as 'fit or faithful'; and Jesus was referred to as the 'one true Prophet' or Messenger of God, and *not* a Son of God.

Paul's letter to the Galatians, on the other hand, is particularly full of sentiments warning his believers to be on their guard, and not to accept any other teaching than Paul's. In characteristically vehement language, Paul insists that even if 'an angel from Heaven should preach to you a Gospel contrary to that which we preached to you, let him be accursed.' (Gal 1:18) He was astonished that his converts were 'so quickly deserting him who called you in the grace of Christ.' He bitterly regretted that, of all people, the Galatians who had been converted by faith and not by the Law, 'having begun in the Spirit were now ending in the flesh.' (Gal 3:2-3) Paul claimed that his Gospel was not a simple reformation of Pharisaism, but had actually been delivered to him by Christ himself: not Jesus the earthly man, of course, but the Risen Lord! Therefore since he had the advantage of a divine origin for his message (which none of the other Apostles could claim) he was entitled to be completely independent of them. Knowledge of the historical Jesus was actually irrelevant to him: what mattered was the mystical communion with the 'Risen Christ'.

The Church in Galatia, however, was in two minds. Why should they be expected to take on trust Paul's statement that he had had a special revelation, if what he was teaching was different from the beliefs of the Apostles who had been trained in their ministry by Jesus himself? If Paul claimed a special revelation, how was it that the gifted seers among the Apostles, possessors of the complete psychic repertory of the Holy Spirit, had not been assured by the Risen Lord that Paul's message was legitimate? In other words: was there anyone to vouch for Paul apart from Paul?

Jesus must have spent a considerable part of his ministry in training the Twelve Apostles to carry on his work when he was no longer with them. Amazingly, if Paul is to be believed, it appears that almost as soon as Jesus left them Paul arrived on the scene with the message that they were on quite the wrong track, and that his own version of the Gospel was the true one. It is hardly surprising that the Apostles were reluctant to accept him, and that a bitter and lengthy controversy should have ensued between him and the 'pillars' of the Church.

If Jesus had really intended to found a new Israel which would cast aside the foundations of the old, is it credible that he would have left his most cherished and intimate disciples in complete ignorance of the conditions under which the Church of the future was to be established? What of the promise that the Spirit would guide these men into the path of truth and justify their teachings? If Paul was correct, these Apostles were very far from being enlightened. But what if they were right after all?[5]

The Clementine Homilies question quite bluntly whether any supernatural vision should take precedence over the personal training given to Peter. Simon Magus, a Samaritan sorcerer mentioned in Acts 8:9, claimed to have obtained knowledge superior to that of Peter. Peter replied to him: 'Why should Christ have remained with his disciples and instructed them even for one year, if it were possible to be made a teacher at once, by a vision? If however, it is true that you have been made an apostle, after having been instructed by him in a brief and momentary manifestation, then preach his words, love his apostles, and do not fight against one who has lived in his society.' (Homilies 17:19.)

It is hardly surprising that many scholars have assumed that the figure of Simon Magus in this document was really a pseudonym for Paul, very thinly disguised.

The Simon Magus of Acts, whose pre-Christian sorcery had earned him the reputation of being 'that Power of God which is called Great', had supposedly been converted and baptised by the Apostle Philip, but he had not 'received the Holy Spirit'. When Peter and John went to Samaria to pray for the new Christians there, Simon Magus showed he was not worthy by trying to *buy* with money the ability to pass on the power of the Spirit by the laying on of hands (Acts 8:10-24).

Early in the last century the theologians of the Tübingen School realised the serious nature of the conflict between Paul and the Apostles, and brought out into the open matters which had until then been concealed or ignored. Baur, one of their chief scholars, supported the theory that Simon Magus was indeed a pseudonym for Paul, since Simon claimed to be the 'Power of God' and Paul gives the Gospel this very title (Romans 1:16, I Cor 12:19). Simon Magus was also called a 'chosen vessel for evil', which recalls Paul's own claim to be a chosen vessel! (Acts 9:15)

Whatever opinion one might now entertain of the Clementine Homilies, it is certain that they circulated freely in the early Church, and must have provoked the anger of Pauline Christians. It goes without saying, of course, that most modern Christians have never even heard of them, or of other Christian books such as these, since they are books that were not chosen for inclusion in the 'New Testament' by the fourth-century Trinitarian bishops who controlled that process.

It has been suggested that despite attempts to filter out irksome views, several parts of the New Testament contain reminders of these early attempts to resist Paul's teachings, especially the letters of James and Jude (perhaps not

Jesus' brothers, but the grandsons of Jesus' brother Jude?), and the first part of the Apocalypse (which may have been written by James' nephew Simeon ben Cleophas).

The first letter of John states that any person who said he knew Jesus but 'disobeyed his commands is a liar, and the truth is not in him.' (I Jn 2:4). Likewise I John 2:6 reproaches those who say that they abide in Jesus, but do not walk in the same way that he walked.

Jude's letter inveighs in very despairing terms about a dangerous heretic, a false Jew, a false apostle, a false Gospel, and those 'who call themselves apostles but are not!' (Rev 2:2); 'the slander of those who say that they are Jews and are not, but are a synagogue of Satan' (Rev 2:9); 'you who have put a stumbling-block before the sons of Israel, that you might eat food sacrificed to idols and practise immorality. So you also have some who hold the teachings of the Nicolaitans.' (Rev 2:14-15)

Who on earth were the Nicolaitans? Scholars have been puzzled here, but one suggestion is that they were Paul's followers.[6] We know that 'Nicolaos', or 'Conqueror of the People', was another nickname for Paul, and hence the Nicolaitans may be those who were despised by Jewish-Christians because they took Gentile liberty from the Mosaic Law to the point of being accused of scandalous behaviour. According to Eusebius they practised 'unlimited indulgence in gluttony and lechery at banquets, drinking bouts and wedding feasts. Nicolaos taught that "the flesh must be treated with contempt" and practised "utter promiscuity", even offering his own wife that anyone who wished might have her.'[7]

One is not to suppose for one moment that Paul himself would have encouraged scandalous behaviour; the very high moral tone of his epistles is a quite adequate guarantee of that! Nevertheless, it must be admitted that various individuals were not slow to take Paul's teachings to their extreme logical conclusions.

Antinomians (those who dispensed with the Law)[8] claimed that if it was true that Christ had been sacrificed and the price had been paid for our sins once and for all, then obviously it no longer mattered a jot what people got up to, so long as they had faith and believed! This was the danger that the Jewish-Christian church could see growing up before them. The epistle of Jude may well be an example of a typical manifesto sent out from Jerusalem in the name of an Apostle to counter the growing and very dangerous heresy spreading in the Church.

The Clementine Homilies advise: 'Remember to shun any apostle or teacher or prophet who does not first accurately compare his preaching with that of James, who was called brother of my Lord, and to whom was entrusted to administer the church of the Hebrews in Jerusalem [...] wherefore He who hath sent us said, "many shall come in sheep's clothing but inwardly they are ravening wolves. By their fruits ye shall know them."' (Homily 12:25)

In the pseudo-epistle of Peter to James prefixed to the Homilies, the unnamed enemy who had falsified the doctrine preached by Peter is clearly Paul: 'I see already the beginning of the evil; for some of the Gentiles have rejected the doctrines taught by me, which are in harmony with the Law, and have adopted a fantastic doctrine and opposition to the Law from the man who is my enemy. Nay, some have attempted, even during my lifetime, to wrest my words by various false interpretations, to the subversion of the Law, as if I also were really of the same opinion!'

If it had not been for the traumatic historical events of 60-70 CE, the teachings of the Mother-Church might well have prevailed, and those of Paul might have perished with him; but in those traumatic years the Jews rebelled against their Roman masters and bloody war engulfed the country. The Romans ruthlessly crushed the revolt, and Jerusalem was utterly destroyed. The Jewish-Christian Church was so involved with (albeit not identical to) Essenism and Zealotism, that when Jerusalem fell, its influence collapsed.

Paul's Trinitarian theology, centred far from Jerusalem, emerged triumphant: sufficient proof in the eyes of posterity that it was no mere corruption of the primitive tradition, but the logical and historical development of what had been inadequately grasped by the 'simple' disciples with their humble origins and lack of high Greek culture. That Paul's 'development' was 'historical' could really mean no more than that certain ideas and ideals then current in the Mediterranean world formed a very congenial framework into which his 'truths' could be readily and successfully incorporated. Anti-Pauline writings current in the churches were either 'lost' or suppressed by his supporters.

By the early second century, Epiphanius and Hippolytus were worried by the success of a group known as the Elchasaites. Hippolytus suggested that the name Elchasai was a version of al-Hesed, the Righteous or Holy One. Epiphanius thought the name meant 'the Great' or 'Hidden Power', and referred to the doctrine of the Christ as a pre-existent cosmic soul, otherwise known as the 'Perfect One' or the 'Standing One'. This Great Soul stood above the created cosmos, and could descend at will upon certain chosen individuals, either through a virgin birth, or as a special 'charisma' that fell upon an adult at a special time, such as baptism. In Elchasaite Gnostic theology, the 'Christ' or 'Perfect One' descended on Jesus in the form of a dove. They taught that 'the Christ [. . .] is transfused into many bodies frequently and was now in Jesus [. . .] Likewise, this Jesus afterwards was continually being transfused into [other] bodies frequently and was manifested in many at different times.'⁹

The teacher Elchasai was apparently a contemporary of Simeon bar Cleophas, and his group was indistinguishable from the Masbutheans. Elchasai was said to have come in the third year of Trajan's reign (i.e. 101), and a book ascribed to him was brought to Rome in the second year of the reign of Hadrian (that is, in 119 CE).

According to Hegesippus (c160 CE):

> After James the Just suffered martyrdom [. . .] Symeon was appointed bishop [. . .] They used to call the church a virgin, for she had not yet been corrupted by vain teachings. But Thebuthis (founder of the Masbotheans) because he was not made bishop, began secretly to corrupt her from the seven sects among the people to which he himself belonged (i.e. the Samaritans); from which came Simon (whence the Simoneans), and Cleobius (whence the Cleobians), and Dositheus (whence the Dositheans), and Gorthaeus (whence the Goratheni) and the Masbotheans. Springing from these, the Menandrianists and the Marcianists.¹⁰

All the first heterodox sects were Samaritan in origin.¹¹ A strong faction of Samaritan Christians lived in Jerusalem in the 50s, following Jesus' successful mission in Samaria in his lifetime (Jn 4), and the later mission of Philip (Acts 8:5-26). Philip is usually mentioned in the gospels along with Nathanael. The only narrative specifically concerning Nathanael included a reference to the vision of the Patriarch Jacob at Bethel, a Samaritan sanctuary (Jn 1:43-51). It is interesting to notice how the name Nathanael is the exact Hebrew equivalent of Dositheus. It is not impossible that the rival missionaries that Paul had to contend with in Corinth and Ephesus were Samaritans.

A fundamental feature of Samaritan theology was the belief that God had withdrawn from history. The era of God's 'good pleasure' with the Jews was the era of Moses to Joshua. After the time of Eli, God turned away. The Samaritans looked forward to a New Age when God would be active among them again. There was a strong dualist element: God the Almighty, the Hidden One, and also God Revealed, spoken of as the Glory or Power, who was an incarnation. Simon Magus claimed to be the 'Power of God which is called Great' (Acts 8:10).¹²

The Samaritan Christians stressed five things: an emphasis on wisdom and knowledge rather than truth and love; the myth of Jesus' pre-existence in the Godhead and his incarnation; a 'Glory' ministry instead of a 'Son of Man' ministry, with Moses and not David as the type; a minimising of the cross and resurrection; and a revealed rather than a futuristic eschatology.

The Elchasaite ideas were certainly pre-Gospel; Paul's epistles speak of the 'First Man' or 'Primal Adam', and Jesus as 'Son of Man' or 'Lord out of Heaven', 'Second Man', 'Last Adam' and 'Heavenly One'.

Marcion of Pontus (d. 144 CE) turned Christianity round completely. He believed that the true Christian doctrine had been *corrupted* by Jewish errors, and needed careful purification from them! The Jewish God, Yahweh or Jehovah, was no more than a jealous and vindictive Demiurge, a sort of renegade power somewhat *less* than the supreme Divinity. The Real God was an Entity far beyond all connection with the world of matter. The creation of the physical world was this Demiurge's vindictive act; it was a lower plane in which pure souls were trapped. Therefore the True God of Goodness sent His son Jesus to release us from the clutches of this fiend. Jesus was the *Chrestos*, the Good One, sent to deliver humanity from the world of evil, by renunciation, poverty, celibacy and mystic communion. He was *not Christos*, an anointed king-Messiah according to the Jewish understanding. [13]

Needless to say, Marcion regarded Paul as the *only* faithful Apostle, and rejecting everything else, took only Paul's ten letters and Luke's Gospel, all in suitably mutilated form, as the Bible of his sect of Christians.

Marcion's views show how far Christian views could move from their original Jewish matrix. Today, at the beginning of the twenty-first century CE, scholars with the courage to challenge inherited opinions are considering a disturbing but increasingly solid possibility: that the Jewish Christian Church had been the correct and true faith all along, in the sense that it preserved the teachings and practice of Jesus himself, and that Trinitarian theology is a tragic and fateful error and heresy. Muslims, observing this transformation, ask the frank and inevitable question: whether to be a true Christian, *one should in fact be a Muslim!*

Chapter Eleven

JESUS THE MYTH?

MOST NEW PAGAN converts cared very little for the Jewish religion that lay behind their new faith. They had little sympathy with its disciplines, and often found it too difficult to relinquish their old native superstitions. Jews were not popular in the Empire; in fact, they were frequently loathed. Where Trinitarian Christianity was taught, however, the transition from the old faiths to the new was easy, often helped by missionaries who deliberately chose the simple procedure of taking over existing holy places, shrines, special days, and even the statues of pagan gods. Often a virgin mother holding on her knee a divine child, was an Isis and Horus, duly 'christianised'.[1]

One can imagine the horror among faithful Jewish Christians who watched this accommodation. Refusal to bow the knee to graven images was the second of the Ten Commandments. This was not just a sign of intelligence (the refusal to acknowledge an object made by human hands as a 'god', or the mediator of a god), it was a deliberate recognition that there *were* such things in the universe as elemental spirits, some of which could gain influence over humans, and many of which could be evil. The temporary rewards or successes people imagined they gained by serving them often resulted in thraldom and a subsequent descent into despair and madness. Those who truly believed in the One God were warned not to be beguiled for a moment by the temptations they offered.

Many of these 'powers' were thought to dwell in remarkable natural objects, such as mountains or springs; others inhabited particular rocks or trees. It was commonplace to represent them with sacred stones or carved wooden pillars, and frequently the carving was extended into an art form in the creation of figurines. For centuries one of the key characteristics of Judaism which marked its adherents off from pagans was the stalwart refusal to make *any* graven or sculpted figure of any description, even as mere decoration, lest it lead the weak and innocent towards idol-worship, or offer any entity less than God the chance of a 'home' and a foothold in their community.

By contrast, pagans who honoured or placated these elemental powers, or wished to have symbolic representations of the great forces of Sun or Moon or Fertility or Success in Battle, created domestic shrines and set up their figurines or stones in every home. A pagan home would not be considered complete without them. The pages of the Old Testament reveal how persistent was the practice; the messengers who revealed the One True God faced constant contact with people who regarded setting up small images of the sacred as normal pious practice.[2] Pagan authorities had huge sanctuaries, complete with priesthoods and gigantic statues, some of which were works of art with world-wide fame.[3]

Involvement with these idols usually dragged the worshipper down into a quagmire of superstitious fear, emotionalism, anxiety and servitude, the chief form of which usually involved the constant flow of blood-sacrifices, either animal or human. Any higher metaphysical thoughts of worship were swamped by the time-consuming, expensive 'factory-line' mentality of desperately feeding and appeasing these dangerous forces. Failure to do so, or not doing so in the most meticulously detailed manner, might bring about appalling consequences.

To any true monotheist, therefore, who had realised the dangers of paganism and broken free of the web of mental servitude and its outcome in moral degradation and loss of individual responsibility, freedom and dignity, the thought of accepting pagan cult objects and statues, even as mere decorations, could never be tolerated.

Many of today's Christians do not realise the scale of the intrusion of pagan practice that accompanies or even compromises their faith. The celebration of the birth of Jesus on December 25th is one obvious example of the christifying of pagan traditions that a pure monotheist would regard as far too close to paganism to be tolerated.[4] Even if a broad-minded Christian was convinced that it was not harmful because it was only an 'official birthday' for Jesus, December 25th would be the *last* day a monotheist would pick, because of its obvious Sun-Baal connotations.[5]

December 25th was in fact the most important of sun festivals, the new birth of the God, rising three days after 'dying' at the winter solstice. One can see how strong has been the hold of pagan elements on the imagination by noting that even now, after twenty centuries of Christian teaching, more people probably celebrate the pre-Christian evergreens, the mistletoe, the kissing, the yule log and the gifts, than throng to Church to pass the night watching and praying, and thinking about the moment when God became man, when the Creator and Guider of all that exists poured His essence into a human baby in a stable in Bethlehem, a baby that was 'begotten of his Father before all worlds, God of God, light of light, very God of very God, begotten not made, being of one substance with the Father, by whom all things were made.'[6]

Vast swathes of humanity that had once been regarded as Christian have now virtually given up that side of things. Specifically Christian Christmas cards are sent almost with embarrassment, the more popular greetings these days being the cheeky robin (with its chest bearing the symbol of the flame), the snowman (who will melt, defeated by the Sun), the fir-tree trinkets hanging (the 'evergreen' symbolising life in the 'dead' part of the year, the hanging trinkets still common world-wide as fertility-prayer symbolism), holly (used by the Celts to deflect evil and goblins at winter solstice time), ivy (the 'female' element of winter greenery as opposed to holly's 'maleness'), mistletoe (used in Druidic worship for occult purposes), the Yule Log sacred to Thor (now usually just represented by a chocolate cake), gift-giving (a diverting feature of the old Saturnalia, along with eating, drinking, and sexual licence) and the 'Red Man' or Father Christmas. Nicholas or Santa Claus is a legendary overlay:[7] the Red Man was probably originally Apollo the sun-god, or Thor whose element was fire, depicted as an elderly man, jovial and friendly, of heavy build with a long white beard, who drove a chariot through the sky. The fireplace in pagan homes was sacred to him, and he was said to descend to it through the chimney.

From time immemorial, the sun has presented the same phenomena everywhere. The same effect is caused by its rise and decline, and its various phases created the same notions in human minds inhabiting all the various corners of the world.

Sun gods had many manifestations, such as Apollo or Dionysus among the Greeks, Hercules among the Romans, Mithras in Persia, Adonis and Attis in Syria and Phrygia, the Osiris, Isis and Horus triad in Egypt, and the Baal, Astarte and Tammuz triad among the Babylonians and Carthaginians. These saviour-gods were typically born at the winter solstice of a virgin mother in a cave or underground chamber or stable. The sun, at the winter solstice, is in the sign of the Bull. They struggled and toiled for the good of humanity and were known by such names as Mediator, Healer, Light-bringer, Saviour and Deliverer. They were conquered, temporarily, by the powers of darkness and descended into

Hell or the Underworld; then they rose again from the dead and became the pioneers of humanity in the heavenly world, and founded communities or communions of saints into which disciples were received by baptism, who commemorated their sacrificial deaths with eucharistic meals.

The pagan Triadic deities were sometimes represented in striking images which show a single head with three faces, three mouths, but only four eyes. Examples of this strange representation have been preserved from many provinces of the former Roman Empire. The evident compatibility of Triadic with Trinitarian theology made it possible for Christians to use the same image to represent the Trinity, disturbingly (for Jews and Muslims) expressing the principle of a God who was simultaneously Three and One, a deity known in ancient times, but among the pagans, not the Jews. [8]

It is therefore very easy to show that the core teachings of the Trinitarian Christian churches today do not come from Jesus. If Jesus had never lived, classical Christian teachings would still have recognisably existed. These dogmas were not invented by Paul, or by the clergy, but were the ready-made essentials of paganism (or Baalism, as it was known to the prophets of the Old Testament), the various ramifications of which spread from Persia to Britain.

Let us probe still further. The name 'Easter' has nothing to do with Christianity, but derives from the spring festival held in honour of the goddess of light known as Oeastra (Astarte, Ishtar). The 'easter bunny' descends from the rabbit that was her animal symbol. Eggs were dyed and eaten at all the spring festivals in ancient Egypt, Persia, Greece and Rome. The 'easter bonnet' was originally a wreath of flowers, the circlet expressing the course of the Sun in the heavens that brought the return of spring.

The spring goddess (Astarte, Ishtar, al-Uzza, Aphrodite and others) not only had a virgin-born son, and wept for his sacrificial death until he rose again, but also had a less pleasant side: an insatiable thirst for blood and sex. Many of her statues depict her with obscenely exaggerated sex organs, or with an egg in her hand or a rabbit at her side. Sacred prostitution was a key part of her cult, and beneath memorials to her in Carthage, archaeologists have discovered brightly coloured urns containing the charred bones of little children.

One of the most popular manifestations of the sun-cult was Mithraism, which reached Rome in around 70BCE and spread wherever the legions marched. Remains of Mithraic temples have been found in Britain, at York, Chester, London, and elsewhere. Long before the birth of Jesus, Mithras was said to have been a great mediator between God and humanity. He was born of a virgin in a cave on December 25th, travelled far and wide with twelve disciples, and died in the service of humanity. He rose again from the tomb, and his resurrection was celebrated with great rejoicing. His great festivals were the winter solstice and the vernal equinox. He was called Saviour, and sometimes figured as a lamb. People were initiated into the cult through the baptism of blood. Sacramental feasts were held in his remembrance.

Bacchus or Dionysus was also born on December 25th. His mother was a virgin called Demeter. The world was enveloped in evil, so the God of gods was beseeched to save humanity. The prayer was accepted by Jupiter who declared that his son would redeem the world from its misery. Dionysus, known as his only-begotten son, was sent as the saviour. The shedding of his blood was symbolised in his gift of wine to humanity.

Attis was born of a virgin named Nana. He was bled to death at the foot of a pine tree, his blood renewing the fertility of the earth and bringing new life to humanity. He rose from the dead, and his celebrations included fastening his image to a pine-tree on March 24th, the 'Day of Blood', with much wailing and mourning. The image was then placed in a tomb, but the coming night turned sorrow to joy: the tomb was found empty, and the festival of resurrection celebrated. His mysteries included a sacramental meal and baptism of blood.

In Egypt, there was the Heb-Sed festival when the powers and sexual prowess of the Pharoah (the incarnation of Horus) were tested annually, and as soon as they showed any sign of being on the wane, he was expected to sacrifice himself and donate his blood to the soil, and allow the next Horus-king to succeed him.

According to Eusebius,[9] a man was sacrificed annually at the feast of Kronos. Justin spoke of a Phoenician ritual in which Kronos had a son, Ieoud, whom he adorned with the emblems of royalty, and then sacrificed. The unfortunate Ieoud (or perhaps he considered himself to be honoured) was known as 'the only begotten son of his Father'.

Another example was the popular Syrian saviour-god Tammuz, who was also born of a virgin. He was killed and rose again every spring. Every year the maidens wept for him and then rejoiced over his resurrection (cf. Ezekiel 8:11-18). Throughout the Near East, wherever Tammuz was worshipped, there was a spring festival in which a human victim in royal robes was killed *and eaten*, so that his body and blood might bring salvation to the community. One of the chief centres of Tammuz worship was Bethlehem, said to have been the birthplace of Jesus.

Another coincidence: Tammuz was sometimes called 'the Carpenter', a title related to 'the Demiurge' or 'Worker', or 'Architect' of the universe.[10] Jesus was supposed to have been called 'the son of the carpenter', which in Baal mythology meant 'son of the Creator'.

A coincidence stranger still: Tammuz was supposed to have entered Jerusalem riding two asses, because this represented the passage of the sun at the summer solstice through the sign of Cancer (in Babylonian and Greek mythology the sign of Cancer was two asses). Christians may know the odd passage in Mt 21:2-7 which specifically states that Jesus entered Jerusalem *riding on two animals.*[11]

Details of the story of the passion of the Babylonian Baal or Bel were found on clay tablets by German excavators in 1903-4 at Kalah-Shargat, the site of the ancient city of Ashur, in the library of King Ashurbanipal of the ninth century BCE.[12] The mystery of Baal was enacted every year in the spring. In places, the Baal-text incidents are so close to the Gospel sequence that one might even wonder if they formed a written source. They include the details of Baal's capture and his trial in the House on the Mount; his torture and being led away to death together with a malefactor; another, also charged as a malefactor, was set free; the city broke out in tumult and fighting; Baal's clothes were carried away; a woman wiped away the blood from the drawn-out weapon thrust into his heart; a goddess sought to tend him, and a weeping woman came to lament at the 'Gate of Burial'; he was brought back to life at the spring equinox.

The early church fathers tried to explain away the similarities by claiming that the Devil had taught these doctrines before, just to cause mischief for the true Christian Church when it came. Tertullian, for example, said: 'The Devil, whose business is to prevent the truth, mimics the exact circumstances of the Divine Sacraments in the mysteries of idols.'

This was presumably the chief reason why the Church Fathers took such pains to destroy and burn as many pagan records as they could lay their hands on; it was deliberate policy to remove this embarrassment by obliterating the evidence of the real origins of their own mythology.

Chapter Twelve

THE KA'BA PANTHEON

SCHOLARS HAVE LONG accepted that there was a time when Yahweh (the Jehovah of the Hebrew Bible) or Allah (of the Qur'an) was thought of as just one god among many. In the Old Testament, we see the long struggle between those religious people who believed that there could only be One True God (the monotheists), and those who believed that there was an entire pantheon of gods and supernatural forces (the polytheists). The natural tendency was to imagine that every aspect of nature had some power or force that could be called upon in connection with that particular aspect; for example, that there was a god in charge of rain, or fertility of crops or cattle, or sources of important springs, and so on. Each of these forces was regarded as a *baal*, or 'lord' of that aspect.

The One True God lay beyond human knowledge and imagination; and but for 'His' revelation of 'Himself', nobody would know of 'His' existence. Those who revealed the truth of this Supreme Being were known as the prophets or messengers. In His mercy, the Supreme God sent such messengers to every society and every place, so that there was no time or region that had not been touched by awareness of the truth, but it was left to individuals to pursue their knowledge and intuitions, as a matter of freewill.

Ancient Arabia had developed a colourful mythology with numerous gods, of whom no fewer than 360 were represented in the Ka'ba sanctuary at the time of the Prophet Muhammad. Every conceivable notion appears to have been represented by a god or goddess, to whom different powers and functions were assigned, and after whom places were named, many of them still existing to this day.

Several of these deities were particularly important to the Arabs. In and around Mecca, the god Hubal had long been venerated as one of the chief deities, and he was invoked with sacrifices all over the Arabian peninsula. The name may have its origins in 'Hu-baal' ('he is the Lord'). He was 'the Great One', the 'Watcher', and he was the head of a triad or trinity of gods, as was usual throughout the Middle East. The chief god in all triads seems to have been a manifestation of the Sun, with the complementary powers-gods of the Moon (or the evening star, Venus); vegetation, grain and harvest; and Fate or Fortune. He had many other names (for example, Dushrat or Dushara at Petra), and his consort was either Atargatis (the vegetation cycle) or Allat (the Moon).

The manifestation of the Supreme God was always known simply as al-Lah, the Almighty One, the Power. Isolated Arab dissidents known as *hanifs* accepted that if there was truly a Supreme God, there could be only One by definition, and the history of religion represents the struggle between those who had accepted the revealed truth of the One God, and those who regarded this Supreme God as simply one among many, albeit the chief of them all. [1]

The three powers the polytheists most associated with al-Lah were either al-Lat (the feminine principle, whose symbol was the Moon; this supreme goddess was also known in many places as Atargatis, the goddess of vegetation and the annual cycle of seasons, believed to be influenced by the moon); al-'Uzza (the 'evening star', who represented human devotion, both romantic and religious), and Manat (Fate). In the Ka'ba pantheon, these three goddesses were regarded as the daughters of the Great One. They were referred to as the *Gharaniq*, 'the exalted (or high-flying) birds', a soubriquet taken from the Numidian cranes that were believed to fly higher than any other bird, hovering, as it were, between heaven and earth, and therefore symbolic of intercessors between God and humanity. [2] These goddesses had several very important shrines, including centres at Petra and Ta'if. [3]

Apart from these great ones, there was an enormous range of other deities, usually associated with various features of nature. [4] These many gods included some whose names have particular significance for Bible scholars. For example, as Kamal Salibi records, there was al-Sadi (cognate with the biblical El Shaddai), a mountain god; al-'Alyan (biblical El Elyon), also a mountain deity; al-Sarah (biblical Sarah), goddess of the Asir highlands, at first barren and then made fertile by Abu Rahm (biblical Abraham), the god of drizzling rain. Their offspring was Dahhak (perhaps a corruption of the biblical Isaac), the 'overflowing one'; a god of wells and irrigation, who married Rebekkah, goddess of fecundity and feminine guile. She bore twin sons, al-'Isa (biblical Esau) the god of unbridled male sexuality, and al-'Uqba (biblical Jacob), the god of domesticated masculinity, regular progeny and family life.

Al-Bashar was the god of live flesh, whose vegetarian cult forbade the eating of meat. Al-Da'ya was the god of ethical knowledge, represented in the Garden of Juhaynah by the Tree of Knowledge. His link with the human world was al-Hanishah, (Hebrew Nahash), the principles of wisdom, cleverness and guile.

Al-Nayih (biblical Noah) was a god of human settlements, his chief allies being al-Thabit (Heb. *Tabut* = Ark), the god of stability, who guaranteed the continuity and regularity of settled community life, and al-Qays, the rainbow god who guaranteed the regularity of the seasons, his main function being to tame the ferocity of the cloud god al-'Inan, who could devastate human settlements with torrential floods.

Al-Lisan (or al-Shafi) was the god of unified speech who tried to promote understanding and co-operation among people; his adversary was al-Balal, the god of misunderstanding and confusion.

There was also al-Ruyah (bib. El Roi) the god of seeing; al-Sham'ah (bib. Ishmael) the god of hearing; al-Yusuf (bib. Joseph) also called al-Yazid, a god of increase and worldly success, the son of the fertility god al-'Uqba; al-Baram[5] a god of male continence and sterility, whose sexual potency could only be unleashed by circumcision; al-Maylah, the god of circumcision who made young men ready for marriage, and al-Damman, the god of marriage who oversaw the 'fusion of the two bloods': that of the male circumcision and the bridal hymen.

The name of the god Yahweh may have originated from the volcanic region of Jabal Alhan in northern Yemen, a place which was once devastated by a great flood, forcing many people to migrate northwards into the Hijaz where the volcanic region around Madina gave Yahweh a second home base. One theory suggests that in the Biblical books of Genesis and Exodus, we may really have the record of the mythological career of Yahweh, as he set out to establish his dominance over the pan-Arabian pantheon.[6] Al-Hayah was a god of the abstract concept of life. The name Yahweh survives to this day as al-Hayah (Ar. *'l hyh*, or the god *hyh*) a village in the Asir highlands. Genesis states that Yahweh used 'dust from the ground' to form the first man; but the words could equally well mean 'dust from the place Adamah'. Eden (Ar. Adanah) and its 'garden' Junaynah are located almost directly east of Wadi Adamah, a short distance downstream from the confluence of Wadi Bistah in inland Asir.[7] The garden's two sacred trees originally represented a god of life and a god of knowledge, whose names survive as those of the present villages al-Hayat (*hyt*, Arabic form of *hyym*, 'life') and al-Da'ya (*d'y*, Arabic form of *d'h*, 'knowledge').

Al-Hayah produced two sons, Hubal (bib. Abel) and Qayn (Cain). Cain killed Abel and went to live in the 'Land of Nod' (Ar. *'rs nwd* – the 'land of wandering' – the open desert to the east of 'Adanah and Junaynah in Wadi Bishnah), where the name Hubal survives as an oasis, and his cult was one of the most dominant at the time of the Prophet Muhammad. Cain's name survived with the Arabic tribe of Qayn, who were regarded as humble remnants of a vanished people. In Arabic tradition, it was considered a grave offence and a disgrace for a member of a respectable tribe to kill or attack one of the humbler desert folk, who were considered to be protected.[8] In the Bible, the Qayn are presumably the Kenites (*h-qyny* – Gen. 15-19; Numb. 24:21 etc). Nod, incidentally, survives as a place-name: Nawdah (*nwd*) is the name of two villages in the northern highlands of the Yemen.

As the Qayn people migrated northwards from Nawdah into the highlands of Asir, place names again link up with the names of the Biblical patriarchs. Cain's son Enoch is represented by Hanakah (*hnk*) near Dhahran al-Janub; his son Irad (*'yrd*) is further north at al-'Irad near Abha. Irad's son Mehujael (*mhwy'l*) is Muhayil on the maritime side of Asir; Methushael (*mtws'l*) is probably Hawd al-Mushayt (the well of *'l myst*, metathesis of *mtws*) near Muhayil, rather than al-Mushayat which is east of Abha. Lamech could be al-Kamil (*kml* being the metathesis of *lmk*) in the region to the north, where his folk formed tribal coalitions with two neighbours, those of 'Idwah in the Bani Shahr hill country to the north (Lamech's wife Adah), and those of Silah (*slh*) in the Rijal Alma' country to the south (Lamech's wife Zillah). Adah became mother of Jabal (*ybl*) and Jubal (*ywbl*), and Zillah the mother of Tubal (*twbl*) and Naamah (*n'mh*); these places could be Buwalah and Buwaylah in the Taif region, and Wadi Tulab and Na'imah both in central Najd. Jabal fathered Topesh, Kinor and 'Ogab (now Shatfah, Qurayn and 'Uqub). Tubal indicates the inhabitants of Wadi Tulab. The village al-Yahil is located at the headwaters of a valley called Wadi Kanahbalah (*knhbl*). This name makes no sense except as a combination of '*kn habl*,' or Cain and Abel.

Most intriguing of all is the fact that there was a fertility deity known as al-'Isa, and in the regions of Hijaz and Asir there are said to be no fewer than seven villages named after him. Other variants of the name are al-'Ays (the god of semen) and al-Ayyash (the life-giving god). Three of the villages are Marwah al-'Isa (*mrwt* or Marut = 'dominion'); Khayal al-'Isa (*khyl* = 'power'); and Misbah al-'Isa (*misbah* = 'dawn light, glory'). It is well-known, of course, that the version of the Lord's Prayer in Matthew's Gospel states, 'For thine is the dominion, the power and the glory, for ever' (Mt 6:13). This trinity of names of the Arabian god 'Jesus' must have antedated the Christian 'Father', 'Son' and 'Holy Spirit' by many centuries.

Inscriptions in the ancient Arabian Thamudic script, discovered in the northern Hijaz and dated between the second century BCE and the second century CE, make three clear references to a god 'S or 'Ays.[9] 'Isa is actually the actual Aramaic form of the Arabic al-'ays, meaning 'the water of the male' or 'semen', and is related to 'aysh, meaning 'life'.[10]

Could it be possible, therefore, that the Jesus of the 'I am' sayings in the fourth Gospel was al-'Isa or al-'Ays, the ultimate source of the fertilising power of the male? Human beings cannot easily make such presumptuous statements as 'I am the bread of life [...] he who comes to me will never be hungry', or 'I am the light of the world [...] whoever follows me will have the light of life' without placing their sanity in question, a matter which the author actually notes (Jn 10:19). Certainly, statements of this type do not fit easily with the Jesus who was the selfless and humble preacher of the Sermon of the Mount, or one who was a political claimant of the ancestral throne of David. The person of the 'I am' sayings was a supernatural figure: 'I have come in order that you might have life'; 'Whoever abides in me and I in him, will bear much fruit; for you can do nothing without me.'

The tribal territory of Shimran (bib. Samaria or Shomeron) close to the place Siqar (bib. Sychar) was the setting of a narrative recorded in the Fourth Gospel in which the god with the power to provide 'life-giving water' requested a female seeker to call her husband and come back: 'for he who drinks the water I will give him will never thirst again; it will become in him a spring which will provide him with the life-giving water and give him eternal life.' (Jn 4:5-16).

What about the narrative of the raising of Lazarus in the Fourth Gospel? Lazarus' Greek name is the Hebrew Eleazar ('ly'zr). In Thamudic inscriptions the Arabicised name occurs as 'Adhr El ('dr'l, remembering that d or dh frequently transforms to z) or Yu'dhir El (y'dr 'l), with the order of the component parts reversed. This indicates what 'Lazarus' really means: the root 'dr ('adhr) or Hebrew 'zr ('ezer) denotes sexual abstinence or virginity: Yu'dhir El was a god of virginity.

The Arabic root 'adhr also denotes circumcision: the cult of Yu'dhir El apparently involved a special circumcision rite in which young men were prepared for marriage, in the belief that the sexual potency of the male could only be properly unleashed by the removal of the symbolically inhibitive foreskin.[11]

Yu'dhir El did not keep men permanently celibate, but watched over them and helped them maintain their virginity until the time came for them to marry.[12]

The connection between the virginity god al-'Adhr or Yu'dhir El and Isa, the god of the life-giving 'ays (semen) can be illustrated, perhaps, by two villages in the Bani Zayd region of Rijal Alma' in Asir: the village of al-'Adhra and the village called al-'Ays bin Hamad, the latter name meaning precisely 'the semen, son of the comforter' (Greek for 'comforter', *Parakletos*). Until very recently young men in the same hill country of Rijal Alma' were circumcised in public, in the presence of their brides. Strabo, the Greek geographer who lived in the first century CE, was one who noted that men of this particular region 'deprived themselves of the prepuce'.

The gospels state that the miracle happened at a place called Bethany, which was near another village, Bethphage; there is a Palestinian village of Bethany-Bituniya near Ramallah, and another village called al-'Azariyyah near Jerusalem, which is traditionally shown to pilgrims as the site of the 'tomb of Lazarus'. However, the Aramaic Beth 'Anya (House of the Echo) could also be extended to mean 'anwaya (ascetic or hermit) or the verb 'ana (to imprison) and the noun 'ani (prisoner). Thus Beth 'Anya could indicate a House of Asceticism, such as a hermitage. In western Arabia many villages are called al-'An or al-'Aniyah, one being in the close vicinity of al-'Adhra and al-'Ays bin Hamad. Luke places his Bethany 'at the mount that is called Elaion' (Lk 19:29; 21:27, Acts 1:12), making a difference between this place and the traditionally-accepted Mount of Olives. In Greek, *elaion* does mean olive grove; it could, however, be the transliteration of the Semitic 'elyon, meaning 'exalted', 'lofty' or 'most high': the Arabicised equivalent would be 'alyan. The other nearby place, Bethphage, would be 'Beth Faga' (the House of the Fig), and north of Rijal Alma' there still exists a village by the name of al-Fajah, near a village al-'Aniyah, at the foot of the rocky crags of the Asir escarpment. Overlooking them from a promontory on the heights is a village called al-'Alyan. This place is associated in Arabic mythology with the fig goddess, Faga, a symbol of miraculous fertility. It may well have been this fig deity, and not just an ordinary fig-tree, that was implied in the narrative of Jesus cursing the fig-tree (Mt 21:17-19; Mk 11:12-14).

Perhaps some sisters in charge of a shrine of al-'Adhr discovered that their god had lost his power to make his male devotees potent, and that he himself was losing potency. So they sent a message to al-'Isa announcing that his dear friend was sick. Al-'Isa assures them that his friend is only 'asleep' and needs to be 'woken up'. He finds him 'tied up' in grave clothes, lying dead in his tomb. (In idiomatic Arabic sexual impotence is often spoken of as a 'tie' or 'knot': Ar. *'uqda*: to break a knot means to nullify an evil spell). Al-'Isa orders that he be untied and allowed to go free; thus his potency is restored, glorifying al-'Isa as the ultimate source of life-giving virility.

So: was there a historical Messianic Jesus who was thought to have died on a cross, but who became identified with the god al-'Isa when he rose from the tomb? He not only had the power to grant eternal life, he also had the power to literally bring back the dead. ('Whoever believes in me will live, even though he die! Jn 11:25).

He may also have been assimilated to Dhu Khulasa, the god of redemption, whose principal sanctuary in the seventh century was at another Ka'ba, the Ka'bah al-Yamaniyah (the Southern Ka'ba), which rivalled the Ka'ba at Mecca and was located in Tubalah, in inland Asir. The idol of Dhu Khulasa was a white stone depicting a phallus topped by a crown. With the rise of Islam, the Prophet Muhammad sent his supporters to destroy this idol.

Another 'gospel problem' is the business of Jesus being betrayed by one of his disciples, Judas Iscariot, with the betrayal money ending up buying a 'Field of Blood'. Such a betrayal was not necessary for the historical Jesus to end up being arrested and crucified: there was no need to track him down, as he was not in hiding. On the night of his arrest, he was enjoying a leisurely supper, after which he went to a 'garden' to which everyone had access. However, all four gospels insist that Jesus was betrayed, and that his whereabouts were kept secret (Mk 14:12-15).

The earliest account, Paul's, did not name the betrayer, and merely suggested that Jesus was 'handed over' (*paradidomi*) from the Jewish religious authorities to the secular Roman court, rather than 'betrayed' (*prodidomi*; cf. I Cor: 11:23). Mark and John make no reference to what happened to Judas; Luke says nothing in the gospel, but in Acts 1:18-19 Peter supposedly reported that Judas bought a field and fell to his death in it: he burst open and all his bowels spilled out, and that is why it was called 'in their dialect' *Akeldama*, Field of Blood. [13]

Akeldama does indeed represent a 'Galilean' dialectical pronunciation of *Haql Dama* (attested in the Babylonian Talmud at *Erubin* 53b). In the dialect of Jerusalem it would have been 'Chakeldama' with the hard 'h'. However, it is possible that the dialect was of the 'Galilee' of the Arabian Hijaz, where large Jewish communities flourished at the time, but 'were not exact in their language,' and not the Palestinian Galilee, which was a leading centre of Jewish religious learning, indeed most of the Palestinian Talmud was compiled in Tiberias, and it was the centre of the Masoretic scribes who studied and vocalised the text of the Hebrew Bible. In the Hijazi 'Galilee', Judas presumably belonged to the village of 'Iskar, and like the other disciples of Jesus who had originated in this general region, spoke with an immediately recognisable dialect (Mk 26:70).

There still exists a valley called Dama, a tributary of Wadi Maysan, in the same Ta'if highlands where Wadi Jalil (Galilee) and the village of 'Iskar (modern 'Askar) are located. There are also places called Nasirah (Nazareth), Sayadah (Bethsaida) Qurazimah (Chorazin) Zubaydah (Zebedee), 'Allaf (Alphaeus), Zel'ota or Zu'lah (Zelotes), and Qinan (Canaan; Qannaim). The tribe inhabiting Wadi Jalil is called Nasirah (nsrt) to this day.

In the Dhu Khulasa cult, the god dies only to return to life, thereby bringing redemption to mankind. For his death to be mystically significant, it cannot be natural – he has to be betrayed and killed by an adversary, normally a close associate. [14] Therefore the god's resurrection represents the triumph of good over evil, of life over death, and light over darkness (cf. I Cor 15:42).

All these precedents force us to confront a fundamental question. Why should people who wished to accept Baal-mythology and the theology of mystical salvation have gone to such trouble to invent yet another new version (i.e. 'official' Christianity), when the old ones already offered such abundant possibilities? Could it be possible that Jesus, as constructed by the Churches, really was no more than a myth?

One answer would be to put the two aspects together: the myth, and the real physical existence of a noble Messenger called Jesus. It could be that the saviour-myth was much more prevalent among the 'people of the land' of Palestine than has been realised. The Old Testament naturally records the history of the One True God and His teachings, not the teachings of the Baal and the Asherah and Tammuz cults, although we can pick out throughout the Old Testament the continued existence of high places, standing phallic stones, and sacred groves. It is reasonable to suppose that the cult persisted as a secret mystery, persecuted by the priesthood and pious kings, and after the destruction of the Jerusalem temple in 70, the central rites and sacraments symbolising the death and resurrection of the saviour-god may have become fused with the prevalent Jewish dream of the deliverer who would put an end not just to the Roman occupation but the entire existing world over, and set up the Kingdom of God.

Did the historical hero Jesus, who really did live at a particular moment of history and in a particular Roman province, a leader of the Nazoreans or 'Keepers of the Law', and was thought to have been crucified as a rebel by Pontius Pilate and whose followers believed would return to establish the Messianic kingdom, become identified with the saviour of this ancient cultic myth?

Stories of dead people returning to life occur regularly in history, but accounts of them do not usually suffice to found a religion.[15] In the case of Christianity, could it be that the story survived *because* it became fused with the myth? No Trinitarian would have invented the story that the founder of their sect had been condemned to death as a human political offender if no such history really attached to him. If Jesus had been no more than a myth, sharp Jewish rabbis and pagan critics would have pointed the finger at that, instead of adopting the tactics they did.

If the Church today had to depend on the letters of Paul, who apparently cared little for the earthly life of Jesus, or his followers or political leanings, who never mentioned Jesus' teachings, never used the term 'Nazarene', never cited the companions trained by Jesus as authorities for any of his facts or doctrines, and never acknowledged any authority or informant but Jesus, the Risen Lord, it would know almost nothing of the earthly career of Jesus. For Paul, the earthly aims of a Nazarene Messiah were totally irrelevant. The surviving knowledge of his teachings, sayings and activities must actually owe a great debt to the Nazarenes, those who presented what Paul called 'another Jesus' (2 Cor 11:4), 'a different Gospel' (Gal 1:6-9), the Jesus accepted to this day by Muslims as one of the greatest of all Messengers of God. These preservers of the reality of the Messenger were the 'pillars of the church', James the brother of Jesus, Cephas (Simon Peter) his chief disciple, and John; possibly not the Galilean fisherman but the Beloved Disciple, perhaps John the Priest (Gal 2:6-9).[16]

Naturally, these monotheist Christians maintained that *they* were the true repositories of Jesus' teaching, and as late as the second century it was still possible for Papias to disparage the heavily-edited written gospels in favour of oral tradition passed down from them, and collected from people who had actually met the disciples of the Lord. He was, inevitably, mocked and jeered at by the Trinitarians.

But is the Trinitarian Church right? In promoting its saviour-myth, has it obliterated the *real* Jesus: Jesus the human prophet, the Messenger of God?

Chapter Thirteen

INSPIRED OR PROHIBITED?

THAT THERE WAS once a great deal more original Christian literature than we have now is stated quite explicitly in Lk 1:1-4 and Jn 21:5. Luke begins his Gospel with this statement: 'Inasmuch as many have undertaken to compile a narrative of the things which have been accomplished among us, just as they were delivered to us by those who from the beginning were eye-witnesses and ministers of the word, it seemed good to me also, having studied all things carefully for some time past, to make an orderly account for you, O Theophilus'(Lk 1:1-4).

How one would love to see those other eye-witness records and memories, the accounts Paul and Luke presumably used as their source material! We know Luke copied large sections of Mark's Gospel, and he and Matthew both seem to have used another document which the scholars now call 'Q'. There must once have existed a very rich fund of historical tradition about Jesus that is now lost.

Gospels other than the finally chosen canonical ones abounded, the most important known today bring those 'according to' Peter, James, the Nazarenes, the Hebrews, the Egyptians, Thomas, and the Ebionites. Christian Gnostics claimed that their teachings had not come from any source other than direct descent from the Apostles. [1]

The Fourth Gospel ends thus: 'Now Jesus did many other signs in the presence of his disciples which are not written in this book' (Jn 20:30); and 'There are also many other things which Jesus did; were every one of them to be written, I suppose that the world itself could not contain the books that would be written.' (Jn 21:25)

According to what principles did the authors of the Christian books make their editorial choices? The Fourth Gospel is quite frank: 'These are written that you may believe that Jesus is the Christ, the Son of God, and that believing you may have life in his name.' (Jn 20:31) All the New Testament writers, including

Paul, presented the truth *as it appeared to them*. They did not simply record everything they knew, every eyewitness account, diary entry, family memory of some notable moment involving the Great Teacher; they *selected* such narratives and teachings as fitted their purpose, and their view of the events that had happened. Our knowledge and understanding of Jesus today is coloured by the choices they made then.

Specialists in religious text-criticism perennially try to discern the truth behind narratives shaped by excessive zeal, personal ambition and the credulity of the pious. The original teaching, the pure unadulterated monotheism that Jesus preached, is now so encrusted with pious embroidery of the truth 'for the greater glory of God', deliberate additions and omissions, falsifications, paraphrasing at the expense of meaning, and mistranslations, that little of it remains discernable.

To scour away all this in order to reveal its original purity is no easy task, and in the past many have paid with their lives for making the attempt. What drives religious scholars to this 'suicidal' desire for truth is not the perverse wish to be a nuisance and disturb the establishment, but the highest moral courage, and the belief that God is concerned that humans should seek and find the Truth.

If this search makes them cruel, vengeful, vindictive, fanatical or infamous, then they are on the wrong path. The 'things of God' encourage intelligence, justice, purity, honesty, mercy, and the spirit of liberty. They are against strife, slavery, greed, ignorance, credulity and superstition. The true 'things of God' develop and satisfy the brain, and civilise the heart. God never says: 'You must believe this, because I say so!' He has no need. As He proclaims in the Qur'an: 'Truth always stands clear from error' (2:256).

Today's theologians, with the benefit of all the latest scholarship, much of it based on new discoveries, should not cling blindly to the past, but should seriously consider by what right they still accept the judgement of the theologians of the fourth century onwards, and still hope to consign to oblivion all that does not fit the received Trinitarian framework; in other words, the evidence of the monotheistic Christianity that predated it. How can the conscience accept all the blatant Trinitarian censorship of venerable texts without a murmur of protest, and acquiesce in all the political skulduggery in those ancient bishoprics? What right have we to ratify the decision that there should be only four Gospels, [2] and that we should discard the Gospel According to Hebrews, or the Gospel of Thomas? Or to toss overboard any writing that smacked of Judaic or

Pharisaic mysticism in favour of the superimposition of a Hellenistic saviour-cult? Or to ignore the sayings and teachings about Jesus in God's revelation to Muhammad?

Hebrew Gospels

As we have seen, the Ebionites (or Nazorenes, or Nazarenes) became separated from the Gentile Church because the Gentiles would not stick firmly to their belief that Jesus was not God, and that circumcision, sabbath-keeping, ritual purity, and refusal to eat *haram* food were all obligatory for all Christians. The Nazarenes saw no reason to set aside the Law of the Torah, any more than Jesus did. In the fourth century, Jerome came across Nazarene Church members in Syria, and made a copy of the only gospel they used, the Aramaic document that was either a version of 'Matthew' written in Hebrew characters, or possibly an earlier 'Matthew'.[3] Since by this time the other canonical Gospels were widely circulated, it must mean that these Christians either did not revere them, or had quite deliberately chosen to reject them.

For a considerable time an extremely large body of Christians regarded a 'Hebrew' Gospel as being no less important, if not more so, than our present four. This Gospel of the Hebrews is known to us from the Neo-Platonic Christian professors of the University of Alexandria in Egypt, Clement and Origen, and may have been one of the sources of the Gospel of Thomas. It was first mentioned by Hegesippus,[4] but Jerome was its principle witness. Both these men recorded that it was written in Syriac, by which they probably meant Aramaic. Epiphanius and Jerome both believed that this was the Aramaic original of our Matthew, but Jerome's quotations from it do not seem to bear this out. However, it obviously bore some relationship to it, and may have been an Aramaic arrangement of it, or a Nazarene version of it.

Unfortunately, Jerome confusingly refers to it seven times as 'According to the Hebrews', twice as 'Of the Hebrews', three times as 'The Hebrew Gospel', twice as the 'Hebrew Gospel According to Matthew', while twice he says that it was called this by the hypothesis of others, and once he calls it the 'Gospel According to the Twelve Apostles.' We can never know for sure, without further discoveries, if all these references were to one document.

Jerome states:

> Matthew in Judaea was the first to compose the Gospel of Christ in the Hebrew character and speech, for the sake of those who came over to the faith from Judaism; the person who later translated it into Greek is no longer known with certainty. The

Hebrew text itself is still preserved in the library at Caesarea, which the martyr Pamphilus collected with great care. The Nazarenes in Beraea, a city of Syria, who use this book, permitted me to copy it. In it, it is to be noted that whenever the Evangelist draws proof-texts from the Old Testament [...] he does not follow the Greek Septuagint translation but the original Hebrew text. [5]

Eusebius of Caesarea also had access to Pamphilus' library. Strangely, he never mentions spotting the original Matthew on the shelves, which is surprising if the library had indeed contained so great a treasure. What Jerome saw was possibly an Aramaic Gospel which he equated, rightly or wrongly, with the original Matthew. He said that it was especially venerated by Jews who had become followers of Jesus, who used it alongside the four canonicals and also *another* Aramaic Gospel. [6] Epiphanius suggests that the Nazarenes had the Gospel According to Matthew in Hebrew in a 'very full version', and that the Ebionites accepted Matthew and called it the 'Gospel According to the Hebrews'; but it was not complete. It was a 'falsified and mutilated version'.

In case the readers of *this* book are now confused, it should be pointed out that although the present Gospel of Matthew is still placed first of the Gospels in our New Testament, the version we read today was certainly *not* the first of the four to be written. Even the most basic examination will reveal that Mark was written before Matthew, and that Matthew copied about ninety percent of Mark's words, and was not an eye-witness.

So, do these references all refer to the same document, or were there two, or even more? Traces of it were still being discovered in the Middle Ages; in certain ninth and tenth century manuscripts there were marginal notes 'from the Jewish' and one of these agrees with one of Jerome's quotations.

One major theory is that the 'Gospel of the Hebrews' was either 'The Gospel according to the Nazarenes', 'The Ebionites' or 'The Twelve Apostles', and that all three were separate texts. Another theory holds that the 'Gospel of the Hebrews' was that of the Nazarenes, while the 'Gospel of the Ebionites' was that of the 'Twelve Apostles', making two books. Finally, some believe that all references are in fact to a single book. Each theory has its doughty advocates.

Extant quotations from 'it' include an interesting version of the story of the Rich Young Ruler (cf. Mt 10:16-30). After Jesus had commanded him to sell all his goods and give the proceeds to the poor, the 'rich man began to scratch his head. And it pleased him not. And the Lord said unto him, "How can you claim that you have done the Law and the prophets, since it is written in the Law that you shall love your neighbour as yourself. Look: many of your brethren, sons of Abraham, are clad in filth and dying of hunger, whereas your house is full of good things, and nothing at all goes out to them".[7] And he turned and said to Simon his disciple, who as sitting by him, "Simon, son of John [Baryonah], it is easier for a camel to enter through the eye of a needle than for a rich man to enter the kingdom of Heaven!"'

The Hebrew Gospel also included an important reference to Christ's appearance to his brother James. Such an apparition had been briefly noted by Paul (I Cor 15:7) but it is ignored by the New Testament gospels. The Hebrew Gospel says: 'And when the Lord had given his linen shroud to the servant of the priest, he went to James and appeared to him. For James had sworn that bread was Corban to him [he would never eat again] from that hour wherein the Lord had drunk the cup until he saw him risen from the dead with his own eyes. "Bring a table and eat" said the Lord. He took up the bread and blessed and broke, and gave it to James the Just, and said to him, "My brother, eat your bread, for the Son of Man is risen from them that sleep."'

What would one not give to be able to read today the full Gospel from which these fragments were taken?

The Shepherd of Hermas

This book was widely used by the early Christians, who regarded Hermas as a prophet. The Muratorian Canon stated that he was the brother of Pius, the Bishop of Rome from c140-155. His book, written between c88-97CE, was discovered in 1922 on a third-century papyrus. Hermas wrote it at Patmos, near Ephesus, probably before the Fourth Gospel was finalised. There is no indication in the work that Hermas had read any of the gospels now in our New Testament, or any others.

Hermas was granted four visions, in the last of which he was visited by an angel dressed as a shepherd, who had been sent to him by the angel Gabriel. This angel had been delegated to live with Hermas for the rest of his life, and his purpose was to oversee the writing down of all the commands and parables which the angel would dictate to him. There are obvious similarities here with the angelic guidance given by the angel Gabriel to the prophet Muhammad.

The book was accepted as inspired scripture until the time of the Council of Nicaea (325CE), when it was banned because it did not teach the Trinitarian doctrine. On the contrary, it held that God was One, and that believers should submit themselves to Him as His servants, and cast out all evil desires and bad manners of life.

It was claimed that Hermas in fact wrote two books, one of which he despatched to Clement. It was accepted as part of the New Testament by Clement of Alexandria, Origen, Tertullian, Irenaeus, and Athanasius, and formed part of the fourth century Codex Sinaiticus. Origen said that this was the instruction Paul referred to in his Epistle to the Romans (15:4): 'For whatever was written in former days was for our instruction, that by steadfastness and by the encouragement of the scriptures we might have hope.'[8]

What is most interesting is that Hermas never uses the name 'Jesus' or 'Christ' of the founder of Christianity, but says simply that he was a man in whom the Spirit of God dwelt; neither does he mention a crucifixion or a resurrection. The fact that this work was regarded as an inspired text and included in at least one canon of the New Testament indicates the breadth of opinion among the early Christians, before the appearance of a self-validated official form of the religion.

Epiphanius

Some information about the Ebionites can be gleaned from the writings of Epiphanius. He reveals that they were Adoptionist, for they believed that 'Jesus was begotten of human seed, but was chosen by God and thus called by election to be the Son of God, the Christ having come on him from high at his baptism in the form of a dove.'[9] They say that he was not begotten by God the Father but that he was created like the archangels, although he was greater than them. He came into this world and taught, as it is written in their gospel: 'I have come into the world to destroy sacrifices, and if you do not give up sacrificing, the anger of God shall not cease!'[10]

One important Ebionite text was a letter from Peter to James, in which he explains that he is sending him an exposition of his doctrine to be used in the training of 'those who wish to take up the work of teaching' in order to ensure the *orthodoxy* (i.e. monotheist orthodoxy) of their ideas. 'For', he says, 'some from among the gentiles have rejected my teaching which is in accordance with the Law, and attached themselves to certain Lawless and trifling doctrines of the man who is my enemy.' The most likely candidate for this 'man who is my enemy' was surely Paul. In the Ebionite literature there was no polite smoothing over of differences.

Other Ebionite works that Epiphanius names include their own Acts of the Apostles, and a text called the 'Ascents of Jacob' (James). This latter infuriated Epiphanius as it gave such a different picture of early Christian affairs to Luke's

Acts of the Apostles by omitting all Paul's mission work, and concentrating on the ministry of James!

Epiphanius also supplies the information that the Jews of Tiberias in the fourth century had in their archives the Hebrew Matthew, the Hebrew Acts, and a Hebrew Book of John (possibly a version of the Apocalypse). A Jewish tradition claimed that all these three works were written by Jesus' cousin Simeon, son of Cleophas, who was the leader of the Nazarenes and who, despite his great age, was apprehended, tortured and executed in Trajan's reign at the beginning of the second century.[11]

Symmachus

Symmachus was an Ebionite Christian whose translation of the Old Testament into Greek was one of those used by Origen in his *Hexapla* (a massive work that compared the texts of six translations Origen regarded as influential and authoritative). Eusebius comments that 'those who belong to the Ebionites (like Symmachus) affirm that Jesus was born of Joseph and Mary, and suppose him to be a mere man, and strongly maintain that the Law, as God's Will, ought to be kept in a true attitude of submission. And commentaries by Symmachus are still extant today, in which he tries his hardest to support the said heresy from the Gospel of Matthew. Origen mentions that he acquired these works, together with others of Symmachus' commentaries on the scriptures, from a certain Juliana, who had received them from Symmachus himself.[12]

Again, therefore, the evidence clearly shows that the Ebionites believed in Jesus as a prophet, a man chosen by God, on whom the spirit descended at his baptism. They rejected the Trinity and any aspect of Christianity which transformed it into a saviour-cult, and instead saw Jesus as the last and greatest of the succession of prophets, the bearers of Torah and spokesmen for God. Like the previous prophets, Jesus had been sent to reform Judaism and lead it back to its true purity.

These men and women were faithful observers of the Law, and considered the suppression of it as demanded by Paul to be nothing less than blasphemy. They claimed that *they* were the orthodox followers of Jesus, defending the real truth against the pagan corrosions to which Paul had subjected it. Jesus was the reformer who was to remove elements that had corrupted the Law of Moses, such as the polluted Temple worship, and especially the sacrificial system.

The Secret Gospel of Mark

In 1958 Professor Morton Smith visited Mar Saba in Palestine, and discovered what purported to be a letter from Clement of Alexandria referring to a secret Gospel of Mark. The existence of this latter text had in fact been noted in antiquity by Bishop Irenaeus of Lyons, who said that the Carpocratian sect had written a commentary on it, but prior to Morton Smith's discovery no trace of it had ever been unearthed. Clement quotes enough to show that it contained interesting material which is not in the Gospel of Mark as we have it today, including a version of the raising of Lazarus, an event which is not in any of the Synoptic Gospels.

In the present-day Mark we have the detail of an unnamed young man who watched the arrest of Jesus, was nearly captured himself, and only managed to get away by wriggling out of the sheet he was wearing and escaping naked. Since this is not mentioned in the other Gospels, many scholars have concluded that this mysterious eye-witness must have been Mark himself, in whose house the Last Supper had been held (Mk 14:51). However, in the secret-Mark, the young man was Lazarus. And he was in a white cloth because this was his initiation ceremony. Jesus had not anticipated his sudden arrest at all, but was interrupted in the initiation ceremony when the troops arrived. [13]

Was this secret document the original Mark (*Ur-Marcus*) from which these narratives had been dropped, or a later version than our Mark to which they had been added? No conclusions can yet be drawn.

Papias of Hierapolis

Two highly influential early Christian leaders, the Bishops Papias of Hierapolis and Clement of Alexandria, both claimed to be familiar with many traditions which had come down to them from the Apostles by spoken word, but which formed no part of the written record which came to be accepted as the canon of scripture.

Unfortunately Eusebius, who quotes tantalising snippets of so many of the writings of the early fathers in his historical works, called Papias a man of 'poor intelligence […] as is clear from his books.' This apparently rather low opinion of Papias influenced many generations and scholars. What Eusebius really intended, however, was not that the venerable Papias was stupid, but that he was of Ebionite frame of mind as regards the non-divinity of Jesus (the word *ebion* meaning 'poor').

Papias had gone to considerable trouble to find out 'from those who had known them, what Andrew, Peter, Philip, James, John or Matthew, or any other of the disciples of the Lord had said, and things that Aristion and John the Elder say'. This indicated, incidentally, that the Apostle John was not to be confused with John the Elder, and that the latter was still alive in Papias' time. He had learned from Philip the Deacon, who lived at Hierapolis with his four redoubtable prophetess daughters, the story of how one of the men put forward as the new Twelfth Apostle after the suicide of Judas, Joseph Barsabbas Justus, had drunk poison and survived (cf. Mk 16:18). He also knew 'some other accounts [...] from an unwritten tradition, and some strange parables and teachings of the Saviour, and some other mystical accounts.'[14] These included ideas of the millennium after the physical resurrection of the dead, and the coming of the kingdom of Heaven in material form on this earth. It was on these grounds that Eusebius concluded that Papias was an Ebionite.

Papias is an important witness, not least because of his insistence that it is a mistake to place too much confidence in the official four Gospels. He mistrusted them, noting that they had left out so many things, and, as our form critics and redaction critics now somewhat belatedly emphasise, the inclusion or non-inclusion of material was very arbitrary, being highly dependent on the aims and motives of the individual writers, or final editors, or the interest of the communities they served. The few quotations Eusebius gives from Papias' works suggest that like the modern scholars, he was critical of the Gospel of Mark as being palpably badly arranged, with an incorrect chronology, and a peculiar sense of geography. He also suggests that the Gospel of Matthew had been faultily translated.

Papias obviously did not regard the 'official' four Gospels as inspired scriptures, but felt free to criticise them, or to pass over them in favour of other sources. He considered that the information that was on offer in these books was not so profitable as that which came from the living and abiding voice.

Irenaeus, who wrote in the late second century, was acquainted with Papias' devout friend Polycarp, and also with Polycarp's information about Papias. He also knew the entire written work of Papias, and unlike Eusebius he prized it highly, since he reckoned that it truly put him in contact with apostolic times. This was quite a different attitude from that of Eusebius, and we are at liberty to decide which of these two eminent fathers' opinions we prefer.

Papias tried to preserve and hand on the doctrines from the Jewish-Christian community, which had been the theology of the First Church. It is a pity Eusebius preserved so little of it for us.[15] Clement of Alexandria considered that it was *vital* to put these oral traditions into writing 'lest they should perish'.[16] He clearly stated that 'This Gnosis came down from the Apostles through their successors to a few of us, being handed down unwritten.'

Justin Martyr

Justin Martyr of Samaria (d.c165 CE) was one of the leading so-called Ante-Nicene Fathers.[17] He composed a *Dialogue with Trypho* (written sometime around 140-145 CE), in which he discusses the respective merits of Judaism and Christianity with a distinguished Rabbi, Trypho, who was a refugee from the Hadrianic campaign against the pseudo-Messiah Bar Cochba in 140.[18]

Justin, who pleaded the Christian case, apparently accepted the Ebionite doctrine of Adoptionism, that the Divine Grace could fall upon a person at any moment of God's choosing, thus elevating that person to the position of being an 'adopted' son of God. In Jesus' case, he believed that this happened at his baptism. The notion of God impregnating a virgin was pagan and abhorrent to him, and quite unnecessary to his scheme. The 'adopting' of the Messiah would be signalled by the reappearance on earth of the prophet Elijah, as foretold in Malachi 3.1 and 4.5.[19]

Now, the Christians claimed that John the Baptist was 'the Elijah who was to come', whether as a reincarnation, or as a representative,[20] but Rabbi Trypho did *not* accept this connection, and therefore since as far as he was concerned John the Baptist was not that Elijah, he concluded that Jesus could not possibly be the Messiah. Justin maintained that John really *had* been Elijah, and that Jesus became the Christ at the moment of his baptism, when the 'Godhead' came upon him. All this reveals that Justin Martyr was not a Trinitarian, although he was stoutly upholding what *he* thought was the absolute truth of the matter, and considered himself to be orthodox.[21]

Trypho was not convinced, and commented that Christianity was 'deserting God and basing its hopes on a mere man [...] You have accepted an idle report and fashioned a sort of Messiah for yourselves; and for his sake, with little consideration of what you are doing, you throw away your lives [...] How can you put your trust in a mere crucified man, neglect God's commands, and still hope to obtain His blessing?'[22]

Trypho derisively and specifically equated the Jesus-myth to the birth of Perseus, son of Zeus and the virgin Danae. 'You Christians should be ashamed to relate such things like the heathen. It would be better if you asserted of this

Jesus that as a man he was born of human seed, and called to be a Messiah on account of his faithful obedience to the Law.'[23]

Celsus

Another influential opponent of Christianity was Celsus, a Neoplatonic philosopher who wrote 'A True Word' sometime around the year 178CE. Unsurprisingly this work has not survived, but Origen published a reply to it in 248, quoting many of his words. In his attack Celsus made two vital claims: that he could 'state many other things regarding the events of the life of Jesus which are true, and not like those recorded by the disciples'; and that the Christians 'have corrupted the Gospel from its original integrity to a threefold and four-fold and manifold degree, and have remodelled it, so that they might be able to answer objections'.[24]

Apparently Celsus knew the story picked up by the Jewish Gemara[25] for he claimed that Jesus was a base-born adventurer, the son of a soldier named Pandera, who had gained magical powers while living in Egypt. A voice had declared him to be the Son of God at his baptism, and thereafter he collected a following of riff-raff, tax-gatherers, sailors, and so forth, and wandered about living on his wits and working magical tricks until he was captured and executed. The witnesses to his resurrection were nothing but crazy women, a handful of dreamers, wishful thinkers or just plain liars. Celsus found the whole business of Christianity ridiculous. Benefactors to the human race such as Heracles and Asclepius were condemned by these fanatics, yet they deified an executed malefactor!

There is a powerful whiff of anti-Christian vehemence in Celsus. His attack was, however, representative of many others. For our purposes, however, it is important to note that he did not attack a Trinitarian version of Christianity but a Christianity of Jewish-Christian Adoptionist stance, a view the official churches no longer consider orthodox! Incidentally, he also regarded Jesus as an impostor, even a malefactor – but not a myth.

Chapter Fourteen

THE DOCUMENT CALLED 'Q'

PAUL'S KERYGMA (or 'proclamation') stated that it was the destiny of Jesus to come into conflict with the rulers of this world, because they were evil subjectors of human souls, and that Jesus the Son of God was the bringer of God's power to release souls. His earthly conflict climaxed with his sacrificial crucifixion, but believers could be confident that everything would soon be resolved when Jesus appeared as Resurrected Son of God to judge the world and establish the Kingdom of God.

The challenge of Q is that the authors of two Gospels which are accepted unanimously as key Christian documents (namely, the Gospels of Matthew and Luke) incorporate sizeable portions of a very different sort of kerygma into their accounts of Jesus' life. Had they not done this, we would never have had access to *written* source material from the earliest followers of Jesus which the writers of those times could not deny was geniune.

So, what was Q? Why is it so important? It was a document written and revered by Christians prior to our existing Gospels, which acquired its 'name' Q simply from the capital letter of the German word *Quelle*, meaning 'source'. How was it discovered? In fact, physical pieces of ancient papyrus with Q-text written on it have never been discovered, not even in fragments; but scholars poring over the Synoptic Gospels, trying to work out which one was written first, realised it must have existed once.

In very simple terms, the reasoning goes like this. The ancient Church Fathers were all unanimous that Matthew was written before the other synoptic gospels, yet over 600 of Mark's 661 verses appear either exactly or almost exactly word for word in either Matthew or Luke or both. This was either the result of a miracle, or Matthew and Luke were both copying, the latter point of view being the one favoured by scholars. Therefore, Mark *must* have been written before both of them, unless Mark was copying either Matthew or Luke. This does not seem possible, for Mark's accounts of things are very much longer than the others, much more vivid, and full of what seem to be eye-witness details. Moreover, if Mark was copying either Matthew or Luke it seems remarkable that he should have left out all the birth and resurrection narratives, and virtually all of Jesus' teaching.

As scholars set the texts side by side for comparison, they noticed something else. There were around 200 verses identical or nearly identical in Matthew and Luke which were not in Mark at all. Again, this was either a miracle, or both Matthew and Luke were copying *something else*: another written document. This, then, is what scholars mean by Q.[1]

There is a problem here: the contents of Q are not clear-cut, since Q by definition *only* consists of verses which are in Matthew and Luke but are absent from Mark. So if Mark had also had access to Q and had copied from it, we would never be able to know, for we could not identify the verses. Verses in all three Synoptics are always assumed to have been copied by Matthew and Luke from Mark. Similarly, verses from Q copied only by Matthew or Luke, but not both, cannot be identified.

However, whether Mark copied from Q or not, it is important to note that since Mark commences with the ministry of John the Baptist and ends with the burial of Jesus, and these narratives in Matthew and Luke hail from different sources, then neither Q nor Mark included the narratives of Jesus' miraculous birth, or the resurrection narratives, the key requisites of Trinitarian theology.[2]

The disquieting conclusion for Trinitarians is that

> the remarkable thing about the people of Q is that they were not Christians (as we understand the term nowadays). [...] They did not take his teachings as an indictment of Judaism. They did not regard his death as a divine, tragic, or saving event. And they did not imagine that he had been raised from the dead to rule over a transformed world. They did not gather to worship in his name, honour him as a god, or cultivate his memory through hymns, prayers or rituals. They did not form a cult of the Christ such as the one that emerged among the Christian communities familiar to the readers of the letters of Paul. This discovery upsets the conventional picture of the origins of Christianity.[3]

The challenge to the popular conception of Christian origins is quite clear. Did these first-hand followers of Jesus fail to get his message? Were they absent when the unexpected happened? Did they carry on in ignorance or in repudiation of the Christian gospel of salvation? And if these first followers of Jesus understood the purpose of their mission in the terms of the Q teachings, is this not proof that the Christ cult, the mythologies of the Gospels, and the eventual establishment of the Christian church and religion are wrong?

Honest consideration of the Q-source challenges the conventional picture of Christian origins in a much more far-reaching way than most people realise. It is not just a variant form of Christianity that can be quietly disposed of, although this seems to be what happened to the document itself when the writers of the Gospels selected by the Trinitarian Church had used what they wanted of it.

The problem is that it undermines the belief that the earliest Christians regarded the 'death and resurrection' of Jesus as a necessity of faith, or even a historical fact. Almost all modern variant forms of Christianity assume that this unique, miraculous, dramatic event was the focus of all early Christian traditions, and their theologies are their several attempts to deduce the mysterious meaning of that divine originating moment. Q's challenge is that the original Jesus movement *was* apparently generated without recourse to such an originating event, religious experience or message of salvation. The Q source had no birth narratives, miraculous or resurrection narratives. Therefore, the originating cause of the Jesus-movement must have been something else, and *not* an atoning incarnation and sacrificial death.

Q forces the issue, for it documents an earlier history that does not agree with the later Christian theology that 'Christ died *for* us', or that his death saves us from our sins, the teaching that undergirds the entire Trinitarian theology.[4]

In the nineteenth century, the quest for the historical Jesus had been driven by a romantic Protestant obsession.[5] The Protestant critique, starkly emphasised in the modern Jehovah's Witness movement, for example, claimed that the official Roman church was a pagan adulteration of true Christianity, a historical development that veered away from the original intentions of Jesus and the earliest forms of Christian community and faith. These Protestants hoped to recover Christianity in the pristine purity of its original form, which was, they considered, far more Protestant than Catholic. In other words, the quest for the historical Jesus was motivated by a Protestant desire to leapfrog over the entire history of Catholic Christianity and land at the beginning again.

A hundred years were spent on painstaking and often brilliant investigations of the four New Testament Gospels (thus omitting all those not in the official New Testament), to get behind the myths and miracles and reconstruct from the given texts the story of the man Jesus 'as he really was'. Few thought to question the main story line, the supposed 'life of Christ', because no-one, until comparatively recently, imagined that the evangelists had intended anything other than a biography.[6]

Q's challenge is absolute and critical, and vital to the Islamic case, for it drives an irrefutable wedge between the story as told in the narrative Gospels and the history they are thought to record. In other words, the narrative gospels should no longer be read gullibly or innocently by anyone as the straightforward record of historical events that generated Christianity. Q put us in touch with the earliest history of the Jesus movement, with the First Church itself, and this was very evidently non-Trinitarian.

Islam endorses the leapfrog, but begs to widen the boundaries of possible conclusions about the life of Jesus. The only answer that makes sense is to accept that Jesus was not just a myth: he really did live, but that he never claimed to be a saviour-god; he was exactly what the Qur'an announces about him: he was a charismatic figure, a Prophet, a Messenger of God, inspired by the same Divine One who had spoken already through so many saintly descendents of Adam.

Chapter Fifteen

SCROLLDUGGERY

(Or: Has there really been a Dead Sea Scrolls Deception?)

HIDDEN AWAY IN caves almost 2000 years ago, the Dead Sea Scrolls are another source of unique insight into Christian origins. But ever since they were discovered by Muhammad al-Dhib in 1947, a controversy has haunted the cloisters of the 'established orthodox' Christian Church. These scrolls were texts which had never been edited or tampered with since they were deposited in their subterranean hiding-places near the ruins of Qumran; and the scrolls have been dated precisely, and promisingly, to the period of Jesus' lifetime.

The Qumran people were thought to be an extremist sect of Jewish mystics and healers usually identified with the Essenes. In view of their date, Christian scholars hoped their scroll library would shed significant new light on the origins of Christianity, and perhaps even contain references to Jesus himself. Enthusiasts assumed that John the Baptist, who lived and worked barely a stone's throw from Qumran, must at least have been known to them, and may have been adopted by them as a youth when his elderly father, the priest Zechariah, died, after which he became a missionary, since Essenes were said to have adopted orphans and sent out trained teachers to call on people to repent before the Day of the Lord arrived.

After the first flush of excitement over the discoveries came disappointment. Nothing. Not a word about Jesus or John at all. It seems that although God had walked around on earth incarnate, the Qumraners had simply not noticed. We read references to baptism, communion meals, groups of twelve disciples, and even to the fact that a 'son of a carpenter' meant 'a very canny fellow' ('Not even the son of a carpenter could do that!'). But Jesus is conspicuous by his absence.

Excitement was, however, rekindled by many references to an eminent leader known as the Teacher of Righteousness. Speculation flared up again: with some experts surmising that Jesus had been a member of the sect, and that in his 'missing years' he had learned secret wisdom in Egypt (where there was a not dissimilar Jewish sect, the Therapeutae). Some speculated that Jesus actually was the Essene 'Master'.

As it happens, this was not a new idea: the versatile Frederick the Great had concluded in 1770 from the few references to the Essenes in Pliny, Philo and Josephus, that 'Jesus was really an Essene, he was imbued with Essene ethics.'[1] In 1863, the 'liberal' scholar Rénan's *Vie de Jesus* proposed that 'Christianity was an Essenism which had largely succeeded.'[2] The eccentric Madame Blavatsky taught that Jesus was an adept or magus who embodied elements of both Essene and Gnostic traditions. A whole host of splendidly imaginative theories were promulgated, not least of which was John Allegro's proposition that the mystic insights of the Essenes were caused by the ritual eating of a hallucinogenic mushroom.[3]

Scholars of more sober predilections waited eagerly for the publication of more texts, and hoped at least for some insights into the world in which Jesus had lived, or preferably unknown textual evidence that would throw light on his life and ministry.

They waited a long time. From 1952, when a team of Roman Catholic scholars under Father de Vaux was appointed to take charge of the scrolls, publication of the translations and findings lay under the control of an elite and secretive clique.[4] Publication was delayed by a series of interventions and inefficiencies, to the irritation of those itching to read them. Allegro, one scholar who was far from happy at this situation, wrote in 1956: 'Already, study of the 1947 scrolls was producing any number of parallels with the New Testament, and these and the materials from this and the later caves were clearly going to change every text-book on this period of Judaism and Christian origins that had ever been written.'[5]

The problem was that these discoveries and parallels were far from what the Trinitarian Churches hoped to find. Frustrated scholars began to wonder seriously whether there was a conspiracy of silence, a 'cover-up', in progress. Were the snail-like Catholic scholars deliberately trying to keep the texts secret, and if so, why? Did they reveal that Jesus was not the Son of God, but a Zealot revolutionary fighter after all, perhaps not even suffering a famous sacrificial death, but surviving his crucifixion to be one of the noble resisters who committed suicide on Mt Masada rather than admit defeat to the Romans, at a time after the Jewish Revolt?

At the same time, 'scroll-duggery' resulted in tragic losses of valuable material as fragile documents were irreparably damaged; other texts mysteriously vanished before scholars could get their hands on them. Two scrolls, for example, vanished from Cave Eleven after being briefly seen by two scholars.[6] There was a thriving clandestine market: one collection of material which was spirited out of the area during the 1967 war was offered to a European government for three million pounds![7]

So much time passed that people could be forgiven their suspicions. Inevitably, this led to speculations that once the full translations of the texts were made publicly available, the Church would be dealt a terrible blow. For de Vaux and his colleagues, working as representatives of the Roman Catholic Church, it must have seemed as though they were handling the spiritual and religious equivalent of dynamite: something that might just conceivably demolish the entire edifice of Christian teaching and belief.

One key factor that would make all the difference was the date of the scrolls. If the Teacher of Righteousness had lived in an earlier century, he could not possibly have been Jesus. It was vital to be clear about this, of course, because the scrolls never depict the Teacher as a divine incarnation, and proof that the Teacher *was* Jesus would be very embarrassing for the Church. Father de Vaux's team insisted that the scrolls were from a period well before the Christian era, and that therefore, although they might show that the teaching of the Gospel of Jesus was perhaps not as original or unique as previously thought, they could not possibly compromise his personal significance.[8]

But was de Vaux correct? If he was wrong about the date, then perhaps Jesus *might* have been the Teacher after all, and the Church was mistaken in believing that Jesus was divine. This would vindicate the faith of the First Church under the leadership of James, who likewise never claimed that Jesus was divine, but was rather a beloved leader and Messiah, a Messenger of God. It became startlingly possible that the Qumran documents would bring us very close indeed to the Jewish-Christian scene; a scene that the team of conservatively Catholic experts was not overly anxious to probe or to publicise.

However, the Teacher of Righteousness (the Righteous One, the Just One, or *Saddik*), was by no means necessarily to be identified with Jesus. The texts implied that the Teacher's ministry was a long one, whereas Jesus had led a strikingly short public career. And on further investigation it soon became clear that alongside this Qumran Teacher there was a second significant person, a Davidic Messiah. Surely Jesus would have been *that* Messiah, in which case the Teacher of Righteousness was someone else, perhaps James, who was a known and esteemed leader of many followers for many years.

The 'Damascus Document', one of the most important of the scrolls, speaks of 'the Righteous Remnant': the Jews who remained true to the Law as opposed to those who were prepared to bow the knee and compromise with Rome. It is called the 'Damascus Document' because their Teacher of Righteousness would lead them to a place called 'Damascus' in the wilderness, where these *Baryonim* ('sons of the wilderness') would enter into a renewed covenant with God.

The problem here is that the biblical Damascus we are familiar with was the Romanised capital city of Syria, and not a place in the wilderness. It now seems virtually beyond doubt that by 'Damascus' they really meant Qumran. Numerous textual references make it clear that this renewed Covenant is the same one cited in the Qumran 'Community Rule', and it is obvious (no scholar disputes it) that the Damascus Document is speaking of the same community as the other Qumran scrolls. In fact, fragments of no fewer than ten copies of the Damascus Document were found in Qumran's caves.

In the Damascus Document many of the regulations are identical to those of the Community Rule, but there are also a few surprises. There are rules for marriage, women and children, which belie the accepted notion that Qumran was a monastery of Essene sectarian monks, although both Philo and Josephus had specifically reported that the Essenes were celibate. Graves of women have been found in the settlement.[9]

Other rules referred to members travelling without being encumbered by provisions, and visiting affiliated communities scattered throughout Palestine, which proves the community was not isolated from the world or obscure, and, incidentally, seems to resonate with the style of missionary work on which Jesus sent his disciples (see Mark's Gospel 6:7-13).

Of particular interest was evidence of a serious split amongst the members. Some had betrayed the sect and deserted to 'the Liar.' 'Those who enter the New Covenant in the land of Damascus, and who then betray it and depart' were bitterly condemned.

After the initial euphoria of supposing that Jesus and John the Baptist must be Essenes because of the many observed similarities, opinion then swung to the opposite point of view. The Scrolls community were now said to be exclusive and hard-hearted, whereas Jesus had been outgoing, merciful and had a message for all. Supposing John and Jesus had *once* been members of the sect but had broken with them because of Essene exclusiveness and rigidity? Their mission was to everyone, including sinners. Could this be the split referred to? Could the disturbing truth then be that it was *Jesus* who was branded as 'the Liar' because he took such a lenient line and this was disapproved of by the extremists, so that he was not the revered Teacher at all, but – in their eyes – a renegade?

Others have been more attracted to the idea that the Teacher was not Jesus but James, so that then the 'Liar' might be *his* rival Paul. According to the Acts of the Apostles, Paul was on his way to 'Damascus' as the instrument of the corrupt High Priest, to ferret out fugitive members of the early 'Church'. Many have wondered on what grounds he could have done so, and what authority he could possibly have had in territory ruled by the Nabataean King Aretas. If 'Damascus' really meant Qumran, then Paul's expedition suddenly makes sense. Unlike the Syrian Damascus, Qumran did lie in territory under the high priest's jurisdiction, and it would have been entirely feasible for the high priest in Jerusalem to have dispatched his 'enforcers' to Qumran, a mere twenty or so miles away.

Father de Vaux's team had tried to maintain that Qumran's Essenes were a pre-Christian pacifist ascetic sect, with no connection either with early Christians or the mainstream Judaism of the time. However, if Qumran *was* 'Damascus', and members of the early church *were* there, then either the first Christians were being sheltered by the Qumran community, which would at least mean that they were sympathetic towards each other, or it might even signify that *the early Church and the Qumran community were one and the same.*

In the autumn of 1991 the monopoly of the Roman Catholic team was at last effectively broken when the Huntingdon Library in California announced it would make its collection of Dead Sea Scrolls photographs public. This epoch-making decision was followed by the issuing of a facsimile edition by the Biblical Archaeology Society in Washington.

When Eisenman and Wise published the previously unseen fragments, it became obvious that they really were not the literature of a passive, contemplative monkish celibate sect, but of a band of Zealots, who, as we have seen, were the Messianic movement in Palestine responsible for the revolt against Rome that led to the destruction of the Temple. They concluded further that the manuscripts offer not merely a picture of the background from which Christianity sprang, but show what Christianity actually *was* in Palestine. It was virtually impossible to distinguish ideas and terminology associated with the Jerusalem community of James the Just from material found in this corpus. Unwary modern readers might not recognise it as Christianity, because it seemed the virtual opposite of the polite, pacifist, tolerant, bland church atmosphere of today. Palestinian Christianity was zealot, nationalistic and apocalyptic.

The serious split cited by the Damascus Document must have been a major and traumatic event in the life of the community, for, as the complete texts reveal, it figures in no fewer than five other scrolls and four further text fragments.

The Habbakuk Commentary, for example, reveals how certain members of the community were urged by the Liar to break the New Covenant and cease to observe the Law. This precipitated a serious conflict between them and the Teacher of Righteousness. The Liar was not the only enemy spoken of in the texts. There was also a Wicked Priest. This miscreant was an outsider, a representative of the corrupt priestly establishment of the Temple, and therefore, incidentally, datable to the time before the destruction of the Temple in the Jewish Revolt. In contrast, the Liar came from *within* the community. He had been given refuge by them and was accepted as a member of good standing, so his subsequent defection made him a traitor as well as an enemy.

The date of the scroll can be set specifically in the Herodian epoch[10] as it alludes to Roman troops making sacrificial offerings to their standards, a practice for which Josephus provided evidence, dating it to 70 CE.[11] In pre-imperial times, Romans sacrificed to their gods, and not to the standards, which were the tokens of the 'deified' emperors.

No ancient description of the Essenes mentions that they possessed a special calendar, but the Qumran community in fact recognised a unique solar-based calendar in preference to the conventional Judaic lunar one; they celebrated the Passover meal the night before the official priesthood did. Could this explain why the Gospels indicate that Jesus held *his* Passover meal on the Thursday, the Qumran night?

Philo states that the Essenes did not perform animal sacrifices; but animal bones have been found ritually buried at Qumran, and are discussed in the 'Temple' scroll. Josephus writes that the Essenes were on congenial terms with the Herods, but the Qumran literature shows a hostility towards non-Judaic authorities in general and towards Herod's dynasty in particular; and there is strong evidence that the commune was abandoned and uninhabited during the reign of Herod the Great. The Essenes are reported to have been pacifists who had 'no makers of armour', yet the ruins of Qumran include a defensive tower and a forge for weapons. Their attitude now seems to have been martial in the extreme, as revealed by such texts as the War Scroll.

> Indeed, the bellicose character of such texts seems to have less in common with what Josephus says of the Essenes than with what he and others say of the so-called Zealots – which is precisely what Roth and Driver claimed the Qumran community to be, thereby incurring the fury of de Vaux and the international team.[12]

One passage in Josephus does ring true, however. He states that 'they despise danger and conquer pain by sheer will-power: death, if it comes with honour, they value more than life without end. Their spirit was tested to the utmost by the war with the Romans, who racked and twisted, burnt and broke them, subjecting them to every torture yet invented in order to make them blaspheme the Lawgiver or eat some forbidden food.'[13]

As we have seen, the community members never referred to themselves as Essenes, but as Keepers or Doers of the Covenant, or the Perfect of the Way. The Habbakuk commentary calls them the *Osei ha-Torah*, or 'Doers of the Law'. As the collective of *Osei* is *Osim*, this may provide the true explanation of the name 'Essene'. Epiphanus speaks of a heretical Judaic sect near the Dead Sea called the 'Ossenes'.[14]

In Hebrew, the 'Keepers of the Covenant' is *Nozrei ha-Brit*. From this term derives the term *Nozrim*, and this is one of the earliest Hebrew designations for the sect subsequently known as the Nazoreans or Nazarenes (modern Arabic/Islamic designation – *Nasara*) – *in other words, the Christians.*

Baigent concludes that the Qumran community must have been a desert community of Nazarenes parallel to the early Church based in Jerusalem, which comprised Nazarenes who followed James, the brother of Jesus. Indeed the Habbakuk commentary states explicitly that Qumran's ruling body, the 'Council of the Community', was actually located in Jerusalem at the time; and in Acts 9:2, the members of the early Church are specifically referred to as 'Followers of the Way': a phrase identical with Qumran usage.[15]

Chapter Sixteen

TWO MESSIAHS: THE SONS OF DAVID AND THE ZADDIKIM

IN ACTS 2:44-46, the faithful are depicted as living together and owning all things in common. They sell their goods and possessions and share the proceeds among themselves according to their need; and go as a body to the Temple every day. The first Christian martyr is said to have been Stephen (Acts 6-8) who alluded in a passionate speech to Jesus as the Righteous One or the Just One, *Zaddik*, a term characteristic of Qumran. In his defence, Stephen showed he was no renegade from the Law, but zealous to keep it in all its purity, as opposed to the corrupt pro-Herodian priesthood.[1]

It was on the road to 'Damascus', perhaps to be identified with Qumran, that the Saul who became Paul experienced some form of vision which struck him blind and brought about his conversion. The community at 'Damascus' healed him. He joined this community as a disciple, and remained under their tutelage for three years (Galatians 1:17-18). According to the Dead Sea Scrolls, three years was the exact probation and training period of a newcomer.

No sooner did Paul launch his febrile missionary activity, however, than his teachings became a flagrant deviation from the 'original' or 'pure' form extolled by the leadership. For Jesus, adhering faithfully to the Jewish Law, it would have been blasphemy to advocate worship of any mortal figure, including himself. Paul's statements about the Law must have been provocative in the extreme, as we have already seen, and constituted the challenges of a self-proclaimed renegade. His 'Christianity' no longer had much to do with Jesus, only with his image of Jesus.

When Paul was arrested and taken into Roman custody, a mysterious group of angry Jews, forty or more 'zealots for the law', met in secret and vowed not to eat or drink until they had brought about his death, an attitude characteristic of the militant Zealots and their special assassination squads, the Sicarii.[2] An important passage in the Damascus Document declares that if a man 'transgresses after swearing to return to the Law of Moses with a whole heart and soul, the retribution shall be exacted from him.'[3]

Whoever they were, the plan of these 'Jews' was thwarted by the appearance of Paul's previously unmentioned nephew, who learned of the plot, and Paul was escorted to safety with a huge Roman escort (Acts 23:23). He was taken to Caesarea, and after appearing (on friendly terms) before the despised enemies of the Zealots, the governor Antonius Felix and his wife the Herodian princess Drusilla, and Drusilla's brother King Agrippa and their sister Berenice, he was taken thence to Rome where he 'disappeared' rather suspiciously, calling to mind some IRA 'supergrass'.

The *Clementine Recognitions*, as we have seen, present copious details about James, and at one point describe an almost fatal attack on him. In this narrative, James was preaching in the Temple when an unnamed enemy with a gang of followers tried to drown out his words with noise, and eventually stirred up a riot by laying about him with a wooden club. James was beaten, thrown headlong down the steps and left when his enemies assumed he was dead. He survived, however, and was rushed by his disciples to Jericho (just a few miles from Qumran) to convalesce. After three days, one of the brotherhood came from Gamaliel bringing secret news that the enemy had received a commission from Caiaphas to arrest all who believed in Jesus, and that he should go to 'Damascus' with his letters.

Is it possible that the Acts account of the martyrdom of Stephen, an obscure figure, supposedly a Hellenist who was nevertheless able to expound to the Jews their own history, is in fact a 'doctored' version of this attack, with James' name deliberately suppressed, and the name of Stephen substituted?

James manifestly survived the attack, (unlike the supposed Stephen) but he did meet with ultimate martyrdom, many features of which resemble the death of Stephen. Josephus' version of it can be dated to the time when Lucceius Albinus was on his way to Jerusalem to take over from the previous governor, who had died. At this time, the High Priest was the hugely unpopular Ananas. James died in 62 CE, only four years before the outbreak of the revolt in 66 CE, and there is genuine reason to think that it was the death of this revered leader which lit the fuse of revolution.

Eusebius states that the whole revolt of Judaea was 'for no other reason than for this wicked crime of which he had been the victim,' and he cites Josephus as his authority for this. Is it not highly suspicious that this passage is no longer in any of the extant texts of Josephus? It was unquestionably there once, for it was also quoted by Origen of Alexandria, who stated: 'These things happened to the Jews in requital for James the Righteous, who was a brother of Jesus known as Christ, for though he was the most righteous of men, the Jews put him to death.'[4] The wicked priest Ananas was one of the first celebrities to perish as a result of the uprising, assassinated by the Zealots as a Roman collaborator. James' death was therefore hardly a 'marginal incident', yet there is no mention of it at all in Acts!

To sum up: in early Christian sources James the Righteous (the *Zaddik*, to recall the Qumran title) was a Nazirite, a leader of Jewish followers of Jesus who were 'zealous for the Law'; he had to contend with two adversaries: Paul, a renegade sect member who preached his own doctrine which drew on that of the community but distorted it, and Ananas the corrupt head of the Temple priesthood, hated by the pious for collaborating with the Romans and with their quisling kings. In the Qumran Habbakuk Commentary we find the Teacher of Righteousness leading a sectarian community which is portrayed as extremely 'zealous for the Law', contending with two adversaries: the Liar and the Wicked Priest.

The Liar flouted the Law in the midst of their own congregation, led many astray and raised a 'congregation of deceit.' Professor Eisenman points out that Paul's letters reveal an almost obsessive desire to exculpate himself from accusations of lying. The Wicked Priest conspired to exterminate 'the Poor' (or Ebionites), those 'Zealots for the Law' said to be scattered about Jerusalem and elsewhere, and harried the Teacher of Righteousness wherever he sought refuge. After the death of the Teacher, his followers killed the Wicked Priest and 'took vengeance upon his body of flesh'. Ananas was indeed quickly killed in reprisal, and his corpse was abused and defiled by those who killed him.

The parallels are surely unmistakable. Eisenman, who has sifted through the scrolls line by line, draws the conclusion that the Habbakuk Commentary and certain other Dead Sea scrolls are definitely and beyond doubt referring to the same events as those recounted in Acts.

Incidentally, Paul's teaching that a person shall live by faith as 'opposed' to living by the Law actually *came from* the Book of Habbakuk (2:4), which would help to explain why the Qumran community found it important to have a commentary on this particular book. It comments that the passage refers specifically to all observers of the Law whom God would deliver from Judgement, because of their suffering, and their loyalty to the Teacher of Righteousness![5]

Belief in resurrection and in the life after death was not a Christian invention. All the Zealots from the time of the Maccabean Revolt in 165 BCE onwards preferred to die as martyrs rather than break the Law, the most extreme proof possible of a person's devotion to a religious cause. They believed in the resurrection of the pure to the point of fanaticism, not because of the resurrection of Jesus, but because of the prior teaching expounded primarily in the Old Testament books of Daniel and Ezekiel, both of which books figure amongst the Scrolls. Daniel had proclaimed that 'of those who lie sleeping in the dust of the earth many will awake, some to everlasting life and some to shame and everlasting disgrace.' (Dan 12:2)

Ezekiel's most famous resurrection passage is the vision of the valley of dry bones. The relevant passage at the end of it was actually discovered buried under the floor of the synagogue at Masada. It reads: 'I mean to raise you from your graves [...] and lead you back to the soil of Israel. And you will know that I am God, when I open your graves and raise you from your graves [...] And I shall put My spirit in you, and you shall live.' (Ezek 37:12-14)

This accounts for the willingness of those 'zealous for the Law' to die as martyrs, by communal suicide if necessary. It was a belief taken for granted by the Hasidim, the righteous 'separated ones' of the time of the Maccabean revolt, who proclaimed 'you may discharge us from this present life, but the King of the World will raise us up, since it is for His laws that we die, to live again for ever.'

Muslim readers curious about the religious quality of the life of the Scroll community will find much here that is familiar and impressive. For instance: here is one fine section of a Dead Sea Scroll hymn:

> I thank you, O Lord, for You have redeemed my soul from the Pit, and have raised me from Hell to the Everlasting Heights. And I shall walk in the boundless plains, and know that there will be a final gathering for those whom You created from clay [...] I am dust and ashes; and what shall I strive to do without Your good pleasure, and what can I do without Your goodwill? How shall I be strong, unless You support me, and how shall I have wisdom unless You create it for me? [...] Nothing is known without Your permission, and there is none other than You.[6]

Readers shaped by the sensibilities of the Muslim community of revelation will jump to but one conclusion: the passage is *muslim*, the latter part of it evoking the Verse of the Throne:

God: there is no God but He, the Living, the Self-Sustaining Eternal; He is overtaken by neither drowsiness nor sleep. Everything in the heavens and on earth is His. Who is there that can plead for another in His presence, except as He permits? He knows what is before or behind them. They cannot encompass anything of His knowledge except as He wills. His throne extends over the heavens and the earth, and He feels no fatigue in guarding and preserving them, for He is the Most High, the Great. (Sura 2:255)

Another fundamental concept of the Dead Sea Scrolls that is familiar to Muslims was that of the 'two spirits', the equivalent of the *nafs*, the good and evil inclinations. The Manual of Discipline states: 'He assigned to humanity two spirits in which they should walk – the spirits of Truth and Perversity; truth, born out of the spring of light, perversity from the well of darkness. The dominion of the children of righteousness (sons of *Zaddik*) is in the hands of the Prince of Light, so that they walk in the ways of light; whereas the government of the children of perversity is in the hands of the Prince of Darkness, to walk in the ways of darkness. The purpose of the angel of darkness (Satan) is to try to lead the children of righteousness astray; all their sin, their iniquities, their guilt and their rebellious works are the result of his attempt to dominate, in accordance with God's mysteries, until His appointed time. All their sufferings and times of affliction derive from Satan's hostility.'[7] This doctrine is a favourite theme in many Jewish-Christian writings. One section of the 'Teaching of the Twelve Apostles' is almost a literal translation of this part of the Qumran manual of Discipline. It is almost identical to the teaching of the Qur'an about the function and role of Satan.

The Manual outlines briefly what conditions will be like in eternity for those who have succeeded and those who have failed. It gives descriptions in physical terms, but these should be interpreted symbolically. It is obvious that our second created life-forms will not be the same as our physical earthly ones. The reward in Paradise will be 'healing, abundant peace, length of life and fruitful seed with everlasting blessings, and eternal joy, a crown of glory and a robe of majesty in eternal light.' Those led by the spirit of perversion (the word Satan means 'to rebel') have become unpleasant, with the characteristics of greed, injustice, wickedness, falsehood, pride, deceit, hasty temper, jealousy, lechery, blasphemy, spiritual obtuseness, obstinacy and 'vile cunning', and can expect 'terror and perpetual disgrace, with the shame of extermination in the fire of the dark regions.'

The description of the qualities of those who will achieve Paradise are also listed in the Manual: to 'enlighten the heart of Humanity and make straight before it all the ways of true righteousness, to urge human hearts to be respectful of the judgements of God; a humble spirit, an even temper, a freely compassionate nature, a goodness that never fails, an understanding and insight and keen wisdom which has faith in all God's words, and a confident trust in His many mercies; a zeal for behaving with justice, and a determined piety with unwavering mind; loyalty towards the children of truth, and a radiant purity which loathes every idol; a humble bearing and a discretion regarding all the hidden things of Truth and secrets of Knowledge.'[8]

Perhaps the most significant fact is that the scrolls refer to two messiahs: the messiahs of Aaron and of Israel, the first being descended on the priestly Levitical line and the latter from King David of Judah. Qumraners wished to restore the purity of the regime of Priest and King, the two anointed leaders of God's community (and therefore both 'messiahs' or 'anointed ones'), a royal or Davidic Messiah, and an Aaronic or priestly Messiah.

Now it is almost automatically assumed that Jesus, 'put to death' for claiming to be King of the Jews, was the Davidic Messiah. However the Davidic claimants known from the scrolls stem from the early days of the Zealot movement, when Judas of Gamala launched his revolt after the death of Herod the Great in 4 BCE. This Judas was acclaimed as messiah, and a public demand was instantly whipped up for the Herodian high priest to be deposed and one of 'greater purity' to be installed in his place.[9]

The priest favoured by Judas was said to have been called Zaddik (or Sadduc, or Zadok). Judas and Zaddik stole weapons from the armoury of Sepphoris, and shortly afterwards Herod's palace at Jericho was burnt down; events which were followed by seventy-five years of incessant guerrilla warfare culminating in the full-scale revolt of 66-73 CE.

Eisenman, following Josephus' reports of the desert holy men active at this time, makes the fascinating suggestion that this Zaddik, the Righteous One, the friend of Judas of Gamala, might have been none other than John the Baptist, whose attacks on the Herodian dynasty (in particular the uncle-niece marriages specifically inveighed against in the Dead Sea Scrolls) led to his martyrdom.[10]

The guerrilla warfare was continued by the sons of this Davidic Messiah Judas of Gamala; his sons Jacob (James) and Simon were both captured and crucified by the Romans in 46-48 CE. A third son, or perhaps grandson, Menahem, was one of the leaders of the 66 revolt, and at one point made a triumphal entry into Jerusalem in 'the state of a king', and later managed to capture Masada.[11]

Since the Davidic messiah was an inherited role, it leads one to ponder the possibility that the Teacher of Righteousness was also a role that was to be passed on, down a particular family line. If this is so, it could perhaps provide an answer to one of the most intriguing of Scroll mysteries. It would mean that one would not have to pick and choose between John or Jesus or James. It is more likely that Jesus was one of a *series* of Zaddiks, or Righteous Teachers, of whom John the Baptist might conceivably have been the first. John obviously had Levitical descent, as we have seen. Jesus was said to have been his cousin; and there are traditions that his mother Mary was raised from infancy at the Temple by the priesthood.

If Jesus was of Davidic descent, and not Levitical, he could not have been a priest. The Gospels present two genealogies of Jesus, and they don't agree. However, for what it is worth, both Matthew and Luke give the family of line of *Joseph* the husband of Mary, who was of the line of David. [12]

If this theory is correct, the John followed by Jesus and then James in his turn were the chosen ones who fulfilled the role of Levitical Messiah of Aaron, the Zaddik or Teacher of Righteousness. This theory would remove the obvious problem of scrolls enthusiasts trying to establish whether it was Jesus or James who was the Zaddik: they *both* were.

It is all speculation. But it provides a credible interpretation of many of the enigmas of the New Testament record which have puzzled scholars for many years.

Chapter Seventeen

JESHU BAR NAGARA AND THE PROPHET 'ISA

IN KAMAL SALIBI's third book *Conspiracy in Jerusalem*, the author deduces that there must have been a combination of *three* sources for the 'person' who became known as Jesus of Nazareth. The first was the prophet 'Isa of the Qur'an, whom he reckons was not the same person at all as the Jesus who was crucified at Jerusalem. He believes that the prophet 'Isa may have lived some considerable time before the Messiah Jesus, and was a genuine Messenger of God. He taught a strict monotheistic Judaism like all the other prophets, and may possibly have been the originator of a parallel Judaism to that kind of Judaism which was propounded by Ezra.

The second was an equally historical personage, whom for clarity's sake he names Jeshu bar Nagara, son of the Carpenter. This person was a descendant of King David, a Messianic claimant, who was persuaded to go to Palestine and start a campaign that resulted in his arrest and execution.

The third element he proposes was not a historical person but the god al-'Isa, (also called Dhu Khulasa), whose cult included the familiar elements of virgin birth, a dying and rising Son, and a secret doctrine which would enable disciples to achieve spiritual enlightenment and a passage to paradise.

In his search for the historical Jesus, Salibi proposes that all notices in the Gospels which refer directly or indirectly back to the Old Testament (the proof-texts) should be discounted as the inventions of theologically-preoccupied scribes. Once this is done, there still remain many facts given about Jesus (the Messiah) that there is no obvious reason to discount. He highlights six.

Firstly: this Jesus is referred to as either 'the carpenter' (Mk 6:3, Greek *tekton*) or 'the carpenter's son' (Mt 13:55). Leaving out Gnostic speculations, this could simply indicate that he did indeed come from a family that practised carpentry, perhaps of a superior kind, or that it was a surname, in Aramaic 'Bar Nagara', similar to our 'Smithson' or 'Shepherdson'. Alternatively, since family names often referred to the place of the family's origin, he looks to see if there was such a village or settlement called Nagara. He finds that to this day there still exist in the Hijaz, near Ta'if, two villages with cognate names, one called Nujar, another called Nujayrah; and that there was a further village, Najr, which no longer exists. All five are 'Ngr', vocalised as 'Nagar' to mean 'carpenter'. He assumes, therefore, that Jesus came from this region.

Secondly, his father was called Joseph. All four Gospels agree to this: Mt 1:16ff, 2:13ff; Lk 1:27; 2:4ff; 3:23; Jn 1:45; 6:42. The Synoptics name his mother as Mary, but the Fourth Gospel leaves her unnamed, while suggesting that she had a sister also called Mary, the wife of Clopas (Jn 19:25), which confuses the issue.

He had four brothers: James, Simon or Simeon, Joses or Joseph, and Jude or Judas, and more than one sister (Mk 6:3).

He attracted public attention shortly after the reign of Tiberius (i.e. CE 28-29 – Lk 3:1), when he was about thirty (Lk 3:23), when Herod Antipas was tetrarch of Galilee (4BCE-CE39; Mk 4:14ff), and when Pontius Pilate was procurator of Judea (CE 26-36, Lk 3:1). He had male and female disciples and friends whose names are cited in the Gospels, though not always consistently.[1] He led a disturbance in the Jerusalem temple, after which he was tried in the presence of Pilate and put to death on the Eve of the Passover. It was highly likely that his career was connected to all the other political intrigues of this period, and seeing that Jesus was commonly claimed to be a descendant of David, why should it not have been true that he really did have a legitimate claim to David's throne?

According to all four gospels, however, the people in Jerusalem who clamoured for his trial and execution were not Romans but Jews, who reportedly presented him as an enemy of the Roman state, and were acting as cowardly collaborators.[2] Moreover, it was someone who was thought mistakenly to be Jesus, but actually was not, who was the one who met this fate (Sura 4:157), perhaps Judas Iscariot, or Simon of Cyrene, or some other person, while Jesus miraculously escaped.

A highly significant fact, for Salibi's hypothesis, is that when Paul decided to become a follower and apostle of Jesus, he did not go to find his information about him in Jerusalem among the original apostles who still lived there: according to his own report he went directly to Arabia instead. 'I did not confer with flesh and blood, nor did I go up to Jerusalem to those who were apostles before me, but I went away into Arabia; and again I returned to Damascus. Then, after three years, I went up to Jerusalem to visit Cephas,[3] and remained with him fifteen days. But I saw none of the other apostles, except James the Lord's brother. In what I am writing to you, before God, I do not lie!' (Galatians 1:16-20). For Salibi, this raises the question of whether he went back to the Nagara region from which Jesus had appeared.

The Book of Acts, however, makes a point of ignoring all this, and gives quite a different account. From Acts 9:19-26, we glean the information that Paul was with the disciples Ananias and his friends in Damascus, preaching openly in the synagogues and amazing them, for they knew he was the man who had 'made havoc' in Jerusalem, and had gone there for the express purpose of arresting Christians and bringing them bound before the chief priests. He confounded the Jews of Damascus by proving that Jesus was the Christ. He then had to escape over the city wall in a basket because the Jews were so angry they plotted to kill him. Then, 'when he had come to Jerusalem he attempted to join the disciples; and they were all afraid of him, for they did not believe that he was a disciple. But Barnabas took him, and brought him to the apostles, and declared to them how on the road he had seen the Lord, who spoke to him, and how at Damascus he had preached boldly in the name of Jesus. And he spoke and disputed against the Hellenists; but they were seeking to kill him. And when the brethren knew it, they brought him down to Caesarea, and sent him off to Tarsus'.[4] (Acts 9:26-30.)

What has happened to the visit to Arabia? Is the author of Acts trying to conceal something? Or had he, perhaps, been kept in the dark about something? There is no further mention of Ananias, but it is Barnabas who initially vouches for Paul and defends him to the apostles. Verse 31 may hold an unconscious irony: having sent Paul off to Tarsus, 'the church throughout all Judaea and Galilee and Samaria had peace, and was built up.'

According to Acts, Paul stayed put in Tarsus until Barnabas was sent by James to preach to the Gentile converts at Antioch, and he went off to Tarsus to look for Paul and fetch him back, to help him. (Acts 11:19-26) They worked together for a year, and then went down to Jerusalem to take famine relief money. Paul's letter to the Galatians stated that he had preached in Syria and Cilicia for fourteen years, and only went back to Jerusalem with Barnabas and Titus, to defend his preaching. (Gal 2:1.)

Salibi next turns to the material about Jesus to be found in the Qur'an.

Firstly, he notes that in the longer suras, where large sections are devoted to the prophets of the People of the Book, a clear distinction is made between the Israelites (Banu Isra'il) and the Jews (al-Yahud). The Israelites are depicted as the past 'chosen' people who were the 'preferred' of God in their time, whose history until the fifth or fourth century BCE was recorded in the Hebrew Bible. The Jews, on the other hand, are spoken of as an existing religious community, specifically the followers of the Biblical monotheism and the laws of Moses as interpreted and developed by rabbinical tradition in post-exilic times, and who paid particular deference to Ezra (identified sometimes with the Qur'anic figure Uzayr).

The Christians in the Qur'an are of two sorts: those who commit *shirk*, and those who are highly commended. Salibi suggests that the latter type of Christians, who are called Nasara or Nazarenes, were Christians of Banu Isra'il origin, who had quite different attitudes to the al-Yahud community of Ezra. They did not call their founder Jesus or Jeshu (standard Christian Arabic Yasu'), but 'Isa, which is an entirely different name, although both 'Isa and Jeshu can be rendered in Greek as Iesous.

The Christians who were considered to be in grave error because they maintained that God was not One but a Trinity, were fiercely opposed to Islam, but the true believers made common cause with the emerging community of Islam, and were absorbed into it. [5]

> You will find the closest in affection to those who have accepted the faith [Islam] to be those who say 'We are Nasara'; this is because there are priests and hermits among them, and they are not arrogant. When they listen to what has been revealed to the Messenger [Muhammad], you see their eyes overflow with tears as they recognise the truth; they say: 'Lord, we believe; enrol us as witnesses.' God rewards them for what they say: in gardens beneath which rivers flow, where they will live forever. This is the reward for those who work goodness. (Sura 5:82-5)

A claim sometimes made of the Qur'an by Christian scholars is that the verses concerning Jesus are no more than a garbled version of canonical and apocryphal gospel accounts. In fact, most of the material concerning Jesus has no clear parallel with the gospels at all, either canonical or extra-canonical.

The two non-canonical Gospels such critics probably have in mind are the Gospel of Pseudo-Matthew and the Arabic Infancy Gospel. In particular it is suggested that as the latter was written in Arabic, its contents must have been well-known to the Prophet Muhammad and other Muslims. It mainly concerns

RIGHT: *The three monotheisms meet here: the tomb of Abraham at Hebron.*

BELOW: *Romanised, wealthy and Jewish: the synagogue at Capernaum.*

ABOVE: *The Herodian temple of Caesar Augustus at Sebasteia. Such pagan structures were lightning-rods for Zealot hostility.*

BELOW: *The caves at Qumran where the Dead Sea Scrolls were discovered.*

ABOVE: *The settlement of Qumran. Several of the structures shown here are ritual bathing pools.*

RIGHT: *Mosque and tomb of Nabi Yahya (John the Baptist), Sebasteia.*

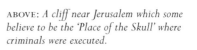

ABOVE: *A cliff near Jerusalem which some believe to be the 'Place of the Skull' where criminals were executed.*

BELOW LEFT: *To forestall disputes, the key to the Church of the Holy Sepulchre is traditionally held by a Muslim, who unlocks it each morning.*

RIGHT: *The so-called 'Tomb of Lazarus' at Bethany, showing the central pit.*

BELOW: *Rolling stones of this type were used to cover the entrances to Jewish tombs in Palestine. The object's great weight is apparent.*

ABOVE: *The 'tombs of the Bene Hezir' at Jerusalem. The structure on the upper left is traditionally known as the tomb of James.*

BELOW: *The Dome of the Rock at the centre of the Al-Aqsa Mosque complex, which occupies the probable site of Solomon's temple.*

ABOVE: *Interior of the Dome of the Rock.*

BELOW: *Mosque of the Ascension of Jesus on the Mount of Olives.*

ABOVE: *Mosque of the Ascension of Jesus on the Mount of Olives. The niche indicates the direction of Mecca.*

BELOW LEFT: *A Triadic deity, from a pre-Christian French altar.*
BELOW RIGHT: *The Trinity (Italy, 19th century).*

three topics: the miraculous birth of Jesus, miracles that took place in Egypt during the stay in that country before the death of the tyrant Herod, and miracles performed by the child Jesus, which also appear in the very early Gospel of Thomas (one of the gospels discovered at Nag Hammadi in Egypt). The Virgin Mary plays a dominant role in this text. The Gospel of Pseudo-Matthew also concerns the birth and infancy of Jesus.

These gospels are of particular interest to Christian tourists visiting various shrines associated with the Holy Family in Egypt. However, if Muhammad was 'borrowing from these sources' as suggested, it is worth noting that the Qur'an never mentions such highlights from Pseudo-Matthew as the interesting data that the Virgin Mary and her infant were protected from dragons, or revered by lions, or that the roses of Jericho blossomed where they trod, or that the idols of Hermopolis Magna (i.e. Ashmunaith, 175 miles south of Cairo) fell to the ground (Pseudo-Mt. 22-24).

As for the Arabic Infancy Gospel, it describes the birth of Jesus in a cave near Bethlehem at sunset; the statement that the visiting Magi came to Egypt according to a prediction of Zoroaster (Gosp 7:1); that it was at Marariayal, a place to the north-east of Cairo, that Mary found shelter and a 'resting-place' (Gosp 24); that they had a home at what is now the site of the church of Abu Sarghis, near the old Synagogue of Cairo; that she made her home for six months at the site now occupied by the monastery of Deir al-Muharraq, near al-Qusiya, some fifty miles south of Hermopolis Magna (Gosp 23); that it was here that they heard of the slaughter of the innocents of Bethlehem; or that when Jesus visited the Jerusalem Temple at the age of twelve, he was 'interviewed' by a philosopher, who was also a skilled astronomer, and who asked him if he had studied astrology (Gosp 50:51). The remarkable boy was able to explain to him the number of spheres and heavenly bodies and their natures and apparitions, their positions, their aspects – triangular, square and sextile – their course (direct and retrograde), and other things beyond the reach of reason.

If these were the Qur'an's 'sources', it seems most odd that none of this comes up in the Qur'an. Those who have studied the Qur'an can only find the narrative of Jesus making birds out of clay (sura 5:113) that could have had any connection with these Gospels.

Therefore Salibi, who is a Christian himself, and who does not accept the Qur'an as the revealed Divine Writ but as the creation of the Prophet Muhammad, nevertheless assumes that it is reasonable to suppose that the Qur'an preserves an *independent* tradition concerning the origins of

Christianity – a tradition that was still current in Arabia in the seventh century. Muslims, of course, would go further and simply state that the revelations concerning Jesus and Mary were true and from Allah, and not mere creations of the Prophet.

What does the Qur'an *not* say about Jesus? It does not refer to 'Isa as a carpenter or son of a carpenter. It nowhere speaks of Jesus as having a human father, let alone calling him Joseph. It is emphatic that 'Isa's mother was called Mary, and he is invariably identified as 'Isa ibn Maryam. It nowhere speaks of 'Isa as having brothers or sisters. It does not specify the period of 'Isa's mission, or associate it with Palestine. It does not name any individual disciple or associate. The Qur'an makes many references to David and his career, but never links 'Isa with him, or speaks of 'Isa as being his descendant. This is particularly noteworthy given the importance of genealogies in early Arabian society. It does not claim that 'Isa ever led a religious or political riot anywhere, and denies the claim that he was crucified or put to death in any manner. The assertion, therefore, is that the Christians had confused two quite different persons.

On all these counts, the 'Isa of the Qur'an has nothing in common with the Jesus of the Gospels. Indeed, the names Yasu' and 'Isa are entirely different names in Aramaic. It is surely unlikely that Muhammad would have 'made up' the name 'Isa in view of the fact that Christianity was long established in his region of Arabia, and many of his actual relatives and close friends were Christians and either remained so, or left Christianity to enter Islam.[6] Muhammad would have been perfectly familiar with the name they used for their Son of God.

Salibi suggests that it is therefore far more reasonable to assume that the 'Isa of the Qur'an really was *not* the Christian Gospel Jesus at all, and was called 'Isa for the simple reason that this was who he was: a prophet who had been revered in Arabia from his own time, some period well before the birth of the Gospel Jesus, until the century when Islam was revealed.

So what does the Qur'an say about 'Isa? It says a very great deal. Born of Mary, he was a prophet whose human person was a living manifestation of the *kalima* or 'word', since he was created by one word from God: 'Be!' (Sura 3:45; 4:171). He was born somewhere to the 'east' of a given place (9:16), the point of reference, on Salibi's view, probably being Mecca; and he emerged from his mother's womb at the foot of a palm tree (19:23). He was a Messenger from God to whom a special 'book' was divinely delivered (19:27-33): the Injil. He was a 'spirit' (Ar. *ruh*) from God, and was assisted by the Holy Spirit (Ar. *al-ruh al-qudus*, identified with Gabriel) (2:87; 5:110). He was called the Messiah (Ar. al-Masih) (3:45; 4:157,171,172; 5:17,71,72,75; 9:30,31). He was born pure (Ar. *zaki*) (19:19), and like Adam, he was a direct creation of God (3:59).

He performed miracles, and was able to raise the dead back to life (2:87; 3:49ff; 43:57), but unbelievers denounced his miracles as tricks and magic (5:110; 61:6). He was himself a miraculous being (Ar. *aya* – miracle, sign or token of God; 23:50). He had the gift of divination (3:49).

He was an apostle to the 'People of Israel' without any indication that he was 'Jewish' or a prophet of the 'Jews' (3:49). He was a consecrated or ordained person (Ar. *muqarrab*), which may imply an association with the priesthood, and his prominence belonged to both this world and the next (3:45). While he accepted the Mosaic Law, he made a point of alleviating some of its rigour in his own preaching, permitting some things which the Torah had forbidden (3:50). The disciples who followed him and were his helpers (Ar. *ansar*) were called al-Hawariyyun (meaning 'the people in white', from the Arabic *hawar* – 3:52; 5:111,112; 61:14), presumably meaning that they wore special white robes. Some Israelites followed him, while others did not (61:14).

Some people, in error, considered him to be the Son of God, just as some Jews mistakenly considered Uzayr to be the Son of God (9:30). Some even imagined 'Isa to be God in person (5:17, 116), but he was in fact human (5:75) and mortal (4:159; 5:17; 19:33, and perhaps 3:55). His followers were known as the community of the *Nasara*.

The Jews opposed his mission and scoffed at his miracles, and there was a claim among them that they had succeeded in having him put to death, either by crucifixion or in some other manner, and this was believed by some Christian sects but not by others. However, this was just an illusion (4:157). 'Isa was not crucified, but someone else with whom his identity was confused. The real 'Isa was taken up by God into heaven regardless of whether or not he died a natural death (3:55; 4:158), and he will come back to bear witness against those who hold false doctrines on the Day of Resurrection (4:159).

He prophesied that another Messenger, called Ahmad, would follow him (61:6). Muslims take this to mean Muhammad: Ahmad and Muhammad deriving from the same Arabic root *hmd*.

The words of the Qur'an insist that the account of him given in this revelation is the correct one, as opposed to other accounts which are hypocritical and false (19:34).

Salibi mentions one tradition preserved in a geographical dictionary written by the fourteenth century North African writer, originally from the Yemen, Muhammad ibn Abd al-Mun'im al-Himyari, that the origin of the religion of the Nasara was in Najran.[7]

Mary the mother of Jesus figures almost as prominently as 'Isa in the Qur'an, and the biographical information about her is also considerable. She was a 'daughter of 'Imran' (the Biblical Amram, father of Moses and Aaron) (66:12), and a 'sister of Aaron' (19:28). The descendants of Amram (Ar. Al 'Imran) are spoken of as being among the elect of God: the Hebrew Bible states that they belonged to the Israelite tribe of Levi. An older generation of Christians who assumed that the Qur'an merely confused the Virgin Mary with Mariam the sister of Moses made a simple mistake, and either failed to notice or ignored the fact that Mary's cousin Elisabeth is called a 'daughter of Aaron' in Lk 1:5, a phrase changed in more modern versions to explain, quite correctly, that this simply means 'of priestly descent'. The phrases indicate that the mother of Jesus also belonged by birth to the Levitical religious aristocracy of Israel.

Mary was a *Siddiqa* (5:17), which possibly signified membership of the community of Zaddikim. Her mother vowed her daughter to the service of God (3:42). She was a quietly obedient believer (21:91), a miraculous being herself (23:50), endowed with the gift of divination (3:44). When the time came for her to serve in the Temple (Ar. *al-mihrab* – in Salibi's theory this was *not* the Temple whose site is pointed out in today's Jerusalem), there was a dispute as to who would have the honour to be her sponsor (Ar. *kafil*), and lots had to be cast to decide the matter (3:44). The person chosen was Zechariah (Zakariyya, 3:37), the prophet who was the father of the prophet Yahya (3:38ff; 19:2ff; 21:89ff), whom the Christians identified with John the Baptist, even though Yahya and Yuhanan (the original Aramaic) are entirely different names. 'Every time Zechariah entered the Temple, he found Mary miraculously in receipt of material provisions' (Ar. *rizq*), and she explained that they were provided to her by God (3:37).

One day she donned the veil (*hijab*), left her folk, and went to dwell somewhere 'eastwards' of her home country (19:16). The Spirit of God (Jibril or Gabriel) appeared to her in male human form, and announced that she would bear a child, 'Isa, although she was still a virgin (19:17-21).[8] She made a point of maintaining her virginity intact, and only became pregnant when God 'blew' His spirit into her (21:91; 66:12), the divine agency being the *kalima* or 'word' (4:171).

She gave birth to 'Isa in a 'distant place', by the trunk of a palm tree, feeding from ripe dates as they fell to the ground (19:25). The word used for these dates is *rutab*, the horticultural term for fully matured dates, which fall between the end of August and beginning of October, suggesting that the birth of 'Isa was in September.[9]

The Jews spoke ill of her, because she gave birth while being unmarried (4:156). Her relatives were appalled when she returned to them with her new-born, and as they supposed, illegitimate child, and rebuked her for what they though she had done. However, the baby was miraculously able to speak to them and assure them that he was no ordinary child, but would be a prophet entrusted with a special divine message (19:27-30). Subsequently, some people misguidedly worshipped Mary and 'Isa jointly as 'two gods' (Ar. *ilahayn*), subservient to the supreme God, although 'Isa had never intended to or wanted this to happen, and considered it a grave wrongdoing (5:116).

'Isa was therefore not a descendant of David but an ordained Israelite *muqarrab*, a Levite of the House of Aaron, and the period of his mission was shortly after the time of a priest called Zechariah. Salibi suggests that this was not the Biblical prophet Zechariah of the time of King Darius of Persia (522-486BCE), but possibly the priest Zechariah son of Jonathan who participated with Ezra in the purification of the walls of Jerusalem in 457 BCE (Nehemiah 12:35,41).

If it *was* this Zechariah, then the 'Isa ibn Maryam of the Qur'an was active in the late fifth or early fourth century BCE.[10] If he was a Sadducee, a strict follower of the original Israelite monotheism, his preachings may have represented an archaic religious reaction to Ezra's innovative reforms. Ezra was also a descendant of Aaron (Ezra 7:1-7), so the two men would have claimed equal religious authority, which sheds light on the bitterness with which the Jewish followers of Ezra opposed the preaching of 'Isa, as we find it reported in the Qur'an.

In short, Salibi suggests there was a 'Christianity' in Arabia: the religion of the Nasara, which was several centuries older than the one which related to the historical Jesus of the Gospels; a 'primordial Christianity' which was monotheistic and survived on its home ground until the coming of Islam. On Salibi's view, this is the true Christianity as understood by Muslims; its founder 'Isa ibn Maryam, was the 'true Jesus'. The other brand of Christianity that elevated to the Godhead a man called Jesus who died on the cross, was false, and in grave error. Those claims were roundly dismissed in the Qur'an as delusions.

The Jesus who was put to death on the cross in c30CE was a descendant of David, not of Aaron, and belonged to the tribe of Judah, not the tribe of Levi.

From where did the canonical Gospel writers (writing in the late first century CE) get the details which really concerned the Prophet 'Isa, and which were incorporated into their material? They obviously could not have been quarrying the text of the Qur'an since that was not delivered until the seventh century CE; they had to have come from a text or tradition which had appeared in far more ancient times.

Chapter Eighteen

THE *INJIL* OF NABI 'ISA

(Was this the Gospel copied by Waraqa ibn Nawfal?)

T HE SAINTLY PRIEST and scholar, Waraqa ibn Nawfal, a relative of the Prophet Muhammad's wife Khadija, was one of the first to recognise and acknowledge the truth of the Blessed Prophet's mission. After he died, the Prophet reported seeing him in his dreams, robed in pure white (perhaps as one of the Hawariyyun) in Paradise. The ninth-century scholar al-Bukhari preserves the memory that Waraqa used to write Hebrew ('*Ibri* – either Hebrew or Aramaic), and used to make copies of the *Injil* in Hebrew. His Gospel, which obviously existed in Arabia long before the coming of Islam and the revelation of the Qur'an in the seventh century, was most probably written in Aramaic, and Salibi assumes that the story it related about Jesus was not enormously different from the one we could reconstruct from the text of the Qur'an. In other words, in this Gospel of the Nazarenes, the Jesus was the Qur'anic 'Isa, and not the Jeshu of Paul and the Greek Gospels.

If this had not been the case, the Qur'an could hardly have made the claim that its account of the career of Jesus was identical with that of the one authentic *Injil*, without facing immediate and serious challenge. It would certainly not have spoken of Christian priests and hermits recognising the truth of the Qur'an and weeping to hear it recited to them.

Islamic traditions recorded as early as the eighth century CE indicated that the same Gospel existed in Ethiopia (known to the Arabs as al-Habasha or Abyssinia). It is well-known that many of the first Muslims migrated to Abyssinia to take refuge from the persecution of the then pagan Meccans with the Christian ruler, the Negus. When relevant verses from the Qur'an were quoted to him, according to the earliest known biographer of the Prophet, Ibn

Ishaq, 'By God, the Negus wept until his beard became wet. His bishops also wept on hearing what was recited to them, until their scriptures became soaked. The Negus then said: 'This and what Jesus taught must come from the same niche of light!' […] Then, smiting the ground with his hand, he picked up a twig of wood and said: 'By God, there is no more to Jesus in addition to what you have said than the measure of this twig!' [1]

The evangelisation of Abyssinia to triune Christianity was credited to Frumentius (CE c300-380), in the wake of the conversion of the Roman Empire, but Christianity already existed there in its older Nazarene form. The new Trinitarian preaching was only successful in Abyssinia and Arabia to the extent that it could secure adequate political and material backing from Byzantium. The older faith was not eradicated; and the diehard Nazarenes stuck to their old ways. The Christian Abyssinians maintained the practices of ritual circumcision, the keeping of Saturday as the Sabbath, the adherence to much of the law of the Torah, and the maintenance of an Ark of the Covenant (a *tabut*) which was carried out by the Abyssinian army when it went into battle.

The Nazarenes may well have been overcome with despondency when they saw their old faith being overwhelmed by the new preaching and theology, but when Islam was proclaimed they were able to reaffirm the veracity of their original Gospel, and they recognised 'Isa as *their* Jesus. [2]

If Salibi is correct, the Gospel of the Arabian and Abyssinian Nazarenes would have been much older than the surviving canonical Gospels, perhaps dating as far back as the fourth or fifth century BCE. Salibi suggests that what prompted Paul to make his visit to Arabia following his conversion experience was that he knew, or suspected, that the son-of-David Jesus who died on the cross in Jerusalem was not the same as the Prophet 'Isa.

Did the authors of the Four Gospels know of the existence of an ancient Aramaic text? Is this what Paul discovered when he went to Arabia? Christian scholars will admit that it is certain that scriptures older than the canonical Gospels existed, but they prefer to speak of the Gospel sources more cautiously and ambiguously as 'traditions'. Paul occasionally mentioned such scriptures, and sometimes quoted from them in his epistles, as he also quoted from the regular Israelite scriptures. In the second epistle to Timothy, reference is made to his 'books […] and especially the ones made of parchment.' (2 Tim 4:13)

Paul never knew Jesus, but he did know his brother James; indeed he repeatedly met and quarrelled with him. He hence certainly accepted the historicity of James' brother, although he appears not to give much credit to the stories circulated about him. He accepted his affiliation to the House of David, but not the genealogies attributed to him. Two epistles make this clear: 'Tell them to give up those legends and those long lists of ancestors, which only produce arguments' (I Tim 1:4); 'Avoid stupid arguments, long lists of ancestors [...] they are useless and worthless' (Titus 3:9).

Christian scholars have long been perplexed by the fact that in Paul's writings the historical Jesus is only a shadowy figure, reduced to unimportance by Paul's vision of the Living Christ. Paul seems to have regarded only his death and resurrection as being especially significant, for theological reasons. Paul's description of *his* Jesus was given in Colossians 1:15-20:

> He is the image of the invisible God, the firstborn of all creation; for in him all things were created, in heaven and on earth, visible and invisible [...] all things were created through him and for him. He is before all things and in him all things hold together. He is the head of the body, the church; he is the beginning, the firstborn from the dead, that in everything he might be pre-eminent. For in him all the fullness of God was pleased to dwell, and through him to reconcile to himself all things, whether on earth or in heaven, making peace by the blood of the cross.

As we have seen, Paul denounced the religious teachings of the Jerusalem leaders where they differed from his own, as worthy of nothing less than outright damnation (Galatians 1:8-9): 'If anyone preaches to you a gospel that is different from the one you accepted, may he be condemned to Hell.' He considered the gospel preached in Jerusalem to be 'legend' (Gk. *muthos* – I Tim 1:4; 4:7), and, even more fearfully, 'Jewish legend' (Titus 1:14). His own gospel was the authentic one, because it was not of human origin, and no human had taught it to him. It was revealed to him by his vision of the Risen Jesus (Gal 1:11-12). He did not validate in any of his surviving epistles the story of his original persecution of the Nazarenes, his vision on the road to Damascus, and his instruction in the faith by Ananias. On the contrary, let us repeat what he says of himself:

> God in his grace chose me even before I was born, and called me to serve Him. And when He decided to reveal His Son to me, so that I might preach the Good News about him to the Gentiles, I did not go to anyone for advice, nor did I go to Jerusalem to see those who were apostles before me. Instead, I went at once to Arabia, and then I returned to Damascus. It was three years later that I went to Jerusalem to obtain information from Peter, and I stayed with him two weeks. I did not see any other apostles except James the Lord's brother. What I write is true. God knows that I am not lying!

Afterwards I went to places in Syria and Cilicia. At the time the members of the churches in Judaea did not know me personally. They knew only what others were saying. (Gal 1:15-23).

He did not return to Jerusalem for fourteen years (Gal 2:1).

The ever-ingenious Salibi suggests that the 'Arabia' he visited was the Hijaz, and that there he learned something concerning the life of Jesus which the Jerusalem apostles never spoke of. Perhaps it was the 'secret wisdom' (as in I Cor 2:7) which formed the basis of his preaching of salvation through faith in the eternal Christ who was the Son of God. It could have included mystical or allegorical interpretations of Israelite scriptures of the sort found in his writings, one of which actually refers to 'Mt Sinai in Arabia' (Gal 4:25), linking it to the story of Abraham's wife Hagar.[3] He may have acquired a copy of the Aramaic Gospel which spoke of the Jesus who was 'Isa, a Messiah of the House of Aaron, not the Davidic Jeshu, perhaps one of the precious books of parchment he was so anxious to have sent to him in prison in his last years (2 Tim 4:13).[4]

Incidentally, according to Paul, those of the original covenant (of Mount Sinai in Arabia) still kept the Law, and were therefore 'still in slavery' (Gal 4:25), along with their descendants. It was only those Christians who accepted the 'Jerusalem above' who were free (i.e. redeemed by the Saviour).

Paul goes on: 'Now you, brothers, like Isaac (Sarah's son) are children of [that] promise. But just as at that time he who was born according to the flesh [i.e. Ishmael] persecuted him who was born according to the spirit [i.e. Isaac], so it is now. But what does scripture say? 'Cast out the slave and her son; for the son of the slave shall not inherit with the son of the free woman!' So, brothers, we are not children of the slave, but of the free woman.' (Gal 4:28-31). He then urged them to stand fast against the monotheists, and to prove their loyalty by refusing circumcision.

'I, Paul, say to you that if you receive circumcision, Christ will be of no advantage to you. I testify again to every man who receives circumcision, that he is bound to keep the whole of the Law. You are severed from Christ, you who wish to be justified by the Law; you have fallen away from grace!' (Gal 5:2-4)[5]

Salibi now connects his thesis to the treatise written in the ninth century CE by Ibn al-Kalbi, who wrote on pre-Islamic Arabian idols of the Age of Superstition (jahiliyya). Heretical concepts of 'Isa as a god were condemned by the Qur'an as false, so it is clear that these concepts were still in the air in seventh-century Arabia. So Salibi suggests that the Fourth Gospel did use an old

Aramaic tradition, and that the synoptic material referred to as M and L[6] were actually Aramaic sources, all probably derived from the Aramaic *Injil* of 'Isa which still existed in the Hijaz of the seventh century CE. If this assumption is made, one can then proceed from the premise that the Jesus of the lost Arabian Gospel (the one used by Waraqa) was identical with the Qur'anic 'Isa, and determine the extent to which attributes of the Qur'anic 'Isa and stories told about him are found in the Gospels of Matthew, Luke or John, but not in Mark.

Neither Mark nor John say anything about the virgin birth or infancy of Jesus. The M source is based on Old Testament proof-texts. But the L source has many points in common with the Qur'anic narrative: for example, the spirit of God appeared to Mary in human form, which greatly disturbed her (sura 3:42-9; 19:17-21); and she was told of God's power in making this possible although she was still a virgin, and her son would be the great Apostle of Israel. The source of Luke, chapters one and two (regarded by scholars as a separate source from the rest of the gospel), repeats this information almost word for word (Lk 1:26-35).

The sura that narrates the miraculous birth of 'Isa immediately follows the story of the miraculous birth of Yahya to the aged priest Zakariyya and his old and barren wife (sura 19:1-5). Luke introduces his version in the same manner (Lk 1:5-25). The Qur'an clearly indicates that Mary belonged to the Levite aristocracy. Luke does not specifically say this, but he says two things about the priest Zechariah which are not in the Qur'an: that Zechariah's wife Elisabeth belonged to a priestly family (Lk 1:5), so she was as much a Levite of the House of Aaron as he was; and she was a cousin of Mary (Lk 1:36), which means that Mary must also have been a Levite of the House of Aaron. If Jeshu the Carpenter was a 'Son of David', his mother could hardly have been a Levite because of the Israelite ban on intermarriage between the tribes.

Many modern scholars think the birth narratives of Jesus were late traditions which found their way into the gospels. But Salibi suggests that on the contrary, Luke's version is an ancient one, originally relating to the birth of the prophet Jesus who was 'Isa, centuries before. This is borne out by textual criticism: Luke's fluent Greek is missing from his nativity account, which suggests that it *was* a translation from a written Aramaic source. Obviously, it cannot have been a 'late' tradition, if Luke had to translate it from an older text which was not Greek.

Paul did not explicitly attribute virgin birth to Jesus, but omitted all mention of his father and left his mother unnamed. This may well have meant that he *knew* (from James?) that Jeshu was the normally-born son of Joseph, descended from David. Likewise, the author of the fourth Gospel avoided all mention of the virgin birth and did not name Jesus' mother. His use of the concepts of the Word and the Parakletos to Come (lit. the future one called aside to help) may well have derived from the Nazarene *Injil*. Paul never mentioned *Logos* or *Parakletos*, but instead gave his Jesus those esoteric attributes of divinity, which, according to the Qur'an, were the erroneous and pernicious concepts of 'Isa preached by false gospels and traditions.

The Qur'an presents the story of 'Isa as the true Jesus of the one and only authentic *Injil*, insisting that the man who died on the cross was someone else. When he went to Arabia and secured copies of sacred writings, apart from those relating to the prophet 'Isa Paul must have found members of the sect of the god al-'Isa. These were the writings that he brought back with him, the 'books of parchment' which he kept strictly to himself while he lived. He, and others after him, used those texts in addition to the Old Testament, to develop his image of Jesus as the eternal Son of God and living Christ.

In other words, Salibi considers that after Paul had those Aramaic documents sent to him in his prison cell, others made use of them. John and Luke at least knew the ancient Aramaic Gospel and made use of it when writing about Jeshu, even though Paul did not care for it, as it presented 'Isa/Jesus as a strict Israelite monotheist in the tradition of Moses and Aaron. Paul preferred the other fusion, that of the historical Jeshu Bar Nagara and the fertility god al-'Isa or Dhu Khulasa, and made no use of the *Injil* of the Prophet 'Isa.

The author of the Fourth Gospel may also have derived some materials from the Aramaic scriptures of the al-'Isa cult, possibly from the same document or set of documents from which Paul constructed his image of Jesus as the Son of God.[7] Assuming that these parchments, which Paul had kept secret during his life, were discovered and translated into Greek after his death, they could have been used either in the Aramaic original or in Greek translation by the authors of the Gospels; it would seem that John went to the Aramaic original, and Luke to a Greek translation for his source. Matthew probably also used the translation, where his quotations are the same as Luke's.

So, the Jesus who died on the cross: 'as to his humanity, a descendant of David' (Rom 1:3) and the 'son of a human mother' (Gal 4:4), became transformed into the ultimate manifestation of the god al-'Isa of Arabia who died and rose from death to give true life to the world forever.

Colossians 1:25-27 indicates how Paul became convinced that the 'secret' that Jesus was really a god must finally be revealed to the whole world: 'I have been made a servant of the church by God, who gave me this task [...] of fully proclaiming His message, which is the secret He hid through all past ages from all mankind, but has now revealed to His people, this rich and glorious secret which He has for all people. And the secret is that Christ is in you, the hope of glory.'

The intriguing question, of course, is whether the fusion between 'Isa and Jeshu was made by the Gospel writers in good faith, in ignorance of the facts. Or was it accomplished by these largely unknown men in full knowledge of the truth, with the intention to deceive?

Chapter Nineteen

DOES THE BIBLE KNOW ABOUT ISLAM?

IF THE ARABIAN prophet Muhammad is to be considered part of the same stream of tradition as the other great prophets of that stretch of desert land, can we identify any mention of him in the Bible texts?

Muslims regard Muhammad as the final prophet, the seal over all who went before him. Can we find any forth-tellings of his coming in the present-day Christian scriptures; or would any such prophecy have been a prime candidate for redaction and censorship, so that at best such anticipations today appear in heavily disguised form, legible only to the expert? This is an important matter. For if it is true that Muhammad must be recognised as a Messenger of God by people of Christian or Jewish inheritance, it would surely be strange if their texts included prophecies referring to the penultimate Messenger, but lacked indications of the later Seal who was to come.

In fact, the Old and New Testaments *do* contain evidence that there existed an expectation not only of a Messiah for the Jewish people, but also of another prophetic figure whose time would come later.[1] One very important prophecy of this type is the one attributed to Moses, and recorded in Deuteronomy 18:

> The Lord said to me [Moses] […] 'I will raise up for them a prophet like you from among their brethren; and I will put My word in his mouth, and he shall speak to them all that I command him. And whoever will not give heed to My words which he shall speak in My name, I Myself will require it of him.' […] And if you say it in your heart, 'How may we know the word which the Lord has not spoken?' — when a prophet speaks in the name of the Lord, if the word does not come to pass or come true, that is a word which the Lord has not spoken; the prophet has spoken it presumptuously, you need not to be afraid of him (Deut 18:15-22).

In these words the author, perhaps Moses himself, sets the criterion for knowing the truth of a prophecy. Needless to say, it would also apply to his own prophecy with which he commenced this passage. If Moses himself, as a man who was himself recognised as a prophet of God, was not 'speaking presumptuously', then one should expect the foretold event to come to pass. Did it? Who was the 'prophet like unto him'? That description would surely signify a prophet who was called to be a lawgiver to the people, setting out God's commandments clearly for the masses to hear and understand. Which prophet fits most closely to one who had the words of God put into his mouth, so that he repeated to the people all that he heard from God? A Christian might like to see a reference to the coming of Jesus in these words, but surely none fits the description more closely than the Blessed Muhammad.[2]

The ministry of Jesus was specifically delivered to convince the people that the Kingdom of God would be set up on earth. Muslim scholars maintain that this would come about through a Messenger of the family of Ishmael, the eldest son of Abraham, and thus heir of the original Covenant with Abraham.

They claim it is contentious editing of history that has falsely presented Abraham's second son Isaac as the heir. Anyone with a knowledge of nomadic sheikhdom would understand that the eldest son was commissioned as 'lord' of the tribe (and therefore he and his descendants ruled from the Arabian region around the ancient shrine of Mecca), whereas the youngest son, in this case Isaac, would have had the role of 'guarding the hearth' (and staying with his father's private tents and herds). The latter's mission is hence local.

Genesis 15 reports the distress of Abraham that he had no son to be his heir, although he had the promise that his 'seed' would inherit from him (Genesis 15:4). God 'brought Abraham outside and said, "Look toward heaven and number the stars, if you are able to number them." Then he said to him, "So shall your descendants be".' Then Abraham asked for some proof, and was told to take three young animals and two birds. The animals were cut in two halves, and Abraham waited as the next day wore on, driving away all the birds of prey that came down on them. At sunset, he fell into a trance-like sleep, and God gave him prophecies about his descendents that would be slaves in Egypt (the descendants of the unborn Isaac). When the sun had gone and it was dark, a smoking fire-pot and a flaming torch passed between the cut pieces of the animal carcasses, and God made a covenant with Abraham: 'To your descendants I give this land, from the river of Egypt to the river Euphrates.' His was the task of subjugating ten different nations between those two rivers (Genesis 15:18-

21).³ This promise of an heir was fulfilled when Ishmael was born (Genesis 16), and in due course, Ishmael's descendants did subjugate all those peoples, an actual and literal fulfilment of one of the conditions of the Covenant which is usually overlooked.

When Ishmael was thirteen years old a further Covenant was made between God and Abraham: the Covenant of circumcision. Abraham circumcised himself, and his son Ishmael, and all his household that very day. All this took place long before Isaac was born. However, it was true that God had also promised that the barren Sarah would bear a son and that there would be an everlasting covenant with him too (Gen 17:15-19).

Sometimes it is argued that Isaac was Abraham's true heir, as his mother was the beloved wife, and Ishmael's mother only a servant, and hence, according to traditional assumptions, to be despised. But Deuteronomy 21:15-17 presents the true legal picture. If a man has two wives, one beloved and the other despised, and each has a son, and if the son of the despised wife is the first-born, *that* son, and *not* the son of the beloved wife, is still entitled to the birthright. The prophecy that 'by Abraham all the generations of the earth shall be blessed', would therefore more clearly refer to the heritage by birthright of Ishmael, and not Isaac.

The text of Genesis 22 now goes on to talk of Isaac as Abraham's 'only son', and records Abraham's famous test of obedience when he was asked to sacrifice him. In the Bible narrative, Isaac is kept in ignorance of what is going to happen until the very last moment. He is saved from the sacrifice when an angel of God stays Abraham's hand, and a ram caught in a thicket is substituted as the sacrifice.

Professor Dawud, the former bishop who has meditated extensively on these themes, comments that 'to efface the name Ishmael from the second, sixth and seventh verses of Genesis 22 and to insert in its place "Isaac", yet to leave the epithet "the only begotten son" is to deny the existence of the former and to violate the Covenant made between God and Ishmael.'⁴

Sura 37:100-113 has rather different emphases: when Ishmael was about fourteen ('the age of serious work'), Abraham had a vision (or dream) that he should sacrifice Ishmael. He asked the boy's opinion, and Ishmael agreed that he would do whatever was God's will, and urged his father to sacrifice him, if that was what God required. However, God does not require the flesh and blood of animals (sura 22:37), much less of human beings: what He requires is the giving of our whole being to Him. The 'momentous sacrifice' with which the youth was ransomed is commemorated in the great annual festival of Hajj and Eid ul-Adha. It was as a reward for Abraham's faith that God granted the son Isaac to Abraham's barren wife Sarah.

Genesis, true to its generally negative portrayal of Sarah, offers the story of her jealousy of Hagar and Ishmael, and her request that he be cast out: a thing which greatly displeased Abraham, although he complied (Gen 21:10-11). He sent them away into the southerly 'wilderness of Beersheba', where Ishmael nearly died of thirst. However, God sent an angel to save him, and Ishmael survived. He lived 'in the wilderness of Paran', and his mother took a wife for him from the land of Egypt, from whence she herself had come (Gen 16:1).[5]

The Qur'anic version does not record a comparable character lapse on the part of either Sarah or Abraham. Ishmael is left with Hagar in the valley-floor of Mecca, where Abraham trusts that God will take care of them. Hagar's desperate search for water is commemorated in the ritual of the *sa'y* during the Hajj; the spring of water revealed by the angel still flows today, and is called Zamzam. Sura 2:124-129 tells of Abraham and Ishmael sanctifying the Ka'ba, and raising the foundations of the House.

Ishmael's firstborn Kedar became the ancestor of the Arabs who from that time until now are the dwellers of the wilderness of Paran. As Dawud notes, this makes passages such as Deuteronomy 33:2 extremely interesting: 'The Lord came from Sinai, and rose up from Seir[6] unto them; He shined forth from Mount Paran, and he came with ten thousands of saints. From his right hand went forth a fiery law for them.' Dawud identifies that Mount Paran with Mount Arafat near Mecca, and claims this passage as a direct prophecy concerning the 'one who was to come', the *Hmd* (or 'Ahmad', or 'Praised one'). Dawud also picks out many possible Old Testament references to this man known as the 'Himada' (from the root *hmd*), which all point to a Messenger from the line of Ishmael.[7] For example, one prophecy in the ever-enigmatic Book of Habbakuk is that the glory of the Holy One from Paran will cover the heavens, and the earth will be full of his praise.

Other interesting passages occur in the book of the prophet Isaiah: 'Let the wilderness and the cities thereof lift up their voice, the villages that Kedar inhabits; let the inhabitants of the rock [Petra?] sing, let them shout from the top of the mountains. Let them give glory and declare his praise in the islands. He shall go forth as a mighty man, he shall stir up zeal like a man of war, he shall cry, yea, roar; he shall prevail against his enemies.' (Isaiah 42:11)

Other prophesies concerning Kedar occur in Isaiah 50:7 and 50:13-17. 'All the flocks of Kedar shall be gathered together unto You, the rams of Nabaioth (the Nabataeans) will minister unto You; they shall come up with acceptance on My altar, and I will glorify the house of My glory.' (Isaiah 50:7)

Ishmael inhabited the wilderness of Paran, where he sired the Arabian patriarch Kedar; and if the 'sons of Kedar' received revelation from God and accepted it, and came to a divine altar to glorify 'the house of My glory', then surely the 'holy one from Paran' of Habbakuk 3:3 is none other than the Blessed Muhammad. And Mecca is the house of God's glory where the 'flocks of Kedar' came to bow the knee. The 'flocks of Kedar' have never come to the Trinitarian church, and have remained impenetrable to any influence of it.

The prophet Haggai, seeing the older generation weeping because of their disappointment that after their exile in Babylon the rebuilt Jewish Temple did not match up to the original one, consoled them with the message: 'And I will shake all nations, and the *Himada* [the treasure?] of all the nations will come; and I will fill this house with glory, says the Lord of Hosts [...] The glory of My last house shall be greater than the first one, says the Lord of Hosts; and in this place, I will give *shalom* [cognate with *islam*].' (Haggai 2:7-9)

The New Testament documents are the work of many hands, many of them quite unknown, and the search for predictions of the world-shaking event of Islam is necessarily fraught with difficulties. However Muslim writers suggest that one should look again at the interpretation of the references of Jesus to the 'Son of Man' who would come,[8] and in John's Gospel to the Counsellor who was to come after Jesus had left them. The Gospel calls this prophesied one a 'Paraclete', with the primary meaning of 'counsel for the defence'. This was later supposed to be the 'Holy Spirit', the third entity in the Trinity. However these passages could be no less credibly read as prophecies of the 'Himada' or 'Ahmad'. Given the defective orthography of the early Gospel texts, it is quite feasible that the Greek word was not *parakletos* but *periklytos*, thus corresponding exactly to 'Ahmad' or the *Hmd*, meaning 'illustrious', 'glorious' and 'praised'.[9]

Therefore Muslims believe that the paraclete spoken of in those 'Farewell Discourses' was not the third being in a Trinity, but the future prophet Muhammad. The words clearly show that the Comforter had to come after the departure of Jesus, and was not with him when he uttered these words. Are we to presume that Jesus was devoid of the Holy Spirit, if its coming was conditional on Jesus' leaving? The way in which Jesus describes him makes him a human being, with a particular role to fulfil.

Even if we include the words that Muslims would regard as Trinitarian edit-ing, the prophecy runs: 'I will pray to the Father, and He will give you another Counsellor, to be with you for ever, even the spirit of truth,[10] whom the world cannot receive because it neither sees him nor knows him [i.e. does not accept him]. You know him, for he dwells with you, and will be in you' (Jn 14:16). 'These things I have spoken to you while I am still with you. But the Counsellor whom the Father will send in my name, he will teach you all things and bring to your remembrance all that I have said to you' (Jn 14:25-26). 'When the Counsellor comes whom I shall send to you from the Father, even the spirit of truth, who proceeds from the Father, he will bear witness to me' (Jn 15:26). 'When he comes, he will convince the world of sin, of righteousness and of judgement; of sin, because they do not believe in me; of righteousness, because I go to the Father; of judgement, because the ruler of this world is judged. I have yet many things to say to you, but you cannot bear them now. When the *spirit of truth comes, he will guide you into all the truth; for he shall not speak on his own authority, but whatever he shall hear, that he shall speak* and he will declare to you the things that are to come. He will glorify me, for he will take what is mine and declare it to you.' (Jn 16:8-16)

Muslims will recall straight away that the Qur'an consists not of the Prophet's own words, but that *which he heard*, which was revealed to him; and it was said of him in the Qur'an: 'Nay, he has come with the truth, and shows forth the truth of the Messengers.' (sura 37:37)

The Prophet Muhammad may have been the one foretold by John the Baptist (Mt 3:11; Lk 3:16). This would certainly explain why John carried on baptising, receiving initiates and disciples and foretelling a coming prophet more power-ful than himself, without joining up with Jesus in Galilee. It is accepted by all Christians that Jesus and John had a parallel ministry until John's martyrdom at the hands of Herod Antipas (Mk 6); but how few have marvelled at the oddness of the fact that John, having spent all his ministry 'crying in the wilderness' to pre-pare the way for the one to come, did not become Jesus' closest and most intimate disciple. Our explanation also accounts for the rather odd remark Jesus made about John when he said that the 'least' in the Kingdom of Heaven would be greater than him. This sounds at first sight like an inexplicable and unneces-sarily unpleasant derogatory remark; but if the word 'least' really meant the 'last' in the long line, the 'youngest', then what Jesus meant was that John had been the greatest of the prophets up to that time, but that the last of the prophets, the one who was still to come, would be greater than him: a remark that was in no way intended to belittle the saintly John. The Pshitta Version (the Aramaic version, which is older than the Latin Vulgate) does indeed use the word *zira* or *zeira* for 'least', meaning small or young, as opposed to *rabba*, meaning great or old.

Professor Dawud offers another interesting suggestion: could it be that the persecution of the true faith after the Council of Nicaea might have been prophesied in the enigmatic Book of Daniel? The 'four beasts' and the conquering 'Son of Man' of the vision in Daniel 7 have always invited speculative identifications; perhaps they represented the Chaldaeans (the eagle-winged lion), the Medo-Persian Empire (the bear), the Empire of Alexander the Great (the tiger with four wings and four heads), and the formidable Roman Empire (the fourth beast, the demon monster). The ten horns might have been the ten Emperors who persecuted the early Christians, down to the time of the so-called conversion of Constantine. So far, the beasts all represented the 'Power of Darkness', or the kingdom of Satan: idolatry itself.

But the nature and character of the Little Horn before which the three other horns fell, and which was finally defeated by a *Bar Nasha* (Son of Man) is quite different. It springs up after the Ten Persecutions under the Roman Emperors. The Roman Empire was then writhing under four rivals, Constantine being one of them. They were all struggling for the purple, and when the other three died or fell in battle, Constantine was left alone as the supreme sovereign of the vast Empire.

The earlier beasts were brutish, but the Little Horn possessed mouth and eyes: a hideous monster endowed with reason and speech. Maybe this was none other than Constantine, and the traditional presentation of him as 'the first Christian Emperor' is really Trinitarian propaganda. He was in fact one of the most dangerous and effective enemies of *tawhid*. The Little Horn was so diabolical and malignant, and his enmity to the faith the more harmful, because it sought to pervert the truth *from within*. This interpretation is on strikingly similar lines to that advanced by modern biblical experts who see Paul as the traitor and 'Liar' of the Dead Sea Scrolls.

This enemy spoke 'great things' against the Most High; the unity of God was openly and officially profaned by Constantine and his unbelieving ecclesiastical cronies as the Trinitarian dogmas of the Council of Nicaea were proclaimed and violently enforced by Constantine's edict, amidst the horror and protests of three-quarters of the Church's members! This Little Horn waged war against the saints of the Most High; so Constantine persecuted those Christians who, like the Jews, believed in the Absolute Unity of God.

> More than a thousand ecclesiastics were summoned to the General Council at Nicaea, of whom only 318 persons subscribed to the decisions of the Council, and these too formed three opposite factions with their respective ambiguous and unholy expressions of 'homoiusion'[11] or 'homoousion'[12], 'consubstantial' and other terms utterly and wholly strange to the prophets of Israel, but worthy of the 'speaking Horn'. The Christians who suffered persecutions and martyrdoms under the pagan Emperors of Rome because they believed in One God and in His servant Jesus were now doomed by the imperial edict of the 'Christian' Constantine to even severer tortures, because they refused to adore the servant Jesus as consubstantial and coeval with his Lord the Creator![13]

The elders and ministers who opposed Trinitarianism were deposed or banished, their religious books suppressed, and their churches seized and handed over to Trinitarian bishops and priests. Merciless legions in every province were placed at the disposal of the ecclesiastical authorities, and a reign of terror against the unitarians lasted in the East for three and a half centuries: until a 'Son of Man' did restore the religion of One God, and Muslims liberated the lands trampled and devastated by the four beasts, from the Pyrenees to the walls of China.

The soul and kernel of what Jesus taught is contained in that famous clause in his prayer: 'Thy kingdom come! Thy will be done on earth as it is in heaven!' Most Christians assume all sorts of illusory or meaningless things about the nature of this Kingdom. It is not a triumphant Catholic Church, nor a regenerated and sinless Puritan State. It is not a kingdom composed of celestial beings, including departed spirits of the believers under the reign of the Divine Lamb. The Kingdom of God *on earth* is a society of believers in One God equipped with faith to maintain its existence against the Kingdom of Darkness.

Jesus referred frequently to this kingdom which would come, and to the *Bar Nasha* or Son of Man who would inaugurate it; but Christians have assumed that Jesus meant his 'church', and that he himself was the Son of Man. Could he really have been referring to Islam and the Prophet Muhammad?

These theories also throw light on another religious group commended by the Qur'an along with certain Christians: the Sabians. Dawud interprets these as the followers of John the Baptist (Yahya ibn Zakariyya), adherents of a parallel movement to early Christianity, who were absorbed into Islam when it came. The Subba, or Sabaeans of the marshes are otherwise known as the Mandaeans in Southern Iraq. Significantly, 'Mandaean' was the name for the rank and file of these groups, whereas the Nazareans were the priestly elite.[14]

The original Aramaic or Hebrew word for the Greek 'baptism' is not certain. The Pshitta (Aramaic) version of the Gospels uses the word *ma 'muditha*, from the verb *aa 'mid* which means 'to stand up like a pillar'. Its causative form means 'to erect, set up, establish, confirm' and has no signification of bathing or washing. Arabic versions of the New Testament call the Baptist 'al-Ma 'midan'.

In fact, the Greek *baptismos* derives from the Aramaic *Sab'utha* or *Sbhu'tha*, (Arabic cognate, *sabagha*), which has the sense of 'to dye, tincture or immerse'. These 'Masbutheans' (also called 'Besmotheans' and 'Subba') existed before the coming of Jesus – as did the Essenes of Qumran – and were either the same as, or strongly similar to, the Daily Bathers/Hemerobaptists and Sabaeans (or Sabuneans) mentioned by Hippolytus, whom we have encountered before. Probably all these names are simply overlapping designations and intertransference of various regions. These 'Baptists', like the Qumraners and Ebionites, led an austere life of self-discipline and prayer. Perhaps they caused their proselytes to stand straight like a pillar in a pool of water or river, in order to be baptised, whence the Pshitta name of *Ma 'muditha*.

Baptism is *not* a purification (*thara*) or washing (*rahsa*) or immersion (*tabhala*), but a dyeing, a colouring (*sab'aitha*). Just as a *Saba'a* or dyer gives a new colour to a garment by dipping it into tincture, so a baptist gives a convert a new spiritual hue. It was a mark of admission into the society of purified penitents who promised loyalty to God and His apostles. It goes without saying that the baptism of John in the river of Jordan was considered sufficient to 'dye' the hundreds of Jewish penitents ('all the country of Judaea and all the region about the Jordan' – Mt 3 : 5) who were baptised by him while confessing their sins. The idea of the shedding of the blood of a God-Man is superfluous.

There is little doubt that until the arrival of Paul on the scene, the followers of Jesus practised the same baptismal ritual as John. It may be significant that the converts of Samaria who had been baptised in the name of Jesus did not receive the Holy Spirit, but had to have an extra ritual: the laying on of hands (Acts 8 : 16-17). The same was said for John's baptism in Acts 19 : 2-7. This appears to indicate that Jesus' baptism was in actual fact precisely the same as that of John, and to provide evidence that the Trinitarian churches wantonly transformed the original rite into a sacrament or mystery. The statement that some twelve persons in Samaria 'had not yet received the Holy Spirit, because they were only baptised in the name of our Lord Jesus' (Acts 8 : 16-17) is surely decisive as evidence.

How was it that the Sabians did not embrace Trinitarian Christianity if their master John had truly and openly declared and presented Jesus as the 'more powerful' Prophet than himself who was to come, and whose shoes he was not worthy to unloose? The followers of John might have been excused if Jesus had come a century later; but they were contemporaries, born in the same year. They *both* baptised with water unto repentance, and prepared their penitent converts for the Kingdom of God that was approaching, but which was not to be established in their time.

The Sabians believed that although Jesus was one of the great Messengers, he was not the one referred to in the prophecy of John as the 'one who was to come'; most of them happily recognised and embraced Islam when it came.

It is all too obvious that those who believe in the doctrine that baptism means an outward and visible sign of an inward and spiritual grace, who believe that the 'inspiration' of the Holy Spirit fills the hearts of those who, in their emotional excitement and ecstasy, believe themselves to be 'new-born,' are suffering from wishful thinking. These 'new-born' frequently slide back and become what they were before. The 'miracle' of the 'Holy Spirit' is a myth.[15] True baptism is that which comes only from submission to the Divine Will, and requires genuine commitment and a great deal of hard work.

> Who turns away from the religion of Abraham but such as debase their souls with folly? [...] 'Oh my sons, God has chosen the Faith for you; do not die except in the faith of Islam' [...] They say: 'Become Jews or Christians, if you would be guided aright.' Say thou: 'Nay! I would rather the religion of Abraham the true – he joined not gods with God. Say ye: 'We believe in God, and the revelation given to us, and to Abraham, Ishmael, Isaac, Jacob, and the tribes, and that given to Moses and Jesus, and that given to all prophets from their Lord: we make no difference between one and another of them: and we bow [only] to God. If they believe as you believe, they are indeed on the right path; but if they turn back, it is they who are in schism. God will suffice thee as against them, He is the All-Hearing, the All-Knowing. [Our religion is] the baptism of God: and who is better than God to baptise? It is He Whom we worship.' (Sura 2:130,132,135-138)

The Baptism of God (*sibghatu'Llah*) does not move Muslims to believe themselves 'made holy'. Every Muslim has to run the race of our short earthly life to the best of his or her ability and effort, in order to win the crown of glory in the next world. Every Muslim needs education and training in accordance with the Word of God: but stands in no need of the intercession of a priest or sacrament. God Himself is quite enough.

Chapter Twenty

DID THE CRUCIFIXION KILL JESUS?

S O F E W P E O P L E actually take the time to examine the origins of the Christian Church that it is hardly ever acknowledged that many early sectarians *never* did believe that Jesus was killed on the cross, even though they did accept that he was crucified.

The Docetists (from the Greek *dokein*, 'to seem') were at the extreme end of this spectrum of views. They were Christians who believed that Jesus was truly God, but that he had never passed a life on earth as a normal human being. What 'seemed' to be his physical or natural body was rather an apparent or phantom body. The Marcionite Gospel (c138 CE) denied that Jesus had been born physically, and taught that he merely appeared in human form. He was not 'real' in the sense we usually mean real. It followed that this Jesus could not feel pain, or such things as hunger and thirst. To Docetics, the crucifixion, therefore, was also only an illusion or appearance, and not 'real'. Elchasaites (somewhat after the manner of Buddhists) accepted the eternal and recurring existence of the Christ-Soul in consecutive bodies.

Docetism was not just a minor heresy that appealed to a few cranks: it represented the far 'right wing' of Trinitarian thought, and was widespread. Some scholars have suggested that it was precisely to counter Docetism that the Fourth Gospel was written (after 100 CE) since it stressed the various physical aspects of Jesus: he wept, he sweated, took bread and fish, and ate. The sect of Basilideans were Docetic in a different sense. They taught that it only 'seemed' to be Jesus who was crucified. To them, Jesus was as physical as you or I, and there was a real crucifixion: but it was not Jesus who was crucified. It was some other person, probably the unfortunate Simon of Cyrene who had been obliged to carry Jesus' cross after he fell on the way to Golgotha (Mt 15:21).[1] Some medieval Muslim scholars suggested that it was really Judas Iscariot who was arrested by the Romans and executed: but they do not usually offer any textual evidence to support this satisfying notion.[2]

Muslims are more aware than most Christians that there is confusion over the events of the end of Jesus' life, because the early questionings are preserved in the Qur'an. 'O Jesus, I will take you and raise you to Myself, and cleanse you of those who disbelieve; and I will make those who follow you superior to those who disbelieve to the Day of Resurrection. Then unto Me you will all return, and I shall judge between you as to that wherein you used to differ.' (Sura 3:55)

The Qur'an teaches that Jesus was *not* killed by the Jews or the Romans; in spite of circumstances which produced that illusion in the minds of his enemies (and also of some of those who revere him):

> They said, 'We killed Christ Jesus, the son of Mary, the apostle of God'. But they killed him not, nor crucified him, but so it was made to appear to them; and those who differ therein are full of doubt, with no certain knowledge, but only guesswork to follow. For of a surety they killed him not – nay, God raised him up unto Himself; and God is Exalted in power, Wise. And there is none of the People of the Book but will believe in Him assuredly before his death; and on the Day of Judgement he will be a witness against them. (Sura 4:157-159)

There is considerable dispute about the meaning of these verses. Some commentators insist that the passage simply means that God did not allow his enemies to kill Jesus, who was instead saved by being raised to Heaven; in other words, they accept the Ascension, but not the crucifixion. Others hold that he did die (see Sura 5:20), but not at the crucifixion. Still others believe that he is still living in the body and will appear just before the Final Day, when the world will be purified of sin and unbelief.

One could argue, alternatively, that what is meant is that even though Jesus *did* die in the earthly sense, he was not *overcome* by death, and through the action of God he became the sign pointing the way to the everlasting life for all believers. For example, the Ahmadiyya sectarians – usually not regarded as Muslim at all[3] – took the view that Jesus *was* crucified, but that he did not die as a result. They suggested that he survived the ordeal and was resuscitated in the coolness of the tomb. He then recovered, and lived on long enough to travel as far afield as Kashmir, where he married and had children, and in due course died. The tomb of this person can be seen to this day at a shrine called the Rozabel in Srinagar. Certainly the shrine, grave and legend exist, but the documentary evidence for the 'Jesus' who came there is tenuous in the extreme.[4]

Here a problem arises. No orthodox Christian can accept that Jesus was not crucified; and no Muslim can accept that even a single word of the Qur'an might be incorrect, since it is the pure and unadulterated revelation of God. However, setting aside the possibility that Jesus was a totally different person from 'Isa, there is one way in which both faiths could concur, namely, if we consider the possibility that Jesus was indeed crucified, but instead of dying, was miraculously saved.

In 1870, a Latin inscription was discovered on a marble slab in Nazareth. This was an edict of the Roman Emperor Claudius (41-54 CE), and read as follows:

> It is my pleasure that graves and tombs remain undisturbed in perpetuity for those who have made them for the cult of their ancestors or children or members of their house. If, however, any man lay information that another has either demolished them, or has in any way extracted the buried or has maliciously transferred them to other places in order to wrong them, or has displaced the sealing or other stones, against such a one I order that a trial be instituted, as in respect of the gods, so in regard to the cult of mortals. For it shall be much more obligatory to honour the buried. Let it be absolutely forbidden for anyone to destroy them. In case of contravention I desire that the offender be sentenced to capital punishment on charge of violation of sepulture.

This decree is not unique, as is shown by the very similar inscription which may be seen at Petra in Jordan, also dating from the time of the Roman occupation. It is not a particularly startling coincidence, and has nothing to do with the mystery surrounding the entombment of Jesus. But the Christian memory is unanimous in holding that Jesus' grave was indeed disturbed, and that his corpse disappeared. Some who are sceptical about the 'resurrection' have suggested that the Romans might have been responsible for taking his body, but this seems unlikely. The Nazareth marble slab well illustrates the genuine Roman reverence for the dead.

What did happen to the body of Jesus? Was he resurrected by the Father to a place of glory? Was his corpse taken by some human agent, to rot away (whether in honour or dishonour) in some unknown resting-place? Was the rolling stone insecure, so that Jesus' corpse was simply eaten by scavenging jackals? Did Jesus really die as a result of his crucifixion? Or could he have been placed, still alive, in his tomb, healed and removed in secret by his friends, and lived to see another day?

For Christians, it was the idea that Jesus died and was physically resurrected that made him unique. Many Messiahs had been and would yet be executed; but no other Messiah had ever conquered death by the will of God, and given proofs of his continued existence. Christians began to search the scriptures for signs and foretellings to account for it. Luke preserves a memory of how on the road to Emmaus, the risen Jesus appeared to two disciples, and 'beginning with Moses and all the prophets, interpreted to them in all the scriptures the things concerning himself.' (Lk 24:27)

Many later Christians have assumed that one key passage Jesus might have referred to was Isaiah 53 with its references to a mysterious 'suffering servant'. He was 'despised and rejected, a man of sorrows, acquainted with grief; we believed that he had been smitten by God and afflicted. [But] he was wounded for our transgressions and bruised for our iniquities [...] *his generation considered that he was cut off from the land of the living* [...] but when he has made himself an offering for sin *he shall see his offspring and prolong his days*; the will of God shall prosper in his hand; he shall see the fruits of his labours, and be satisfied [...] he shall divide his portion with the strong, because he poured out his soul to death [...]' (Isaiah 53:4-14, my italics).

Modern scholars, however, tend to be sceptical about the traditional Christian reading of this passage as a reference to Jesus' 'sacrificial' death. Look again at those last verses: isn't there something about them that reminds the reader of an earlier famous sacrifice, that of Abraham offering up his dearly-loved firstborn son (Genesis 22)? The important message in Abraham's willingness to slay his son was that God was *testing* him. Having proved his obedience, God intervened and the son lived to see his offspring and the prolonging of his days.

It is often claimed that Jesus himself gave a clear sign in advance of his death and resurrection after three days on at least two occasions. 'An evil and adulterous generation seeks for a sign,' said Jesus, 'but no sign shall be given it, except the sign of Jonah.' (Mt 16:4) 'For as Jonah was three days and three nights in the belly of a whale, so will the son of man be three days and nights in the heart of the earth. The people of Nineveh will arise at the Judgement Day with this generation, and condemn it! For they repented at the preaching of Jonah, and behold, something greater than Jonah is here, and yet they did not believe!' (Mt 12:38-41).

This has always been taken by Christians to refer to the 'three days and nights' that Jesus spent in the tomb between his death and resurrection. Of course, anyone with a little maths can work out that from the time of his purported death at 3pm on a Friday, to his resurrection before 5am on a Sunday, three days had *not* elapsed at all, but the much shorter interval of about 36 hours. It could even have been less, since we are not told the hour the resurrection occurred. Once again, we have an Aramaic idiom here: the phrase 'three days' doesn't necessarily mean three literal days. It implies 'a short time', as opposed to 'a long time' which was usually referred to as 'forty days'. A *very* long time was 'forty years'.

Christians are therefore wrong to emphasise the three days as the meaning of the sign. The time is not the significant factor. Indeed, Luke's version mentions every part of the quotation except the business of the three days.

What was *really* the sign of Jonah? Surely it was that here was a man who 'went down into the depths', who was swallowed up *alive* by his dire fate, and who was then restored to the world again *alive*. (Lk 11:29; Jonah 2:4-5)

John's Gospel has an interesting passage which relates to this. After he had cleansed the Temple, the Jews asked him what sign he had to show for doing this. Jesus answered: 'Destroy this Temple, and in three days I will raise it up.' The Jews then said: 'It has taken forty-six years to build this Temple, and will you raise it in three days?' But he spoke of the temple of his body. When, therefore, he was raised from the dead [but not before, one notices!] his disciples remembered that he said this, and believed the scripture and the word that Jesus had spoken.' (Jn 2:18-22)

What was the scripture referred to? The most relevant passage that might have been used by our Gospel writers, but surprisingly was not, read as follows: 'Come, and let us return to the Lord; for He has torn, and He will heal us; He has smitten, and He will bind us up; After two days He will revive us; in the third day He will raise us up, and we shall live in His sight.' (Hosea 6:1-2)

Surely we have here the key to the whole matter, not only of the sign of Jonah but also of Jesus being accused of threatening to destroy the Temple. He was simply predicting the impossibility of his human body being overcome by death, because it was not the will of his Father. The smitten one will be revived. What the sign of Jonah does *not* imply is the ritual of a dying-and-rising virgin-born god of the Baal/Adonis/Horus/Mithras type.

Muslims have always maintained that Jesus did not die, not because they have carefully studied all the evidence, but simply because the words of the Qur'an have this interpretation. They *do* believe he was 'raised to heaven', in an Ascension. Unknown to Christians perhaps, they insist on it.

Remember when God said: O Jesus, I will raise you to Myself, and clear you of the false errors of those who blaspheme. (Sura 3:55)

Who could have the least power against God, had it been His will to destroy Christ the son of Mary, his mother, or all the people that are on earth? The heavens and the earth and all that is between belong to God. He creates as He pleases, and He has power over all things. (Sura 5:19)

Jesus said [...]: 'I said not a single word except as You did command me, which was to worship God, my Lord and your Lord; and I was witness over them whilst I dwelt among them, and when You took me up. You were the Watcher over them, and You are the Witness to all things.' (Sura 5:120)

There is a clear and enormous difference between 'rising up' and 'resurrection'. As we have seen, the Trinitarian Christian belief included the necessary factor that the saviour-hero should actually die, and then be triumphant over death, in order to save humanity. However, we note at once that the original disciples had evidently not been anticipating anything of the kind.

The grave of Jesus was hardly a secret place. On the Sabbath, according to the apocryphal Gospel of Peter, multitudes visited the tomb out of respect or curiosity.[5] The Coptic *Book of the Resurrection* attributed to Bartholomew[6] names the gardener as Philogenes, with the engaging detail that he was upset by the crowds trampling on his lettuces. When the women friends of Jesus discovered the tomb empty just before dawn on the Sunday following the Sabbath, their conclusion was that human hands had removed the body for some reason or another. Perhaps the irate gardener had cared more for his *caulibus* than he had for the deceased holy man. The odd and frightening thing was that although the body of Jesus had gone, his burial wrappings were still there. The corpse must have been stolen naked!

They did not assume that the glorious resurrection of their saviour-god had occurred as predicted. The earliest version, Mark's, tells of a young man dressed in white who informed the women that Jesus was not there any more, and that the disciples would see him if they went back to Galilee. However, the women were so shocked and upset that they did not feel that they could speak to anyone.

The teachings about Jesus' resurrection appearances in the material still left in the New Testament is really twofold: that of the 'intimates' and that of Paul. The testimony ascribed to individuals who knew Jesus intimately indicates that he was not expected to have survived death, and that there was no thought in their minds of resurrection in any shape or form. Those early Christians were devastated, downcast and depressed, rather than excited by the prospect of his imminent return to life.

The belief generally accepted by all pious Jews was that certain dead people *could* be raised to renewed and real physical life if they were lucky enough to be prayed for by certain saints and 'holy ones' (Elisha, for instance, raised a widow's son, and Jesus raised Jairus' daughter); many also believed that there would be a general resurrection of the dead at the onset of the Time of Judgement.[7] Neither of these beliefs would apply to the case of Jesus following his tragic crucifixion. The Apostles, although they had been granted certain healing powers during Jesus' lifetime, obviously did not think that *they* would be able to resurrect him, or that he could resurrect himself.

John 20:1-10 explains how Peter, the Beloved Disciple, and Mary Magdalene all saw the empty tomb, and their natural reaction was that the body of Jesus had been moved. The Gospel explains: 'As yet they knew not the scripture that he must rise again from the dead.' Having made the unwelcome discovery of the empty tomb, they went away sadly to their homes.

Now, when Jesus did appear to his intimate friends, they were amazed and overjoyed, and in no sense assumed that he was a 'spirit', but fully alive, in a body of solid flesh and bone that could be touched, whose wounds were painfully visible, and who had the ability to eat solid food. They did not assume that his spirit had floated through the stone that sealed his tomb, but that it had to be rolled away before he could get out. Now that they could see him, they assumed he was very much alive.[8]

It is noteworthy that Jesus did not make any dramatic appearances to his enemies (when surely the temptation for the Risen Lord to stage an embarrassing arrival to spoil the evening dinner of Caiaphas or Pilate or Herod would have been overwhelming), unless he still had something to fear from them.

The surviving Gospel accounts present the physical reanimation of Jesus, not the manifestation of an undying and triumphant god. We are told nothing of where Jesus was, or how he was maintaining himself at times other than at his few recorded appearances. The Acts of the Apostles merely states that people saw him for a period of forty days (Acts 1:3), after which he was taken from them and seen no more.

Paul's letter to the Corinthians, written some twenty years after the crucifixion, shows how belief in Jesus' resurrection was well established by then. Paul listed several people who had seen him, some of whom were still living, and added his own name to the list. However, Paul had certainly *not* seen the resuscitated physically-living body of Jesus, but had experienced the apparition of a non-physical entity, which is not the same thing at all. Moreover, this weakened his claim to be an apostle, so that he was obliged to argue his case.

In fact, most people who had any thoughts at all on the subject of life after death assumed that the physical corpse of a deceased person would rot away, and that which was resurrected would be the *soul* or spirit of that person, perhaps in a special new kind of body created for the purpose. This belief was a commonplace all round the Mediterranean pagan world, and elsewhere, and is what most Christians regard today as their own fate, sharing with the Corinthians a scepticism about the resurrection of the body. Paul's Corinthian converts accepted the raising of souls quite readily, but the notion that Jesus' actual body had left the grave and 'physically ascended to heaven' they regarded as a very dubious prospect.

Paul's answer was that one body was succeeded by another: the natural body by the spiritual body of the same person. The first body perishes, but the second is indestructible. Paul did not seem to distinguish between the post-mortem experience of Jesus and that which is coming to the rest of us; but in Jesus' case it happened on the spot, and for us it will occur at Judgement. His thesis called for the instantaneous transformation of believers who were still alive when it occurred. There seems to be no back-up support for this theory.

Belief in the physical resurrection of human beings was a fairly recent development in Jewish philosophy, accepted by groups such as the Pharisees and Qumraners. In Isaiah 26:19-21 we have the beautiful passage: 'Thy dead shall live, their bodies shall arise. O dwellers in the dust, awake and sing for joy! For Your dew is a dew of light, and on the land of the shades You will let it fall [...] the earth will give back the blood shed upon her, and will no more cover her slain.'[9]

In the Age to Come, *all* the dead would be resurrected, some to find blessing, and some to taste extreme punishment or purgation. In the case of the Messiah, his corpse would not be allowed to see corruption (Psalms 16:6-11), he would sit 'at God's right hand' with his enemies as his footstool (Psalm 110:1), and reign forever on the 'throne of David'. (Psalm 132:11; Isiah 9:7.) None of this implies Trinitarian saviour-doctrine. What it does imply is the wonderful and comforting teaching that there will indeed be a raising for all of us after our deaths, and that what was done for Jesus will also be done for us.

The fact that Paul taught that 'flesh and blood cannot inherit the Kingdom of

God' really eliminates Paul as a witness to any physical resurrection of Jesus. In all other New Testament records of people raised from the dead – Jairus' daughter, the widow of Nain's son, Lazarus, and the widow Dorcas raised by Peter – the return to *normal* existence was stated or implied. We even have mention of a mass exit from sepulchres in Mt 27:51-53; a suspect verse, but still evidence that it was a real physical return to life that was expected.[10]

Sherlock Holmes used to eliminate the possible before he went on to consider the impossible. Let us consider the simplest theory, that Jesus was able to rise and meet his friends 'post-mortem' for the simple reason that he was not dead when he was laid in his sepulchre. Was there a desperate yet deliberate plan to rescue the crucified historical Jesus *alive* from his crucifixion? Was it this that was hinted at by the 'beloved disciple' who wrote one draft of the Fourth Gospel, for those who had eyes to see? The identity of this disciple remains a mystery: the only certainty is that it was not John the Galilean fisherman. Some have wondered if it was Lazarus, Jesus' much-loved friend; but the most likely candidate is someone who was intimately connected with the Jerusalem priesthood.

He knew the High Priest Caiaphas personally (Jn 18:15); he was probably a man of means, maybe the owner of the house where the Last Supper was held, where he reclined in a place of honour; he was first associated with John the Baptist, and there are many resonances of the Dead Sea Scrolls in his work; he alone reported the parts played by the Sanhedrin members Nicodemus and Joseph of Arimathea (see Jn 7:45-53); he knew the name of the High Priest's servant whose ear Peter cut off, and that it was a kinsman of that man who challenged Peter in the courtyard of the High Priest's palace (Jn 18:26). Peter was only admitted because he was in the company of this disciple 'who was known to the High Priest', and who spoke on his behalf to the doorkeeper. When he reached the grave with Peter, he would not enter in: presumably because he would incur defilement from contact with the dead.

Since the house in which Jesus took his Last Supper has been associated so strongly with the house of John Mark's mother, is there not a strong possibility that this unnamed disciple was the very man in whose house Jesus had just partaken of that supper? The man who took the seat at the supper next to Jesus, in his capacity as the host? The man who sent another man, probably young Mark, to carry a pitcher of water (usually women's work), for the disciples to follow in order to come to the right place? That person was Barnabas the Levite, the brother of John Mark's mother, who was the probable owner of the house.

Jesus was crucified with two others. And all of them would have had their lives terminated before the beginning of the Sabbath (see Deuteronomy 21:23). Deaths were normally expedited by the Roman officer breaking their legs, and normally the malefactors would then be cast into a common grave. But two eminent members of the Jewish Sanhedrin, Nicodemus and Joseph of Arimathea, had asked Pilate for permission to take Jesus' body, and after requiring burial linen and an enormous amount of spice-material, they interred Jesus separately, in a cool ventilated tomb above ground. This may not have been intended as a permanent internment: the important thing was speed, and this tomb was ready nearby. What upset the women who found the tomb empty was not that the body had been removed, but the fact that it had been removed secretly, during the night, and they did not know where they had laid him. 'They' most likely denotes Joseph of Arimathea and Nicodemus.

Could Jesus have survived crucifixion? The torture of the cross normally lasted for several days. The Romans used two quite different methods, one 'fast' and the other 'slow'. The slow death was designed to inflict even worse suffering on a particularly heinous criminal such as a traitor, and the victim could take up to six days to die. A *sedile* or little seat was fitted to the upright post so that it projected between the victim's legs and supported his body weight, and the wrists were then nailed to the crossbar. In the 'fast' method, when it was simply death that was required rather than prolonged torture, the *sedile* was replaced by a tiny platform under the feet, and his wrists were bound to the crossbar by leather thongs. He was exhibited thus for the purpose of humiliation. When the time came to kill him, the executioner broke his legs with a *crucifragium*, a blow from a reinforced club, and the entire weight of the body was thrown upon the thongs, which promptly proceeded to strangle the circulation. In a matter of minutes paralysis, suffocation and heart-failure would bring the victim to a merciful release in death.

In neither case were crucified persons expected to die rapidly. Indeed, when the soldiers went to check, the other two crucified men were still very much alive and had to be finished off. Just before Jesus died he was given something to drink: Jesus deliberately called out for it. Was this a drug that gave Jesus the appearance of having died?

Did the soldier's spear-thrust upset all the secret plans, and kill Jesus after all? That was surely the intention of the soldier who speared him. The eyewitness of John's Gospel insists that he saw blood and water come from the spear-wound. Did this mean that the vicious stab had really killed him, or on the contrary, did this emission from the spear-wound suggest that Jesus was still alive?

If the whole 'death' of Jesus had been an arranged sham, he had still gone through the torture of the scourge and the crucifixion. Jesus' resuscitation would have had to be done at night since it would be a serious criminal act designed to defeat the ends of justice. If it worked, the term 'resurrection' would hardly apply, since Jesus had not in fact died.

Is it beyond the bounds of possibility that Jesus thought out the entire plan himself, knowing that he would have to face crucifixion, but intending to escape death if at all possible? We *do* have several Gospel clues that are presented as examples of Jesus' superhuman knowledge, but might in reality indicate his far-sightedness as a strategist. There are so many important details *missing* from our narratives. For example, did Jesus really know by some psychic means that there would be an ass with its foal tied outside a house in Bethphage, and that the owner would calmly let two strangers take it away when they said the magic words 'the Lord has need of it'? Or does it make more sense that he previously organised this with the owners, so that he could make his triumphal entry into Jerusalem in fulfilment of that prophesy in Zechariah? (Mk 11:1-10; Zech 9:9)

When he intended to visit Jerusalem after dark to celebrate the Passover at a place unknown to the disciples, did he know psychically that there would be a man carrying a pitcher of water who would lead them to a host who was expecting him to come, or had that also been privately arranged beforehand? (Mk 14:12-17)

What about the part played by Judas Iscariot in bringing the troops to the Garden of Gethsemane to arrest him? (Jn 13:21,27) Was it just a lucky guess on Judas' part that Jesus and his friends would stay up all night in the garden instead of going back to their hosts in Bethany to sleep as they had done every other night that week? Why did Jesus say to him 'What you have to do, do quickly'? Why did he sit there waiting for him to come, when if he suspected Judas' betrayal, it would have been so simple to have got away?

Let us return to the strange affair of the mysterious character Barabbas, who was set free by Pilate just before the execution of Jesus. 'Bar' simply means 'son of' and 'Abbas' means 'father'. According to the Sinaitic Syrian, Harclean Syriac, and Armenian versions of this passage, plus the *Codex Koridethi* and the Lake Minuscules for Mt 27:16-17, Barabbas' first name was *Jesus*. An important coincidence this, for it means that the man set free by Pilate was therefore actually known as 'Jesus, son of the father'. Does this mean that we could turn the whole thing round? Who should Pilate release: Jesus, the Son of the Father, or

Jesus who is called the Messiah? (Mt 27:17) Surely then *our* Jesus would be the 'Son of the Father' or 'Barabbas', and the Jesus called Messiah would have been the rebel or zealot leader? That would leave us with the stunning possibility of real confusion, for it would mean that Jesus Barabbas was really our Jesus of Galilee, who was released; and it was the unfortunate rebel leader (who was not called Barabbas) who died. And that would mean that the Jesus of the Christian church was not crucified at all.

There is yet another theory, uncountenanced by any Christian church, but interesting nevertheless. It was commonplace for sons to be named after their fathers. Supposing Jesus had been a married man, and had a son also called Jesus? Supposing this son had been captured in the rising in Jerusalem, and was being held under sentence of death? That would explain why Jesus did not make his getaway, but remained in Jerusalem and seemed almost to negotiate his own arrest. Maybe Judas was offered money to betray him: but threw it down contemptuously in the priests' faces. Was the true scenario behind the arrest narratives really an exchange, so that Jesus would give himself up, and hand over his life for that of his son?

Perhaps he timed it very precisely, in order to have the best chance of a clever plan for his survival. We will consider this further in the next chapter. Were there really angels in the tomb, or was he deftly rescued by friends from the Qumran community, with the help of Joseph and Nicodemus?

Chapter Twenty-One

WAS JESUS BURIED ALIVE?

R EMARKABLY, SEVERAL PIECES of 'archaeological' evidence have survived that provide scope for a range of theories concerning what actually happened at the crucifixion and burial of Jesus. These include a fourteen foot long piece of cloth known as the Shroud of Turin, another piece of cloth known as the Sudarium or 'sweat-cloth' kept in a special shrine in Oviedo in Spain, and a further piece kept in Peter's Cathedral in Rome known as 'Veronica's handkerchief.' Of these, the Handkerchief was said to have wiped the blood and sweat from Jesus while he was still alive, the Sudarium to have covered his head just after his death, and the Shroud has been regarded by many faithful Christians as the very cloth in which Jesus' dead corpse was wrapped and buried.

Veronica's miraculous cloth (known as the Vernicle) used to be displayed every Sunday afternoon. It was reported to be a fragile, almost transparent veil of silk bearing the features of a bearded man.[1] It was said to have been seized by the troops of Charles V who sacked Rome in 1527, and sold by drunken soldiers in the tavern.[2] In fact, the silver reliquary still preserved in the sacristy of Peter's was opened by art expert Monsignor Joseph Wilpert in 1907 (and, I believe, examined again in the 1960s), and the cloth was there, although people were disappointed to discover that there was no 'miraculous face' visible. Wilpert removed the metal covering and two glass plates, and saw a square piece of cloth yellowed with age. Upon the cloth were two dim stains, rust-brown in colour, joined together. There was no image, or remnant of any image.[3]

However, any disappointment is surely misplaced, for if we drop the dubious concept of the miraculous face appearing, we are left with the far more interesting possibility that the 'image' represented genuine marks caused by the actual blood and sweat of Jesus. The relic despoiled by Charles V's soldiers was probably only a painted cloth depicting the face of Jesus, credulously believed to be the actual relic, but which was only one of the many pious and devotional paint-ings and painted cloths produced by artists who venerated the relics, and were frequently used to drape the reliquaries as covers. These icons were often also regarded as holy in themselves, since they had touched the real relics, and absorbed something of their sanctity.

Another famous relic was the Mandylion of Edessa, yet another miraculous cloth, closely linked with a tile known as the Keramion. The Mandylion was also said to have on it an image of Jesus' face, not made with hands, which had been sent to King Abgar of Edessa, and the Keramion (the tile which was laid over it to protect it) somehow picked up the same image.

The fourth century Syriac manuscript 'The Doctrine of Addai' tells how Abgar sent a letter to Jesus, begging him to come to Edessa and cure his leprosy, or at the least to send him a portrait. Instead, Jesus washed his face, wiped it on a towel, and sent Abgar that.[4] A tenth century version of the legend agreed that the Mandylion was the cloth with which Jesus wiped away his sweat, but it was the sweat of his agony in Gethsemane just before his arrest, which 'became like great drops of blood falling down upon the ground.'[5]

Either way, the 'miraculous face' seems not to have been a face at all, but yet another cloth thought to have been impregnated with the genuine blood and sweat of Jesus, the 'face' once again being a pious work of art used as a cover, and assumed by the innocent to be the important object itself.

At least two 'Shroud scholars' (but not this author, or the historian Runciman who believes that the Mandylion perished in the French Revolution when the ship carrying it sank at sea) regard the Shroud and the Mandylion to have been one and the same object.[6] Some illustrations of the Mandylion show it as a face surrounded by a criss-cross grille-like pattern, assumed to be typical of the Parthian region, which acted as a framework. One interesting suggestion, made by Noel Currer-Briggs,[7] is that this actually depicted a gold lattice-work casket which had been created to contain the folded Mandylion in such a way that only the face part showed in the middle, as in a frame; and he suggests the further possibility that this may have been the mysterious object revered as the Holy Grail.

It would have been a flat casket, more like a tray than a box, some four feet by two feet by no more than six inches deep. If this theory is true, the Holy Grail container of the Blood of Christ was not a cup or a chalice, as commonly thought (neither the cup of Christ's blood at the Last Supper, nor the cup in which the blood of Christ was caught at the crucifixion) nor even the *Sang Reyal* or 'royal blood' of supposed descendants of Jesus.[8] Currer-Briggs suggests that the word 'Grail' simply came from the mediaeval French word for 'grill': 'greil' or 'greille' derived from the low Latin 'gradella' or 'craticula'. He suggests that the folded Shroud was taken out and displayed fully by the Knights Templar at certain times to favoured dignitories. The sheet may even have been placed reverently on the altar to serve as the altar-cloth, and the holy communion wafers (the 'body of Christ') served from the Grail – or grille – which on these occasions served as a tray.

Was it the Shroud, which was folded up and kept in this golden grille, with the Keramion placed over the top for protection, which after various adventures, ended up being known as the Shroud of Turin? The Shroud actually bears a visible depiction or marks of a man's whole body, back and front, and not just a head. The notion of it being only the face of Jesus arose simply because it was only the face that was visible when shown to the public.

The Shroud is no ordinary cloth, but has upon it faint marks of the outline of a tall, dignified man, with all the wounds of a crucifixion, and a piercing of the side. Arguments have raged for centuries over whether or not this cloth could possibly be genuine. When photography was invented towards the end of the nineteenth century, a further amazing fact was discovered: when a photo was taken of the marks on the Shroud, the negative of the *photograph* acted as a 'positive', and for the first time a 'photographic' likeness of the dead man could be seen by anyone. It should be made very clear (since the pictures are now so famous) that this positive likeness *cannot* be seen by the naked eye looking at the cloth, but only on a photographic negative of it, and obviously had never been seen thus before the invention of photography. It seemed like a miracle, a piece of evidence that had been almost meaningless until the technical advances of the century made it possible to see its full significance.

The medieval church revered numerous relics of dead saints, and any object connected with Jesus, such as the nails of his crucifixion, the crown of thorns,[9] the lance with which he was pierced,[10] and so on. We are told that some of Jesus's blood shed at Calvary was taken by the centurion Longinus after piercing Jesus' side. This was kept by the Patriarchs of Jerusalem, until given to Henry III of England to be presented at Westminster Abbey.

Other relics of Christ's blood were or are preserved at the Basilica of Sta Maria Maggiore, Rome; the Abbey of Fécamp in Normandy; the Abbey of Hailes in Gloucestershire (this sample was removed by Thomas Cromwell); while at St. Basil's in Bruges is a piece of lamb's wool saturated with blood which was said to have been used to clean Christ's wounds before he was buried. Since we know his body was not cleaned, the supposition is that it may rather have been a cotton-wool plug such as is still used to close body orifices after death. The Patriarch of Jerusalem gave this piece to Count Derrick of Alsace after the Second Crusade.

However, the Middle Ages was a time of a great deal of unscrupulous deception in which dealers in false relics did a roaring trade. Even as early as c400, Augustine deplored hypocrites in the garb of monks who went about hawking what they claimed were the body parts of martyrs. St. Vigilantes of Toulouse condemned all veneration of relics in any case, as being sheer idolatry. It is well known that Calvin particularly despised relic-honouring. He suggested that enough bits and pieces of the 'True Cross' were available to build a ship, if not an entire fleet. What is less well-known is that one Charles Rohault de Fleury took objection to this cynicism, and in 1870 investigated all the known fragments and concluded that whereas it would take around 188,000,000 cubic millimetres to make one cross, only the modest total of some 178,000,000 cubic millimetres of 'True Cross' were actually being claimed in shrines around the world: which explains why the Vatican still has fragments to give out.

Despite all the controversy, and the roaring trade in ridiculous false relics sold to the gullible, the few cloths with personal stains from the body of Jesus were and are regarded as being in a totally different category from other relics. Among these, the Shroud took pride of place, eventually becoming the personal property of King Umberto of Italy.

Science marched on, and people begged to be allowed to prove the authenticity of the cloth by subjecting it to radiocarbon dating. Eventually this permission was granted; and in 1988 the Shroud was declared to be a medieval fake, and was removed 'in disgrace' from its shrine of veneration. That should have been the end of the matter, were it not for the fact that many people who have studied the shroud are still convinced that it *is* genuine, and that the image really was made by the body of Jesus. They are highly suspicious of the handling of the evidence.

Some have gone so far as to challenge the whole procedure of the carbon dating as a deliberate deception by all or at least one of the scientists involved. For example, one claim is that the co-ordinator of the operations substituted a piece of cloth from the cape of St. Louis of Anjou, who died in 1297, so as to secure a medieval dating.

Others feel that the entire process of carbon dating is not as reliable as the public think it is. The Archbishop of Turin himself commented in April 1997 that the carbon 14 tests were not definitive,[11] although no further testing by the same method would be carried out as long as he was in charge. He would no doubt prefer the evidence of dating the Shroud by the pollens on it, which do appear to go back to the time of Jesus, and also show the route of the travels of this relic, as do the pollens on the Oviedo cloth.

Others have come to the conclusion that the Church authorities actually wanted the Shroud to be proved a fake, because, although it really was genuine, the latest evidence now proves that the person wrapped in the cloth was *not dead* when he was buried. They wished to conceal the real truth. As with the Dead Sea Scrolls discoveries, the Shroud conclusions might have had enormous implications for the Church.[12]

Hidden in the text of the Fourth Gospel, for those who have eyes to see, are hints that something very unusual indeed happened at the crucifixion of Jesus. Reading through the text, one immediately has the feeling that one is listening to a genuine eye-witness account. Now this Gospel is the only one to give us also a description of the raising of Jesus' friend Simon Eleazar, better known to us as Lazarus of Bethany.

John 11:1-45 presents a precise description of the burial customs of his time. Lazarus was bound hand and foot in grave clothes, for which the Greek word *keiriai* is used. This denotes long bands of linen, which would be wrapped round the whole body. Hence we should not take this passage to mean that Lazarus was only tied at the wrists and ankles, but rather that his whole body was wrapped in linen bands up to the hands and feet. If his feet had been tightly bound at the ankles, it would be hard to see how he could come out of the grave by himself (Jn 11:44). (The Greek poet Nonnos who made a paraphrase of John's Gospel said he was 'wrapped in linen bands from head to foot'.)

When describing the burial linen of Jesus, however, the gospel writer calls the cloths *othonia*, and these are definitely not bands.

Lazarus' head was 'bound about' (*peridedemenos*) with a *sudarium*. The word, implying 'sweat band', may suggest the band traditionally tied round the head and under the chin to prevent the lower jaw from sagging. However, Jesus' head was not bound with a *sudarium*, but 'covered' (*entetyligmenon*) by it. John says quite clearly that the cloth was 'placed on or over the head' (*epi tes kephales*).

This is claimed to be the cloth which is kept in Oviedo in Spain. Mark Guscin, in his fascinating book on the relic,[13] suggests that contrary to the old theory that the *sudarium* was a cloth that was laid over Christ's head after his body had been shrouded and laid in the tomb, it represents a far more traumatic and interesting relic, similar to the sort of hood one might place over the head of someone about to be executed, but in this case a cloth that was pinned at the back of Jesus' head and wrapped over his face and nose, after he had died but before the body was taken down from the cross. It served the purpose of hiding the contorted features of the deceased's face and rendering the corpse more decent.

Guscin's conclusions are that the stains (one part blood and six parts pulmonary oedema fluid) reveal that Jesus did indeed die on the cross, from asphyxiation. There was then a time lapse of about an hour, during which the body was still on the cross; then it was taken down and laid at the foot of the cross for around forty-five minutes. When the body was picked up again and moved to the tomb for burial the *sudarium* was again held to the nose to absorb the fresh flow of liquid.

Following the latest research, it appears that the blood on the cloth is of the same blood-group as that on the Shroud (AB, which is common in the Middle East), and that the frontal stains on the *sudarium* showed 'seventy points of coincidence' with the Shroud. Guscin concludes that since it is impossible to deny that the *sudarium* has been in Oviedo since 1075, a great shadow of doubt is cast over the results of the Shroud's carbon-14 dating. 'There are two irreconcileable conclusions,' he says, 'one of which must be wrong. All the studies on the Sudarium point to its having covered the same face as the Shroud did, and we know that the Sudarium was in Oviedo in 1075. On the other hand, the carbon-dating specialists have said the Shroud dates from 1260-1390. Either the Sudarium has nothing to do with the Shroud, or the carbon-14 dating was wrong – there is no middle way, no compromise.'[14]

John used quite different words to describe the burials of Lazarus and Jesus; he probably wished to make clear to the attentive reader that fundamentally different things had taken place. The raising of Lazarus was clearly that of a dead body; but in the case of Jesus, everything suggests that this was not an ordinary burial at all.

Lazarus came forth without any help. He ascended from the grave and was then released from his linen wrappings. The typical Jewish tomb was a chamber cut into the rock, in which oven-like cavities (known as *kokim*) were cut. These were usually around 50cm across, 80cm high, and 200cm deep, and the bodies were inserted length-wise. The burial of Jesus was quite different. He was not pushed into a tomb cavity, but laid out on a bench. Mary was able to observe 'angels' one at the head and one at the feet, where the body of Jesus had lain (Jn 20:12). No-one could have sat at the head end of a *kok*.

Kokim tombs were reached through an entrance below ground level, which was often closed with an old millstone or grinding-stone. They consisted of an inner chamber, with a number of *kokim* cut into the sides, each designed to take one body. At the centre of the inner chamber there was usually a square pit which served as a drainage area, and also facilitated the management of the corpses. The bodies would be laid out for washing and oiling on the side of the pit, at the same level as the entrance to the tomb-hole, but at a comfortable height for the convenience of those preparing the corpse, who were standing in the pit. Lamps were placed in niches. When the beloved disciple reached the grave, he 'stooped down and looked in' and saw the linen cloths; Mary stooped down and saw two angels where Jesus had lain. If Jesus had already been lying in a *kok*, he would not have been visible from the tomb entrance. The implication must be that Jesus was still lying on the ledge around the central pit of the tomb chamber, and had not been placed inside one of the tomb holes.

John records that they 'took the body of Jesus, and wound it (*edesan*) in linen cloths (*othonia*) with the spices (*meta ton aromaton*), 'as the manner of the Jews is to bury' (*entaphiazein*).[15] Normally the word *edesan* was used in connection with the bands of fabric (*spargana, keiriai*), cords or thongs (*desmoi*), but not with cloths. In Mark 15:46 the verb *eneileo* is used, which suggests that the body was not only covered with a cloth, but closely wrapped: one might almost say 'packaged'. The term is that used in cookery for wrapping morsels of food in fig or vine leaves. It does not suggest winding round as one wraps a mummy: the word for that is *kateilisso* (as used by Josephus for wrapping mummies and bandaging wounds).

Nicodemus brought a hundred pound weight of aromatic substances, a mix of myrrh and aloes (Jn 19:30). Was this intended to embalm Jesus? It is an enormous quantity: a whole row of sacks. Rabbinical texts only suggest that bodies be washed and oiled, the hair cut and tidied, the corpse dressed decently and the face covered with a cloth. The addition of spices is nowhere mentioned, let alone in these quantities. Either John was mistaken, or he did not know Jewish burial rites, or he was misinformed as to the practicalities of embalming. Alternatively, these herbs and spices had some different purpose.

Older commentators on the New Testament state that Jesus was buried in a hurry as the Sabbath was commencing, and no burials could be performed on the Sabbath: but this is now known to be untrue. One Rabbinical rule allowed complete burial on the Sabbath, while another merely suggested that a corpse should be covered in sand to preserve it until the Sabbath was past.[16] In all synoptic Gospels it is recorded that women went to the tomb after the Sabbath intending to oil the body and inter it properly, something that would seem quite superfluous after all the work put in by Nicodemus and Joseph of Arimathea.

Nevertheless, in recording Jewish customs the Fourth Gospel appears to be more accurate. Instead of the 'women' who go to the tomb (such as Mary Magdalene and Mary the mother of James and Salome who brought spices so that they might go and anoint him; Mk 16:1), we have only Mary Magdalene and no spices; and she only went to the tomb to weep. Jacob Neusner points out that scholars familiar with the Judaism of that era are somewhat surprised to discover women expecting to tend the dead body of Jesus: as in Islam, it is normal for men to take care of male bodies, and women of females.[17]

John writes that they buried Jesus according to the custom of the Jews, and then proceeds to describe a burial that had nothing to do with their custom. Didn't he know? Of course he did, as is demonstrated in his description of the burial of Lazarus.

What was the significance of the huge consignment of herbs? John tells us that they were myrrh and aloes. The aloes were probably *aloe vera*, a plant native to south-western Arabia used in medicine and for incense as far back as the third millennium BCE. The sticky gel had been known to be efficacious for healing wounds from very early times,[18] and is still important in traditional Islamic naturopathy. Both substances could easily be made into ointments and tinctures, and the Jews often mixed myrrh with labdanum, the resin of the rockrose, for plasters and bandages. Could the binding in cloths really have been the placement of a heavy healing plaster round the body of Jesus? Myrrh was used in the mummification of corpses; but it is worth making clear that at the time of Jesus, these substances provided the greatest possible efficacy against infection, and the promotion of healing, that money could buy.

John, it would seem, is trying to reveal a secret event to the reader while concealing it from the eyes of the ignorant. Intentional secrecy? Why not – there are other intentional secrets; as we have seen, the Gospels also never mention the Qumraners,[19] although there were thousands of them doing mission work throughout Judaea and Galilee, with practices and teachings remarkably similar to those preached by Jesus.

Let us take a look at the actual moment Jesus passes away on the cross. Jesus apparently dies just after drinking a bitter drink (Jn 19:29-30). Luke does not mention this, while Mark and Matthew state that a 'bystander' ran up and gave it to him, after hearing him cry out (Mk 15:34-36; Mt 27:46-49). He had cried out the opening words of Psalm 22: 'My God, my God, why have You forsaken me?', but Mark and Matthew report that the crowd thought he had cried out for Elijah the Prophet to come and help him get down off the cross. Someone dips a sponge in vinegar, [20] puts it 'on a hyssop' and holds it in his mouth. Most commentators explain that since the *hyssopos* on which the sponge was placed was a flimsy piece of shrubbery which would hardly have served, the word should rather read *hyssos*: a short spear. This would then suggest that it was a co-operative soldier who actually administered it. [21]

The commentator-editor of John's Gospel states that this fulfilled a prophecy, presumably Psalm 69:10-21: 'Insults have broken my heart, so that I am in despair. I looked for pity, but there was none; and for comforters, but I found none. They gave me poison for food, and for my thirst they gave me vinegar to drink.'

However, in John's narrative, it does look as if the bitter drink was not just fortuitous. It appears in the narrative as if it had been prepared and fetched to the crucifixion for this very purpose. Maybe it was not just the sour Roman wine or *posca* given to the soldiers. It was Jewish custom to offer a condemned person some wine mixed with myrrh or incense. 'The one departing to be put to death was given a piece of incense in a cup of wine, to help him fall asleep.' [22]

Kersten and Gruber suggest that the drink may also have included the milky juice of the seed-heads of the poppy widespread in Palestine: in other words, opium. The narcotic effect of opium can be so strong as to lead to a state of stupor, in which the person is completely without external sensation. One ingredient, morphine, has a sedative, narcotic and breath-inhibiting effect; another, the alkaloid papaverine, has a pronounced cramp-relieving influence. The Gospels report that after drinking it, Jesus lost consciousness and hung on the cross as if dead.

Neither Luke nor Matthew mention the thrust with the lance. Mark records that Pilate, surprised that Jesus was already dead, summoned the centurion to confirm this. John records that the soldier pierced his side with his spear, and from the wound flowed blood and water, and he particularly bore witness to this. The centurion then released the body. This same centurion also praised Jesus as 'a son of God' (Mk 15:39), or as 'an innocent man' (Lk 23:47).

Was this centurion a secret follower? According to the *Acta Pilata* he was called Longinus, and a tradition testified to by Gregory of Nyssa suggests that he later became a bishop in Cappadocia.

The term used for the stabbing was *nyssein*, which in fact signifies a light scratch or puncture, rather than a forceful thrust or deep penetration. The procedure was merely to confirm that death had occurred if the corpse did not show any reaction to it. It was not a death thrust: an experienced soldier would hardly make a fatal thrust through the side, but into the heart. The eyewitness at the cross makes special mention of the blood and water that flowed from the wound. (Jn 19:35)

Again: is this in fact a testimony that Jesus was still alive? Corpses do not bleed,[23] apart from the slight natural flow downwards due to the law of gravity. They cannot pump blood upwards and out, and blood serum is not seen on the wounds of a body which has just died. Incidentally, 'blood and water' may not mean blood and water, or imply serum; it was an Aramaic idiom meaning 'a considerable quantity of' blood. The point was rather that the stab of the lance produced a copious flow: and that is what surprised the eye-witness, for Jesus was supposed to be dead.

We are told that the women, arriving later at the tomb with their oils and spices, were shocked to find the stone moved out and the body gone. Mary's comment 'they have taken the Lord out of the tomb, and we don't know where they have laid him' makes no sense if she is talking about grave-robbers. One obviously would not know where thieves had taken their stolen loot. Mary then supposes the 'gloriously resurrected Lord' to be the gardener! This sounds ridiculous, but Jesus would hardly have wished to make his escape in the nude. It may well have been the gardener's clothes he was wearing. He may even have had a garden implement to lean on as a walking stick. An interesting detail in the Gospel of Peter is that the guard at the tomb described *three* men emerging, two of them supporting the other: was this two angels and the glorified Lord, or two helpers and the badly wounded Jesus?

The burial cloths were left in the grave. The synoptics use the word *sindon*, meaning 'robe' or 'dress'. In the Talmud, *sindon* denotes a simple burial robe.[24] In Mark, the *sindon* is wrapped around the body (*peribeblemenos*). The original Hebrew was probably *sadin,* with connotations of both robe and cloth. The Greek *sindon* signifies a precious cloth, used to make sheets of linen. In Latin, it can mean either a large cloth or a large cloak; in other words cloths of different sizes for different purposes. In reality it is the generic term for linen in general; John uses *othonia*, or just 'cloths': cloths made from *sindon*.[25]

The fourth evangelist writes that they saw the cloths lying there, and the *sudarium* that was about his head was not lying with the cloths but was wrapped together in a place by itself (Jn 20:4-7). Normally *sudarium* is translated as 'towel' or 'napkin'; but, as we have seen, this was presumably the cloth placed over Jesus' face after his death, perhaps preserved or represented by the Oviedo relic. When Jesus was placed in the tomb, the first thing to be done would have been to remove this healing cloth, fold it, and lay it to one side.

The author of John then comments that the disciples still did not know the scripture that Jesus must rise from the dead. What scripture could that be? The most likely candidate is Psalm 16:8-11: 'My heart is glad, and my glory rejoices; my flesh shall rest in hope. For You will not leave my soul in hell; neither will You allow Your holy one to see corruption. You will show me the path of life; in Your presence give us fullness of joy; at Your right hand there are pleasures for evermore.'

The psalmist speaks of *saving from death,* not resurrection. And there are no signs of *rigor mortis* on the Shroud-man. There is nothing bent, skewed, distorted, crooked or stiff about him. He looks like a peacefully resting person. [26]

The blood-like marks also reveal life. Blood freshly flowing is surrounded by a 'halo' of serum fluid. Dried, coagulated blood has quite a different appearance, with no serum border (seen most clearly in photographs under ultraviolet light). Even today, doctors sometimes determine death by making a small cut in the heel or wrist artery. If arterial blood spurts out, the circulation system is still operating. In the case of the shroud-man, it has been estimated that there were some 28 wounds that continued to bleed after his removal from the cross. In other words, he was not dead when he was placed in the tomb.

Herein lies the whole mystery. If the Shroud, and the other 'sweat and blood' relics, *are* false, there is no more to be said. If, on the other hand, the Shroud is not a fake, it matters very much whether or not it can be proved that it touched or covered the body of a living or a dead Jesus.

For if Jesus was not dead when he was buried, it makes no difference to the beliefs of Jews or Muslims, but for a Christian it means that Jesus did *not* die for the sins of humanity after all.

Chapter Twenty-Two

IMPERIAL MANOEUVERING AND WAVERING

T HE FATHERS NOT only disagreed over theological doctrine, they also disputed as to which of the holy writings should be included in the scriptures. Should one simply choose books that had been written by Apostles, or at least those who had been eye-witnesses to the ministry of Jesus? That would immediately rule out everything by Paul, and would plunge the scholar into fierce arguments over the authenticity of many books, given that it was common practice for writers to assume an apostolic pseudonym. For example, Simeon ben Cleophas the leader of the Jerusalem Church after James, was said by the *Toldoth Yeshu* to have been the author of the second and third epistles of John and at least part of the Apocalypse, as we have noted.

Or should the criterion be to select only those books that had been written during the first century? That would allow the inclusion of all manner of works that were eventually ruled out, like the letter written by Clement, regarded as the third Bishop of Rome, who died in c96, and whose work predates much of our present New Testament. It would also allow such works as the *Shepherd of Hermas*.

The Rabbinic scholars had themselves engaged in editorial decision-making between 323 and 198 BCE, when they sorted out which books were to be included in the Septuagint (the Greek translation of the Old Testament). Many other writings were put together by Pharisaic rabbis between 70-73 CE, as they voted to reduce the number of books in the Hebrew scriptures, and style the remainder the 'Apocrypha'. Most Christian authorities accepted the earlier and larger selection, but Jerome in the fourth century chose the shorter version with the addition of Judith and Tobit when working on his Latin translation, the

Vulgate. To this day Roman Catholic scholars still accept the Apocrypha as being of equal status to the Hebrew canon; whereas the Reformed scholars largely reject them.

Modern scholarship largely acknowledges that the ability to mangle and distort the truth, or even to eliminate or fabricate it wholesale in the cause of theological expediency, was a skill ably exercised by the Gospel authors, the intention not being to deceive, but to glorify. This well-meaning tampering in the first three centuries has proved an acute embarrassment to its inheritors ever since, because no scholar can today escape the realisation of how insecure the whole edifice of the 'historical' Jesus is, [1] and how fragile is the Trinitarian doctrine, and how immediate its vulnerability not only to the evidence of the past, but also to the fresh wind of scholarly Islam (as opposed to anti-scholarly Islamic radicalism) which is now beginning to make itself felt in traditional Christian strongholds.

It is fascinating that even Josephus admitted that there were people writing 'histories' in the turbulent Roman Imperial period, and that 'persons with no first-hand knowledge, accepting baseless and inconsistent stories or hearsay, wrote garbled accounts of it; while the narratives of eye-witnesses *have been falsified either to flatter the Romans or to vilify the Jews,* eulogy or abuse being substituted for accurate historical record'. [2] Josephus himself, of course, is a prime example of a man guilty of precisely this sin!

It should now be accepted as a fact, no matter how inconvenient, that for the first three centuries CE there had been consistent and truculent opposition on Biblical grounds to the developing idea that Jesus was God. The struggle to impose a religious uniformity (especially for Byzantine rulers whose subjects lived from Italy to the borders of Persia, and from the Crimea to Upper Egypt) was made formidably difficult by one simple but awkward fact: the age-old psychological differences in approach which made it impossible for believers to see each other's point of view, let alone agree with it.

In essence, the subject of all the theological battles was the nature of Christ. Did he have two natures, one human and one divine, co-existing side by side? This issue split the whole Christian world. Many in the East preferred to believe that although Christ had been both God and man, his human nature had been absorbed into his divine nature during his life on earth. Since this could be presented as a belief that Jesus had only one nature, those who took this view were called Monophysites, from the Greek *monos* (single) and *physis* (nature).

They were cruelly persecuted by the Orthodox: monasteries were closed by force and often with great barbarity, bishops and priests were murdered or hounded into the deserts, while monks and nuns were subjected to repulsive indignities by Imperial troops.[3]

In fact, *none* of the Ante-Nicene Fathers were genuinely Trinitarian. Irenaeus, (died *c*200 CE), said that the pre-human Jesus had a separate existence from God and was inferior to Him. Jesus was not equal to Him who was the 'One True and Only God' who was 'Supreme over all, and besides Whom there is no other.' He took a petition from Bishop Pothinus of Lyons to the Pope, begging him to stop the persecution of dissenting Christians. Pothinus and his followers were all killed while Irenaeus was in Rome, and Irenaeus took over as bishop. When the next Pope, Victor, came to office, he wrote himself, trying to curb the massacres, only to meet the same fate as Pothinus.

Clement of Alexandria (died *c*215 CE) called Jesus 'a creature', whereas God was 'the Uncreated and Imperishable and Only True God'. The Son might be next in glory to the only Omnipotent Father, but he was certainly not equal to Him.

Tertullian of Carthage (died *c*230 CE) taught that 'the Father is different from the Son, as He is greater; as He is who begets is different from him who is begotten; He who sends is different from him who is sent.' He also said: 'Before all things God was Alone.'

Hippolytus (died *c*235 CE) said, 'God is the One God, the First and Only One, the Maker and Lord of all [...] who had nothing of equal age with Him; Who, willing it, called into being that which had no being before.'

Origen (died *c*250 CE) insisted that Father and Son were two separate essences, and that the son was inferior to the Father. Origen's father Leonidas had founded the theological college in Alexandria and appointed Clement to his position. Leonidas refused to accept the 'new' Christianity, and was murdered in 208 CE. Origen sought martyrdom too, but was prevented from leaving his house when his mother hid his clothes. Origen became head of the Alexandria College, and was ordained priest in 230 CE, in Palestine. Bishop Demetrius deposed and exiled him, so he started a new school in Caesarea. He was condemned in 250CE by the Council of Alexandria for rejecting the doctrine of the Trinity.

Lucian of Antioch (died *c*312 CE) believed Jesus was not equal to God, and was tortured to death. His two leading disciples were Eusebius of Nicomedia, originally bishop of Beyrouth, who had great influence over the Emperor Constantine's sister, and Arius of Libya; two men who were staunch Unitarians.

It is hence clear that many leading writers in the first three centuries, even among those who did believe in Jesus as divine, and who did speak of Father, Son and Holy Spirit, did *not* think of them as co-equal, nor as one numerical essence, nor as Three in One in any sense intended by Trinitarians.

In 303 the pagan and anti-Christian Emperor Diocletian persecuted the Christians and issued an edict to have all holy books and bibles destroyed. The Rescript of Milan in 313 gave the Church the opportunity for a massive re-write, and there was immediately an urgent demand for copies of any texts still available. (Later, Lucinius of Boetica in Spain, for example, sent six scribes to Palestine in order to copy everything Jerome had written up to that time (391), especially his revised texts of the gospels in Latin.)

As for Eusebius, the only New Testament books he would accept as being genuine and authoritative were the four usual Gospels, Acts, the epistles of Paul, I John and I Peter. He disputed the genuineness of the epistles of James, Jude, 2 Peter, and 2 and 3 John, and declared that the Acts of Paul, the Epistle of Barnabas, the Teachings of the Twelve Apostles, the Revelation of St John, and the Gospel according to the Hebrews were all definitely to be excluded.

One extremely suspect feature of New Testament study is that although a diligent search has been made for original source-material for centuries, through hundreds of ancient monasteries and other likely repositories of antique documents, not one gospel manuscript older than some time in the fourth century CE has ever been found; not even in the Vatican Library, which has some 25 *miles* of venerable papers.

The reason for this cannot just be the accident of time; it is an obvious fact that thousands of ancient manuscripts of *other* faiths *far older* than Christianity still exist. It appears to have been the outcome of the public conversion of a Roman Emperor to the faith[4] and his subsequent interference. Before Constantine, a work such as the original Hebrew Gospel had reached as far afield as India, and was more popular in many churches than the gospels we have now, but not one full manuscript of it now exists. How is this possible?

It must have been due to Constantine's deliberate policy to clarify the 'true faith', unify the bishops, and establish one form of Christianity as the official religion of his Empire. Upon his accession, the wild beasts in the arena were treated to their first taste of the blood of pagan heroes who refused to be baptised, instead of the Christian heroes who had previously refused to burn incense to the *divi filius*, the Emperor.

At that time churches were more or less autonomous under their own bishops, whose differing theological viewpoints about Jesus and his significance in the eternal scheme of things evolved from (or generated) the large variety of texts then in circulation. Not only that, but bishops were quite happy to scavenge other notable writings to suit their purposes: Virgil's *Aeneid* and the Sybilline Oracles, for example, were used frequently as books of prophecy.

Constantine was hardly a model for the faithful. He had killed his own son Crispus, and then had Crispus' stepmother found guilty of the crime and executed by immersion in boiling water. Their supporters sought revenge, and the Roman priests of Jupiter would not absolve him; which was the main reason why he moved his capital to Byzantium. Christianity was now no longer illegal, but was the faith granted imperial favour, with the result that many people now claimed conversion for political reasons: and on the whole they preferred the Pauline church as it was a good deal less demanding. In Byzantium, now renamed Constantinople, the Emperor was permitted to do penance in the Pauline church, and was 'forgiven'. He therefore gave this church his full support, but found his plans opposed by the Libyan Arius, and Donatus, a Berber bishop of North Africa, who insisted that Jesus was a Messenger but not God, and that there was no reason why they should be obliged to accept rulings from Rome. Donatus was a bishop for forty years (from 313 CE). When the bishop of Rome sent his nominee Caecilian to take over in Carthage, the Donatist Schism was precipitated. Both sides sought the patronage of Constantine, who decided in favour of Caecilian. The followers of Donatus would not give way, and his popularity did not diminish.

Constantine tried many times to encourage them to unite, but to no avail. Eventually the Roman army was sent in, there was a mass slaughter with bishops murdered in their churches, so that the Donatists became known as the 'Church of Martyrs'. As far as they were concerned the Roman Catholics were evil priests working with the 'kings of the world'. After the death of Donatus, the people of North Africa continued to follow his 'rule' for the next 300 years, after which they accepted Islam.[5]

Arius (250-336CE) was a priest of Alexandria. He insisted that while Jesus was the highest under God, he was not himself divine. His argument was that if Jesus truly was the Son of God, then clearly the Father existed before the Son, and there must therefore have been a time when the Son did not exist. The Son must have been a created being, since he had not always existed. And if God was eternal and had always existed, this meant that Jesus could not be part of the eternal Godhead, as only God was eternal. He could be *like* the substance of

God, but not of the same substance.[6]

Moreover, if Jesus was a created being, then he was subject to change, whereas God is unchanging; therefore Jesus was not God, having himself taught 'The Father is greater than I' (Jn 14:28). Jesus *was* the Word (*logos*), but the Word was itself a creature. Arius had been Lucian's pupil, and so knew very well that his teachings were dangerous. When he was around sixty-eight years old he was a presbyter of one of the oldest Alexandrine churches, the Baucalis, as a famous teacher with a huge following. He was ordained priest, then excommunicated and reinstated twice, and was only just defeated as Bishop of Alexandria by his Pauline rival, Alexander.

Alexander could not overcome him in debate, and excommunicated him again. Arius wrote to his friend Eusebius (of Nicomedia, not the historian of Caesarea of the same name), complaining that Bishop Alexander was only trying to expel him from the city as an 'impious atheist' because he and his friends did not subscribe to the bishop's outrageous Trinitarian doctrines. The letter still exists, and shows that Arius had no desire to divide the church, but could not give way on his beliefs. Eusebius rallied to his support, and tried to get him accepted back by Alexander, but this only served to make Eusebius and Alexander enemies. As the conflict became personal, the Emperor himself intervened to try to make peace.

Meanwhile Constantine clashed with his brother-in-law Licinius, who was killed, and the latter's widow Constantina (the Emperor's sister) arrived to live in the imperial palace. Both Licinius and Constantina were close to Eusebius, and had given Arius their support. Constantine decided to settle the whole controversy with a council of all Christian bishops, over which he (still claiming at the time to be a 'neutral' pagan) would preside. It was a grand occasion, but matters did not fall out according to his plan. To his embarrassment, most participants were suspicious of his motives, and such was the reluctance of the majority to agree to teachings they considered wrong that only some four hundred bishops actually turned up, a fraction of the total.

Alexander despatched the young priest Athanasius as his representative. Hundreds of hours were spent on vocabulary: defining *ousia* (being or essence), *hypostasis* (substance), *physis* (nature), and *prosopon* (person or self-presentation). The Emperor's Christian mother Helena supported the Trinitarians, but Constantina used her own influence, pointing out that the Emperor wanted a peaceful solution, and that if no agreement was reached he might lose patience with Christianity altogether.

In the face of imperial and Trinitarian vehemence, Arius and his side agreed to adopt a peaceable and passive stance, but to disassociate themselves from the conclusions that seemed to hover perilously close to sun-worship: the Roman Sunday which replaced the sabbath; the sun-god's birthday, December 25th, which was adopted as the birthday of Jesus; the sun-god's emblem (a cross of light) which was chosen as the Christian emblem; and the key features of the Sun-god's birthday celebrations which were incorporated into the developing Trinitarian ceremonies.

The Nicene Creed was drawn up, outlawing Arianism and its understanding that Jesus was subordinate to God, even though this view was not considered heretical at all by the majority of bishops attending.[7] The crucial formula expressing the relationship of Jesus to God in the creed issued by the Council was that he was 'of one substance with the Father'. The bishops, with two exceptions only, consented to sign the Creed, but it was much against the inclinations of many of them; they signed only after two months of furious debate, and many did so with great misgiving.

Jesus was officially declared divine, and the Only-Begotten Son of God, and the creed proposed by the brilliant Trinitarian deacon Athanasius became the official belief of the established church. The Emperor, for his part, resorted to requesting a miracle from God to support the Council. All the books referred to the Council (one source specifies some 270 gospels and another source indicates no fewer than 4000 texts) were placed under the communion table, and the room was locked up for the night. The Lord was besought to levitate the inspired volumes on to the table, and to leave the spurious ones underneath. In due course, those favoured by Athanasius were found to have risen upon the table, and Constantine ordered all the rest to be burned.

Yet the matter was hardly settled. After the bishops had gone home, they simply returned to their old and cherished beliefs, and it soon became clear that the bitterness had actually increased. Bishop Alexander escaped it all by dying in 328, and Athanasius was promoted to replace him. Meanwhile Constantina continued to support Arius, and managed to secure the recall of Eusebius from exile.

Constantine intervened again. For his second move, a mere six years later in 331, he 'caused to be prepared under the direction of the notable church historian Eusebius, fifty copies of the gospels for use in the churches of Byzantium'. Why? What does that ominous phrase *cause to be prepared* mean? It is certainly most suspicious that *every one* of the many copies of other gospels in use in the churches right up until the time that Eusebius produced his new edition are now lost without trace.

In 335, at the Council of Tyre held to celebrate the 30th year of Constantine's reign, there occurred an extraordinary turn-about of events. Athanasius was accused of episcopal tyranny and was condemned, and Arius was received back into the church. Arius suddenly found himself accepted as Bishop of Constantinople, but his satisfaction was not destined to last long. He almost immediately perished (in 336), from poisoning. The Emperor suspected Athanasius, and loudly condemned him.

It was not until shortly before his own death that Constantine at last officially became a Christian: but what is not often made clear is that it was, amazingly, as an *Arian* that he was baptised. To Constantina's delight, the officiating bishop was Eusebius of Nicomedia. Constantine died a year later, in 337, in the faith of all those he had allowed to be killed. The Council of Antioch in 341 confirmed unitarianism, as did the Council of Sirmium in 351. But the argument was not over. When Damasus was elected Bishop of Rome in 366, the election was so hotly contested by opponents of his beliefs that at the end of an eventful election day a hundred and thirty-seven corpses were counted.

Chapter Twenty-Three

HAVE THE CHRISTIANS REALLY GOT IT ALL WRONG?

THE 'PROBLEM' STILL refused to go away. Trinitarian doctrine was gaining ground in the west. St Basil of Cappadocia and St Theophilus of Antioch were the first to employ the word Trinity or Triad. At the Council of Nicaea there was not yet a Trinity as such: at this stage the Holy Spirit was not even considered to be a separate entity. Those who believed that Jesus was not equal to God even came back into favour for a time; but the later emperor Theosidius decided against them. He imposed the Nicene Creed as the standard for all his realm, and convened the Council of Constantinople in 381 to clarify the formula: and *that* council decided to make the Holy Spirit another separate entity in the Godhead, instead of just the 'action' of God, and to place the spirit on the same level as God and Christ. So in 381, for the first time, there was officially a Trinity.

In 387 Jerome, a Trinitarian hard-liner, took up residence in the caves of Bethlehem and translated the scriptures (of his choice) into Latin, thus establishing the text known as the Vulgate. Once this became accepted, all the books not included in his selection had even less influence. Yet even then Trinitarianism was not widely accepted, even though those who opposed it brought upon themselves more persecution.

Much material not considered to be orthodox was deliberately destroyed, or falsified by Christian censorship, a censorship officially authorised in the reign of Constantine I, and reinstituted in the reigns of Theodosius II and Valentinian III.[1] The present-day New Testament came into being as we have it today as late as 397 CE, when the Council of Carthage, after much wrangling and disagreement, fixed the number of books at sixty-six.

As regards the many writings which lived on the fringe of Christian acceptance, Eusebius writes with a sweeping and grandiose dismissal of the many who disagreed with him: 'To none of these [apocryphal writings] has any who belonged to the succession of the orthodox ever thought right to refer in his writings. Moreover, the type of phraseology differs from the Apostolic style, and the opinion and tendency of their contents is widely dissonant from true orthodoxy [i.e. Trinitarian theology], and clearly shows that they are forgeries of heretics. They ought, therefore, to be reckoned not even among opinions, but shunned as altogether wicked and impious [...]'

The library of one ancient Egyptian Christian community was found in 1945, in the sands of Nag Hammadi in Egypt. It consisted of thirteen volumes, containing a total of forty-nine works, and is now the chief treasure of the Coptic Museum in Old Cairo. The texts presumably show what was acceptable to *this* community: three versions of the Apocrypha of John, three Apocalypses of James, an Apocalypse of Paul and one of Peter, and three Gospels none of which are in the present-day New Testament: Valentinus' Gospel of Truth, the Gospel of Philip, and the Gospel of Thomas. [2]

There was a time when the official New Testament included such material as the subsequently abandoned Epistle of Barnabas, the Epistle of Clement, the Shepherd of Hermas, the Preaching of Peter, the Didache (or Teaching of the Twelve Apostles), the Apostolic Constitutions, and even the Sybilline Oracles. [3]

For the first six centuries the Syrian Church omitted four of the presently accepted epistles, and Revelation. In the fourth century, Syria and Armenia recognised a third epistle to the Corinthians by Paul. To the present day, the Ethiopian Church has eight more books in its New Testament than are recognised in the West. It is evident that the process of the selection of books was determined simply by the victory of one Christian party over another. Had a different party won, then the 'New Testament' would have been different too.

One of the main controversies was over a subject called Patripassianism: a particularly complicated piece of doctrinal jiggery-pokery. The argument runs like this: if the Logos (the pre-existent Christ) has the nature of God, is perfect, incapable of change, and so forth, then 'he' is no more able to mediate for the inescapably inherited 'original sin' of man than a Transcendent God, so the problem of Atonement remains unaltered. If, however, Jesus, although divine, suffered as we do, and experienced the same temptations, then this must mean that since he shares the essence of the Father, the Father must also suffer. Athanasius could not accept this. In any case, it did not touch at all the vexed question of how it was possible for any spiritual, non-physical entity such as a non-material Logos to be involved in matter and become incarnate.

In Antioch, they plumped for the theory that Christ was a human being uniquely endowed with the Logos. He was, as it were, a human used as a receptacle for that which is divine. The Christ was God *in* a man, and the Virgin Mary was his mother as regards his human body, and not of Christ as God. In Alexandria they preferred to think of Christ as an incarnation of a supreme figure. In Antioch, led by Theodore of Mopsuestia (c350-428), they stressed the differences between the two natures, and since the divine and human natures were essentially separate, they could not give a satisfactory account of their union; in Alexandria they compromised the distinction between the divine and the human, and emphasized the divinity of Jesus at the expense of his humanity. The formula *Apathos epathen* was mooted: 'he suffered without suffering.' (That is, his body suffered, and the Logos suffered in sympathy because it was his body!)

One of the chief thinkers was Apollinaris of Laodicea (active 360-380), who taught that the *physis* or nature of Jesus was divine, and therefore that Christ was God become a man. Therefore Christians were quite entitled to call the Virgin Mary *Theotokos* or 'Mother of God' and to address intercessory prayers to her in that capacity.[4] This was the doctrine known as Monophysite, implying one nature.

In fact, *both* doctrines compromised the Trinitarian theory, for if one conceded that Christ was essentially God in human form, one necessarily accepted that he was incapable of true human suffering and death on our behalf, this being the essence of the redemption doctrine. On the other hand, if one accepted the separateness of his two natures, it implied it was only Christ as a man, and not as God, who died on the cross, which again compromised the concept of redemption.[5]

The leading theologian of the Antioch school was Nestorius, an Aramaean Arab from Mesopotamia, who openly denied the union of the 'natures' in Christ. Nestorius' view was anathema to Orthodox and Monophysite alike. Not only did Christ have two natures, human and divine, but two persons had been combined in Christ, and therefore Mary should not be called *Theotokos* or Mother of God. She was no such thing, having been no more than the mother of the man Jesus, so that therefore she could only be entitled *Christotokos*.

Nestorius was angrily opposed by the staunch Monophysite Cyril of Alexandria (412-444). It was to settle the Nestorian controversy that the Council of Ephesus was called in 431, which, through the majority vote of the bishops, confirmed the Virgin as *theotokos*, branded the two-person or Nestorian view of Jesus as a heresy, and banished Nestorius to die in exile in the eastern desert of Egypt. However, even today, his view is *still* accepted as orthodox in the Assyrian Church.

Cyril's success, however, provoked alarm in Rome, and Pope Leo I (440-461) attacked the Monophysite position, summoning the another council in 449. Cyril's successor Dioscorus (444-454) arrived with a bodyguard and intimidated his opponents into deciding in favour of the Monophysites: the reason why it was nicknamed the 'Robber Synod'.

In 451 the Council of Chalcedon again came out against the one-nature or Monophysite view of Jesus engendered by many, specifically attacking its teaching that in the Incarnation the human-ness of Jesus was completely absorbed into his divinity (the opposite position to that of Arius). However, this view is still regarded as orthodox amongst the Egyptian and Ethiopian Coptic Churches, and the Armenian and Syrian Churches. The formula of Chalcedon, in which the Council was backed by the Emperor Marcian (450-457), was really only a compromise, not a solution, achieving no more than the anathematising of several rival positions.

The formula asserted that 'Jesus was consubstantial with the Father in Godhead, and with us in manhood; like us in all things except sin; begotten before the ages of the Father in the Godhead; the same in the last days for us and for our salvation born of the Virgin Mary, *theotokos*, in manhood – acknowledged in two natures without confusion, without change, without division, without separation – the distinctive character of each nature being preserved and not confused.' By 'confused' they meant 'running together' like salt dissolved in water: not the ensuing mental state of the scholars![6] Each nature was perfect in itself and distinct from the other, yet perfectly united in one person who was God and a man at the same time.

In 494, Pope Gelasius I finalised the work of the censors of the preceding two centuries. The Gelasian decree was a catalogue of prohibited books, proscribing no less than sixty-one volumes and thirty-six authors, whose supporters were to be 'damned in the inextricable shackles of anathema forever.' It became a serious offence to own forbidden texts, and many thousands of Christians were put to death by other Christians for keeping such books.

As regards the writings of those hostile to Christianity, or any historical material presenting Jesus as a human leader (maybe even a troublemaker or political activist) these were systematically censored or destroyed. Thus, there is nothing in Josephus; the relevant portions of Tacitus are missing, and the works of Celsus and his like were wiped from the face of the earth.

But the evidence suggests that they really had quite a lot to say: they knew the story of Jesus the Saviour-Son of God, and rejected it. The basis of their rejection was not that Jesus had never lived, but that the Christian assertions of his divinity were a misunderstanding or a deception, and the Christian accounts of his life and teaching were false.

The Nestorians formally broke relations with Antioch in 498 and became an independent communion with their own supreme bishop in Ctesiphon, in Iraq.[7]

In 506, the Armenian Council of Dvin rejected Chalcedon and openly declared itself Monophysite. In 512 the Monophysite patriarch of Antioch, Severus (d.458), was overthrown and exiled. The Monophysites refused to accept a bishop foisted on them, and elected their own new patriarch, St Sergius of Tella. Severus was given support and protection by the Empress Theodora, wife of Justinian 1 (527-565), and the Syrian Monophysites became another independent communion. In 553 the Second General Council of Constantinople affirmed again the doctrine of Trinity and the Motherhood of the Virgin Mary, and in 680 the Third General Council, also at Constantinople, affirmed that in Christ there were two natural wills and two modes of operation.

Theodora had been visited by Sheikh al-Harith ibn Jabalah, a Ghassanid king, who came to tell her of the plight of his Christian Arabs. They had suffered appalling horrors at the hands of the imperial commissioners who had been sent east to extirpate 'heretics'. The Sheikh told the Empress they needed a new bishop to ordain men to replace the priests who had been arrested or martyred by their 'orthodox' oppressors. They were sheep without a shepherd. He would have to be a very remarkable person, tough and fit, speaking Syriac and Greek if not Arabic, and should be willing to accept that he would be hunted all the time like a wild beast. The Empress' inspired choice was Jacob Baradaeus (d.578), a monastic recluse, who was consecrated Bishop of Edessa. His name Baradeus was actually a nickname meaning 'rags' or 'tatters', which he acquired because he spent so much time in disguise as a beggar.[8]

Baradeus was an amazing preacher who was said to have travelled many thousands of miles, mostly on foot, knowing all the time that he was evading a vast manhunt. He is said to have ordained thousands of priests and consecrated eighty-nine bishops and two patriarchs. So firmly did he build up his church that it still exists today throughout Syria: the Jacobite Church.[9]

The full development of Christian Trinitarianism, really an ancient belief that can be traced back thousands of years into the dim and misty pagan past, in fact took place in the West, in the scholasticism of the Middle Ages. The Athanasian Creed – that 'We worship one God in Trinity ... the Father is God, the Son is God, and the Holy Spirit is God; and yet they are not three gods, but one God' – was unknown in the Eastern Church until the twelfth century. The Eastern Churches, for their part, still regard as heretical the phrase in the Nicene Creed that the Holy Spirit proceeded from the Father *and the Son*.

What about the present century? At the Mariological Congress at Lourdes in 1958 it was proposed that Mary be proclaimed 'causa efficiens': the agent or cause that produced redemption, without whose intercession and mediation no grace could fall on the faithful. This proposal failed, but only temporarily, for in 1964 Pope Paul VI elevated her to the status of 'Mater Ecclesiae': 'Mother of the Church', and automatically she became 'causa efficiens', hence being elevated (as many Protestants pointed out) to a form of divinity. It should be noted that Pope Paul's decision was personal and somewhat solitary, for it was made in the face of the almost total opposition of the Second Vatican Council, which saw little hope of any ecumenism with the Protestant churches if Mary were further glorified.

It is clear that it took hundreds of years for the Trinity to become widely accepted by Christendom: and what guided the decisions? The Word of God; or clerical and political considerations? It was in truth largely a matter of Church politics. All patristic theology was conducted within the framework of contemporary politics and philosophy and was therefore culturally determined. The doctrinal controversies were shaped not only by the qualities of the arguments, but also by personalities and politics. The cases of Cyril, Nestorius, Arius, Eutyches and Athanasius are particularly illustrative.

'Deep emotions and profound intolerance stirred up councils, churches, and armies of monks into horrific attacks upon one another, and to the excommunication and exile of upright and sincere church leaders. It is a distressingly human story': and not the gradual dawning of the truth inspired by the Holy Spirit![10] The Emperor Heraclius (610-641) made another attempt to unify the churches, but was preoccupied with the Persian invasion, the Persians being themselves supported by the Monophysite Christians. The Byzantines managed to defeat the Persians in 628, but by this time the Arab tribes to the south had united under the banner of Islam. The Monophysites widely rallied to Islam, welcoming the Muslims as liberators.

Heraclius attempted to reconcile the Monophysites with a new formula: that there was one 'energy' and 'will' emanating from the union of divine and human natures in Christ. This new idea was dubbed 'Monothelite' ('one will') Christianity. Heraclius attempted to secure its acceptance for twenty years, and finally issued a decree imposing it. The decree was meaningless, as both sides rejected it, and it was roundly condemned as a heresy in 680 by the Sixth Council. By this time the Monophysite, Coptic, Jacobite, Armenian, Maronite and Nestorian churches were no longer subject to the Emperor of Constantinople.[11]

We can surely conclude, then, that the history of Trinitarian theology was not therefore especially 'divine', but depressingly similar to other sacerdotal schemes, and has no right to be regarded as more 'timeless', 'providentially guided,' or 'possessed of the eternal truth' than any other scheme.

Sadly, it has a very bloody record in the annals of world history. Charlemagne, for example, convinced the pagan Saxons of the 'reasonableness and truth' of Christianity by having over four thousand people beheaded in one day; the sur-vivors were immediately convinced! He was canonised in 1164. In 1215 Pope Innocent III called for the extermination of non-Trinitarian heretics; in 1252 Pope Innocent IV sanctioned their torture in heresy trials. The Inquisition was set up to investigate and eliminate any traces of deviation.

In 1563 the Council of Trent declared that the Church alone was the sole arbiter of spiritual revelation, the Bible was to be interpreted only according to the opinion of 'orthodox fathers', heretics were to be anathematised, and all books purporting to be sacred but not approved by the Holy Office were pro-hibited. On St Bartholomew's day in 1572 some ten thousand Protestants in France were massacred in a single bloodbath to save France for Catholicism. After this horror, Pope Gregory XIII had a Te Deum sung and struck a special gold medal.

Protestantism was no less cruel. In fact, all branches of the church can pro-duce examples of repellant tyranny, cruelty and intolerance, giving no quarter to anyone. Down the centuries, over a million unitarian Christians were put to death: the consequence of hierarchical religious power believing that it alone had divine authority.[12] It is an interesting thought that had this author lived in Spain a mere two centuries ago, this book could not have been written without her life being, quite literally, at stake! Although scepticism was already stirring in other parts of the 'civilised' world where the fearsome Inquisition had fallen into a decline, those who challenged the accuracy of the Gospels still had to walk with care.

> In Spain those monstrous men of God still ran a pretty tight torture chamber until, in 1816, the use of torture to force heretics to confess was forbidden by the Pope. Eighteen years later His Holiness disbanded the Inquisition and, after some 600 years, Europe could at least breathe clean air, untainted by the stench of burning corpses. No longer awed by the sinister greasy black stains in a thousand marketplaces where heretics had writhed at the stake 'for the glory of the Lord Jesus Christ', thinking men all over Europe began to wonder whether the truth expounded by the Gospels was literally the historical truth. [13]

To be a member of a particular church is already to have accepted the fact that somebody, or some committee, has made a decision, a choice between viewpoints, and thus defined an orthodoxy that suits that individual. No more than that.

Despite widespread revisionism among professional New Testament scholars and theologians, many ordinary churchgoers still accept and repeat the creeds set out in the prayerbooks as a sheer act of trust. Muslims, who do not know these creeds and have not studied the histories that generated them, are frankly baffled when they come across the statements of official Christian belief for the first time. A simple Muslim can understand, if not agree with, the devotion of believers that had caused them misguidedly to elevate a servant and messenger of God to divine status. Many Muslims innocently think that if they sit down together with Christians, and talk things through calmly and reasonably, the Christians will soon see the error, and revert to the logical belief in the supremacy of the Deity. When they come across a theologian, they are instantly out of their depth in a morass of linguistic hair-splitting, illogical assertions, and elaborate attempts to justify time-bound patristic dogmas.

Paul triumphed, and Trinitarian Christianity spread over the face of the earth. But was it right? Was it what Jesus ever intended? Can any Trinitarian Christian really be sure? Or have they really got it all wrong?

True orthodoxy is a different animal to throw a net over. The line of thought which reduces to a vanishing point the amount of Christology traceable to Jesus himself, is a grave loss to Christianity. No doubt it would be a departure from orthodoxy, but if the history of Christianity offers any clear lesson, it is that 'a nearer approach to truth is *always* a departure from orthodoxy.' [14]

Let us refresh ourselves by asking a simple question. Why, for thousands of years, did *none* of God's prophets ever teach His people about the Trinity? Why didn't Jesus make it clear? Would God have inspired hundreds of pages of scripture and yet not used any single phrase of this instruction to teach the Trinity, if it really was the vital doctrine of faith and the means of human salvation? Why did all the Old Testament prophets campaign so tirelessly against the cultus of the Baalim and Ashteroth, in all their manifestations? And why should God, centuries after Jesus, and after having inspired the writing of the Bible, back the formulation of a doctrine that had been unknown to His servants for thousands of years, that was an 'inscrutable mystery beyond the grasp of human reason', that had a pagan background, and whose victory took place at the hands of imperial and church politics?

Surely it is time to admit the possibility that it is in fact *not* the truth, but apostasy? 'God is not a God of confusion' (I Cor 14:33). Surely it is time to consign to its proper place a doctrine so complicated and unnecessary that no major scholar of the past or present has proved capable of properly explaining it, or making it intelligible to the ordinary person. Indeed, while the Church was busily eliminating unitarian dissenters who were branded as heretics, Islam rapidly gained converts. The hatred and venom felt for unitarians was turned against the Muslims: the Crusades being in this sense an extension of the massacre of the Arians.

The fact that today thousands of Christians are leaving their faith is surely proof that the Trinitarian religion is not as satisfying and persuasive as is claimed. Any ideology or faith that is based on the tenuous foundation of blind belief cannot last, and sooner or later its adherents will begin to wonder, and will leave it for a more solid and rational persuasion. Faith can be created in a flash by an illusion, and destroyed in a second by disappointment.

Faith might demand total allegiance to the Bible, with its faults and absurdities, its sometimes immoral ethics, and its uncertain origins. Reason, on the other hand, is loath to accept matters that constitute an abuse of the human intelligence. The mind thinks, the heart believes. If belief is arrived at without thinking, it really is blind. But if we arrive at belief *through* the God-endowed process of thinking and reasoning, then no-one can shake or destroy that belief.

Faith is a necessary thing, and an integral and natural part of human life on earth, but we must know and understand in what our faith is vested. If the object of our faith has been exposed by scholarly research to be fallible, man-made, spurious and fabricated, and if our religious beliefs have been exploded by analysis, then we must re-examine and re-assess our whole religious outlook and reorientate ourselves spiritually in the light of what is true and what is false.

> We have entered a new era, which is bound to be very disturbing to those who have pinned their faith on the veracity of the New Testament version of the Christian story. Much will have to be reformulated and reappraised, and what the outcome will be cannot be predicted with any assurance. Yet it must be better to adjust, however painfully, than to try to hold on to concepts, however precious, which truth demands should be abandoned.[15]

Let us walk again on the hills of Galilee, or in the wilderness of sand where the sun hammers down by day and the light of great stars guides the wayfarer at night, in the fresh desert air. Let us try, if we can, to keep company for a while with the nomad herdsman Abraham, the shepherd David, the tree-tender Amos, the carpenter Jesus, the honest merchant Muhammad, and feel a kinship with their disciples, common folk who were so certain of the simplicity, the truth, the logic, the rightness of what these Messengers taught that they could share it easily with others, and were so prepared to hand over their lives in love to the God Who was being revealed to them. Let us blow away the tangle of cobwebs from the mind, and submit to His will as being the most reasonable and right way of life that there could possibly be!

> I will lift up my eyes to the hills. From whence does my help come? My help comes from the Lord, who has made heaven and earth. He will not let your foot be moved; He who keeps your will not slumber [...] The Lord is your Keeper; the Lord is your shade on your right hand [...] The Lord will keep you from all evil; He will keep your life. Your Lord will watch over your going out and your coming in from this time forth and for evermore. (Psalm 121)

> In the name of God, the Most Compassionate, the Most Gracious [...] God: there is no deity but He, the Living, the Self-Subsisting, the Eternal. No slumber can seize Him nor sleep. His are all the things in the heavens and on earth. Who is there who can intercede in His presence, except as He wills? He knows what is before them and what is behind them. None of His creatures can know anything of His knowledge, except as He wills. His throne extends over the heavens and the earth, and He is never tired in guarding and preserving them, for He is the Most High, the Supreme. (Sura 2:255)

Chapter Twenty-Four

LIFE WITHOUT AN ATONING SAVIOUR

WHAT LIES BEHIND all the saviour cults is a sense of the utter helplessness and hopelessness of humanity. Humans are in a terrible predicament, held fast in the clutches of sin, the Devil and all his powers, unable to save themselves without the aid of Divine intervention, and following that, a cultic priesthood.

In the Christian tradition, the situation is briefly as follows: every human child is born with the taint of Original Sin, its origin being the sin of Adam and Eve, when in disobedience to the Lord they ate the fruit of the Tree of Knowledge, and in punishment for this were expelled from Paradise. After this, God decreed that every single descendant born from the time of Adam to the end of the world inherit their sin. It was for this reason that the Son of God was not conceived by Mary through the seed of man, but through the agency of the Holy Ghost, so that he might not be tainted by this original sin.

Since humans are therefore all born in sin, the consequence of which is punishment in Hell, it is necessary that a Christian should sincerely believe in Atonement. God, in His infinite mercy, wants to see that humanity is saved; but how can His two attributes of Justice and Mercy be reconciled? The problem is solved by the Son of God who willingly offers himself as the punishment on behalf of all humanity. The doctrine of Atonement is the most important pillar in the whole superstructure. Knock down this pillar, and the whole edifice is razed to the ground.

Does it make sense? Did Jesus teach this? Let us look at the Parable of the Wicked Husbandmen (Mt 21:33-41). An earthly landowner sustains wrongs committed by his tenants. Does he offer to forgo his right of recovery for the damage with full forgiveness and remission of all penalties, so long as his only son and heir gives his life and dies the death of a felon in satisfaction of the claim? Far from it. He sends his son as a messenger, and the villains kill him too. The result in the end is not their forgiveness, but the loss of the vineyard which is taken from them and given to others who are more worthy.

The doctrine of killing the son to save the villains infringes the very concept of justice. How all criminals would really enjoy being taken to court for their crimes, if they could relax in the knowledge that the judge's son was going to bear the fine or the flogging or even the execution! If the aim and the motive of punishment is the correction and reform of the wrongdoer, how can this purpose be served if the judge punishes his own son instead? Would that really make the criminal better: or would it encourage him to go out and cheerfully commit more crimes? One does not have to believe in Original Sin to recognise that most criminals are lacking in moral conscience or the feeling of shame. In any case, such a judge, cruelly executing his own son, could hardly be called merciful.

The famous case of a Muslim leader, Schamyl, being flogged in the place of his mother comes to mind, a moving incident which touches the heart: but nobody regards it as real justice, and it probably had very little effect on the activities of the criminals of the Schamyl's time. The sons of royalty or wealthy nobles who could afford to have a 'whipping boy' to take floggings on their behalf were rarely moved to noble morality by this device, and nobody thought it just.

If it is argued that Jesus was the master of his own life and that he gave it willingly, that is not really true. We read in Matthew 26:39 of his agony, that 'he fell on his face and prayed, saying, O my Father, if it be possible, let this cup pass from me!' before he agreed to do God's will. Luke's version adds that he was 'in agony … and his sweat became like great drops of blood falling to the ground.' (Lk 22:44). His later cry: 'My God, my God, why have You forsaken me?' expresses his sense of abandonment when he realised that he really was going to die.

In short, the doctrine presents God in a negative light. God is not really loving and compassionate at all, but cruel and merciless: a God who cannot forgive the sins of humans without exacting His 'pound of flesh'. A God Who is truly loving will always accepts human repentance directly, and can never reject it on the grounds that it is not accompanied by faith in the Atonement. Moreover, if one takes the system seriously, it makes Jesus unjust also. Humans commit two kinds of sins, those against God and those against their fellow humans. If A steals something from B, and is then forgiven by God because his sins have been taken away by Jesus' sacrifice, where is justice to B? Islam teaches that whereas God is so compassionate He may indeed forgive a human any sin, no matter how great, the human who has sinned against a fellow human is obliged by the Divine Command to seek forgiveness from that fellow human first. If the wronged person grants forgiveness, well and good, and reparation could perhaps be made in some way to put right the offence. If the wronged person refuses to forgive, then at least the wrongdoer has done his or her best to appease, and has satisfied the Divine Requirement. The sinner could then do something positive to put right the sin anyway; and the burden of not-forgiving falls on the person who was wronged.

When one looks at the Gospels, one can see that this was exactly what Jesus taught too. If a person had sinned against another, it was quite pointless him standing before the altar making prayer to God, until he had put right that sin. 'Leave your gift and go!' said Jesus. 'First be reconciled to your brother, and then come and offer your gift' (Mt 5:23-24).

Moreover, the supposed Atonement of Jesus does not in actual fact save humans from the things that were the consequences of their sins, according to the Adam and Eve story – they still die, bear children in pain and toil, and go to prison for their crimes. There is no evidence that belief in Atonement has made human beings any better in general terms at all. A student of the Middle Ages, for instance, might even put forward evidence that crimes of all sorts are more prevalent in Christian societies than in other societies that do not have this convenient false hope. If belief in Atonement is supposed to remove from one's heart the power of doing evil, the evidence for this is lacking.

In short, the doctrine of Atonement is absurd and preposterous, and offends human reason. It was positively refuted by the prophets of the Old Testament, who revealed God's mercy and compassion. 'If My people humble themselves and pray, and seek My face, and turn from their wicked ways, then will I hear them from Heaven and will forgive their sin.' (2 Chronicles 7:14) 'Let the wicked forsake his way, and the unrighteous man his thoughts, and let him return to the Lord, and He will have mercy on him, and to our God, for He will abundantly pardon' (Isaiah 55:7).

It was likewise not taught by Jesus, and is not found in the Gospels. A rich young ruler is represented as asking Jesus point blank what he has to do to gain eternal life. Jesus does not even mention the doctrine of Atonement, but tells him to keep the commandments. The rich man replies that he had, and asks if he still lacks anything. Jesus then suggests that he sell all his possessions and donate the proceeds to the poor (Mt 19:21).

The epistle ascribed to James (which Luther used to tear out of Bibles, calling it 'an epistle of straw') may well have been written to counteract the argument of Paul in his epistle to the Romans. The subject is broached in Chapter One: 'Religion that is pure and undefiled before God is this: to visit orphans and widows in their affliction, and to keep oneself untainted from the world.' (James 1:27) His theme reaches its climax in chapter 2:

> How does it profit you, brothers, if you say you believe, but you do not do good works? Do you think your beliefs will save you? If someone clad in rags with an empty stomach comes in, and you say 'Go in peace, be warm and full' without giving them anything – how have you helped them? Belief not accompanied by deeds is worthless. Someone may say – 'you have faith and I have works'. Show me your faith apart from your works, and I by my works will show you my faith [...] Do you want to be shown, you foolish fellow, that faith apart from works is barren? As the body apart from the spirit is dead, so faith apart from works is dead. (James 2:14-6)

Nothing could be more emphatic, more moral, or more clear. James taught:

> Draw near to God, and He will draw near to you. Cleanse your hearts, sinners, and purify your minds. Humble yourselves before God, and He will lift you up [...] O you who say 'Today or tomorrow we will go into such and such a town and spend a year there, and trade, and get gain', you do not know about tomorrow! What is your life? You are a mist that appears for a little while and then vanishes. Instead, you ought to say 'If the Lord wills, we shall live, and we shall do this and that!' (James 4:8,10,13-15)

Insha'Allah. Insha'Allah (Sura 18:23-24).

What does the Qur'an say about justification by faith? It says this:

> It is not righteousness to turn your face towards east or west; but righteousness is to believe in God and the Day of Judgement, and the angels, and the Book, and the Messengers; and to give from your wealth out of love for God to your family, to orphans, to the needy, to the wayfarer, to those who ask, and for the freeing of slaves; to be steadfast in prayer and to practise regular giving; to fulfil all the promises which you have made; to be firm and patient in pain and suffering or any other adversity, and through all times of panic. Such are the people of truth, the God-fearing. (Sura 2:177)

Another passage discusses the fate of various persons on Judgement Day.

LIFE WITHOUT AN ATONING SAVIOUR 215

What was it that condemned those who had 'failed'?

'They of God's right hand will ask of the wretched – "What has cast you into hellfire?" They will say, "We are not of those who prayed or those who fed the poor, and we wasted our time with many empty arguments, and we rejected as a lie the Day of Reckoning – till we were forced to accept the Reality." (Sura 74:40-47).

'Who shall teach you what the steep highway is? It is to ransom the captive, to feed the orphan or the poor man who lies in the dust.' (sura 90:12-16).[1]

Here is one teaching from the Rabbis: 'And so the Holy One, blessed be He, said to Israel – "My children, whenever you feed the poor, I count it up for you as if you fed Me".'[2] Jesus taught the parable of the Two Foundations, one on rock and the other on sand. The firm foundation for any human being wishing to please God is not some complicated esoteric belief, but to hear the words of Jesus and the prophets, *and do them* (Mt 7:24).

In another of his most famous parables Jesus gave an account of God the Almighty sorting out who was to inherit eternal life and who was damned to punishment. He did not divide the 'sheep and goats' according to their beliefs, or their faith in Jesus as saviour, but according to how they had lived.

> The King will say to those on His right hand: 'Come, O blessed of my Father, inherit the kingdom prepared for you from the foundation of the world; for I was hungry and you gave me food, I was thirsty and you gave me drink. I was a stranger and you welcomed Me, I was sick and you visited me, I was in prison and you came to me.' Then the righteous will say, 'Lord, when did we ever see Thee [like this]?' And he will answer: 'Truly I say to you, inasmuch as you did it to one of these the least of my brethren, you did it to me.' (Mt 25:34-40)

The Hadith Qudsi give a very similar teaching:

> On the Day of Judgement God will say, 'O son of Adam, I fell ill and you did not visit me.' The man will answer, 'O Lord, how could I have visited you when You are Lord of the Worlds?' He will say: 'Did you not know that My servant had fallen ill, and you did not visit him? Did you not know that if you had visited him, you would have found Me with him?'[3]

In Pauline theology,[4] Jesus the crucified was presented on the one hand as 'God [...] in Christ, reconciling the world to Himself', but also by implication as a sacrifice offered *to* God *in order* to reconcile God to humanity, and thus to enable humanity to obtain His forgiveness. However if a person who believes in

God rejects the need for atonement, he or she rejects the whole edifice of Trinitarian theology as to *why* Jesus was born, and this is why it is such a serious step for a Christian. But what is the basis for this doctrine? Christians are supposed to accept that humanity is trapped by sin because it is somehow passed down genetically from Adam's original disobedience, and that God for some reason is unable to forgive it until a being greater than a human pays it off by dying! Therefore God Himself must be born as a human in order to pay the price Himself.

Article II of the Thirty-Nine Articles of Faith follows precisely this line of reasoning. 'The Son [...] truly suffered, was crucified, dead and buried, to reconcile his Father to us, and to be a sacrifice, not only for original guilt, but also for the actual sins of men.'

Many Christians, once they start to reason things through, find they cannot accept this tortuous logic. Most do not believe in the real existence of Adam and Eve anyway, but have accepted the Darwinian theory of evolution. Some have turned completely from belief in God simply because the system seems so archaic and absurd, and they accept that evolution has been proved. The problem only exists because Christians have always been obliged to think and reason *within the confines of this ancient saviour-cult ideology*. They think that if they give up *this* belief, it means giving up *all* belief in God! Broaden the horizons, however, and new light is available.

Islam presents the whole story of Adam and Eve with an entirely different slant. Firstly, Adam, and his partner Hawwa (Eve) are said to be the first created beings, *intended* khalifas (or vice-regents) of God on earth. They did not 'fall' to this position, but were created for this purpose. They were equal partners. The angels were concerned that physical beings with free-will would cause chaos, and Shaytan, the chief jinn, refused to bow to Adam (15:28-31). His pride and disobedience were the origin of evil. On being rebuked by God, he determined to prove his point by tempting them into disobedience, and thus became the enemy of humanity.

Adam and Hawwa originally lived in a state of innocence and happiness, described as a 'garden', in which they were set one limit: a tree whose fruit they were forbidden to eat. Shaytan deceived them by falsely suggesting it was the 'tree of life' that would give them immortality (20:120), and tempted them to try to live forever on earth: a wishful desire to avoid death, and a lack of faith in life after death. In Islam, it is not suggested that they originally inhabited the state of Paradise to which the successful go in the Afterlife, or that there *was* such a thing as a 'tree of life' or 'tree of the knowledge of good and evil'.

Humans lost their innocence through disobedience; and, in hoping to be free of dependence on God, they lost the real meaning and purpose of life itself. Adam and Hawwa fell for Shaytan's temptations and were driven out of their garden (2:35-39; 7:19-25; 20:120-122). However (and this is the great doctrinal difference), as soon as they realised their loss, this brought *tawba* (repentance); they turned back to God for forgiveness, and were reunited and forgiven at Mt Arafat. This is the event remembered in the *wuquf* or 'Standing' at Arafat during the Hajj.⁵ God taught that all humans who repent of sins and turn back to belief will be forgiven, no matter how great those sins; and only those determined to reject Him and not repent will be punished in the life to come.

So Islam differs radically from Christianity in that it has no doctrine of inherited original sin; every individual human faces Judgement Day for their own decisions and actions, and not those of their parents, or forefathers, or anyone else. Consequently there is no need of a 'saviour', still less any possible justification for God to 'incarnate' Himself in order to sacrifice Himself.

'He is that light by which you will walk straight in your path; if you come to the light and walk in it He will forgive your past deeds, for *He always forgives* and is merciful.' (Sura 57:18)

There is one vitally important passage in the Old Testament which is consistently ignored by those who advocate the Atonement theory of the death of Jesus. It is the revelation to Ezekiel (in the Qur'an, Dhu'l-Kifl) in chapter 18 of his book. The word of the Lord came to Ezekiel specifically concerning this subject of inherited sin. It is such an important passage that it is worth giving the text almost in full:

What do you mean by repeating this proverb concerning the land of Israel, [that] 'the fathers have eaten sour grapes and the children's teeth are set on edge'? As I live, says the Lord God, this proverb shall no more be used by you in Israel. Behold, all souls are Mine; the soul of the father as well as the soul of the son are Mine; only the soul that sins shall die. If a person is righteous and does what is lawful and right [...] he shall surely live, says the Lord God. (Ezek 18:1-9)

You say: why should the son not suffer for the sin of the father? When that son has done what is lawful and right, and has been careful to observe all My laws, he shall surely live! The soul that sins shall die. The son shall not suffer for the sin of the father, nor the father for the son [...] and if any wicked person turns away from sins and keeps My law, that person shall live; he shall not die. None of the sins which he has committed will be remembered against him. 'Have I any pleasure in the death of the wicked?' says the Lord, 'and not rather that he should turn from his way, and live?' (Ezek 18:19-23)

'I will judge you, O House of Israel, every one according to his own ways,' says the Lord God. 'Repent and turn from your transgressions, lest your sin be your ruin. Cast away from yourselves all the sins which you have committed against Me, and get your-self a new heart and a new spirit. Why will you die, O House of Israel? I have no pleasure in the death of anyone,' says the Lord God. 'So, turn and live.' (Ezek 18:30-32)

What could be clearer? I humbly suggest that this was not just the belief of the Jewish prophets and the prophet of Islam; it was also the belief of the Blessed Jesus.

What of his virgin birth? Doesn't that prove he was Son of God? Although Muslims accept the virgin birth of Jesus, they do not accept that this denies his real and essential humanity. Muslims do not find it difficult to accept any of the miracles of God, including Jesus' virgin birth, but they do not use this miracle as an argument to prove that Jesus was divine: simply that God can perform what-ever miracles He wills.

'The likeness of Jesus before God is that of Adam: He created him from dust. He said to him "Be" and he was.' (Sura 3:59)

'Mary said: "O my Lord, how shall I have a son when no man has touched me?" And He replied: "Like this: God creates what He wills, and when He has decreed any plan, He says only 'Be' and it is so."' (Sura 3:47)

Mary's uniqueness in giving birth to a son by a special miracle did not mean that she was any more than human, or that her son was more than human. The full, normal, uncomplicated humanity of Jesus is unacceptable to Trinitarians because it emphasises that Jesus was not 'begotten' but was a created being, like you or I. Miraculously created, yes, but still created and not 'God from God', 'emanated' or 'of one substance with the Father.' To Muslims, Mary's virginity – although accepted – is not really the key issue, and the extraordinary specula-tions that some Church Fathers were prepared to accept to explain it, are quite superfluous in Islam.

Islamic theology drew entirely different conclusions. If Jesus was born with-out a human father, what did that prove? Why, the first prophet Adam was created with neither father nor mother. As far as *all* the physical bodies of humanity are concerned, they are no more than dust. The greatness of Jesus, or of any prophet, arises from the divine command 'Be!' Trinitarian Christians who have elevated Jesus into the ranks of a Triune Godhead obviously make him quite different in kind from any other representative of humanity: and herein lies the theological dividing line between Christianity and either Islam or Judaism.

What the Qur'an taught was that even the truest, the purest, the greatest of humans was no more than human. The closest to God is the most aware of his humble status as a creature, and his great privilege: of being beloved by the Father.

> They do blaspheme who say God is one of three in a Trinity; for there is no God except one God [...] Christ the son of Mary was no more than a Messenger; many were the Messengers that passed away before him. His mother was a woman of truth. They both used to eat food [...] Will you worship besides God something which has no power either to harm or benefit you? God: He it is Who hears and knows all things. O People of the Book, do not exceed the bounds of what is proper in your religion, nor trespass beyond the truth; do not follow the vain desires of those who went wrong in times gone by, and strayed from the straight path. (Sura 5:76-80)

As Imam al-Busiri says of the Blessed Muhammad:

> Leave aside what the Christians say of their own prophet,
> But say what you will of him, and say so beautifully;
> For the most that can be said is that he was mortal man,
> And that he was the best of God's creatures without exception.

One Qur'anic passage depicts Jesus standing before the Throne of God and giving account of himself, like any other mortal.

> And behold, God will say: 'O Jesus, son of Mary! Did you tell people to worship your-self and your mother as gods, in derogation of God?' He will say: 'Glory to Thee! I could never say what I had no right [to say]. Had I said such a thing, You would indeed have known it. You know what is in my heart, though I know not what is in Thine. For You know in full all that is hidden. Never said I to them anything except that which You commanded me to say, which was "Worship God, my Lord and your Lord." And I was witness over them while I dwelt amongst them; and when You took me up, You were the Watcher over them, and You are the Witness to all things.' (Sura 5:119-120)

A further passage attributes the following words to him, spoken miracu-lously in his cradle:

'I am indeed a servant of God; God has given me revelation, and made me a prophet. And He has blessed me wherever I may be, and has enjoined prayer and charity upon me as long as I live. He made me kind to my mother, and not overbearing or miserable. So, peace is upon me the day I was born, the die that I die, and the day I shall be raised up to life [again].' Such was Jesus the son of Mary; [it is] a statement of truth, about which they [vainly] dispute. It is not befitting to the [majesty of] God that He should beget a son. Glory be to Him! When he determines a matter, He only says 'Be', and it is. (Sura 19:30-35)

Although Muslims react strongly against the notion that God could have, or need, a 'Son', they feel the strongest kinship with devout and compassionate persons, and are so sorry that, in their opinion, Christians choose to believe according to emotion rather than reason.

Nearest among mankind in love to the believers you will find those who say 'we are Christians'; because among them are people devoted to learning, people who have renounced the world, and are not arrogant. And when they listen to [and understand] the revelation received by the Apostle [Muhammad], you will see their eyes overflowing with tears, for they recognise the truth. They pray 'our Lord, we do believe! Write us down among the witnesses'. (Sura 5:85-86)

Muslims maintain that Jesus' teaching was never anything but monotheism in all its purity. They are now in the strange position of being able to claim that it is *they* who are the true Christians, for they follow the true teaching of Christ. No doubt many of the Christians who feel so 'at home' when being drawn into Islam today are those whose hearts have never felt at ease with the Trinitarian dogma. All controversies about dogma and faith will of course disappear when we appear before God, who judges us not by the words that fall from our lips, but by what we are and how we have lived according to what we knew.

The grace of God calls, and the mercy of God forgives, but all people are responsible for their own salvation. *Akhira*, or life after death, is the real reason for our earthly existence. Muslims believe that human life is divided into three sections, the creation and pre-human existence of each individual soul, a relatively short human life-span, and the eternal life to follow. Details about pre-human and post-human existence are part of what is *al-Ghayb*, the Unseen. However, it is obvious to a believer that the eternal life is far more important than whatever happens on earth.

Chapter Twenty-Five

JUDGEMENT

O people of the Book! You have no ground to stand on unless you stand fast by the Torah, the Gospel, and what has come to you from your Lord. (Sura 5:68)

AFTER CENTURIES OF arrogance, it has become a commonplace of modern science that the settled truths of today are rarely true tomorrow. It is important that theologians throw off restricting shackles too, to preserve the right of fresh minds to come to bear on matters so that there is the possibility of changes of opinion and the airing of fresh theories.

As a Muslim scholar might say, 'the gates of *ijtihad* must be kept open'. This has been a blind spot of organised religion: the conviction that one inherited format or framework is entirely right, and all other ways are wrong. People of insight have always had to find the courage to stand out against the complacent inertia of centuries, and point to a new path. 'Above all', says Shakespeare's Polonius to Hamlet, 'to thine own self be true; then it must follow as the night the day, thou canst not then be false to anyone.'

Galileo and Copernicus knew this; and stood firm. And among scholars of religion, theories about Jesus, Christianity and the canon of scripture have always been changing. Science makes progress in leaps of insight, several scientists often spotting the new link or novel twist all at the same time. Transformations occur when the time is right. Perhaps this is so in all fields of insight. Many honest thinkers reached the point of disillusionment with Christian theology in the past, and in the last few centuries some have bravely dared to put forward the possibility of living a good life without a saviour.

The intellectual élite were the first to withdraw their support, and found an exciting sense of freedom in their new-found independence from the monopolistic priesthood of the Christian Church. Religion of any kind was soon seen not only as outdated superstition, but as a restrictive force and a hindrance to the quest for further scientific knowledge. Thus many 'Christians' who gave up their faith did not feel sinful or villainous: they reasoned that their creed had been no more than a man-made philosophy which had simply been expedient in the past for the maintenance of law and order.

Moreover, having fought so hard to free themselves and their countries from the domination and jurisdiction of the clergy, and to replace them by civil government and civil law, many of today's followers of atheistic materialism inevitably fear the spread in Europe and America of Islam, with its return to a belief in a Divine Almighty Being, and what they assume must be mediaeval nonsense best forgotten.

This attitude follows on from a more ancient prejudice, which is itself far from defunct. For centuries Christians have characterised Muslims as the enemy, the arch-rivals, the infidels, the savage deniers of their God, and not as deeply devout believers in *the same God*, who also respect and accept the Messenger Jesus.

Suddenly, with the advent of fair-minded literature about Islam in the West, and the increasing number of translations of classical Muslim works, it has become possible and permissible to study Islam properly. And it follows, as night follows day, that as soon as devout lovers of God who are baffled and bored with Trinitarianism make a real study of Islam, many are led to the same conclusions as myself.[1] It is the *theology* of the churches that is wrong, not the love of Jesus or the Christian way of life. God has not gone away, and Jesus the moral guide is still an inspirational presence. It is just that for centuries church people have never dared to admit that the Trinitarian choice made by the fourth century church might have been wrong, and that Jesus might not have been the great blood-sacrifice of propitiation, but exactly what the Muslims have patiently said he was: a sublime Messenger of God, one of a series of chosen prophets, of whom Muhammad was the seal and the last.

The first step to this liberating knowledge is the realisation that the world extends far beyond the confines of a Chosen Race, or an élite Church, and that God's love is widely-bestowed: it has no need to be limited. As Islam believes, there have been 124,000 perfect prophets. Just as today's principal versions of Christianity are *not* the real truth, so too Christ was *not* the only way to God. God's plan was to send many, as befits His generosity and love; and not just to rely on the action in history of one 'only-begotten son'.

Secondly we must drum out of our brains the obsession with narrow doctri-

nal conformity. Since God lies far beyond the reach of human reason, any condemnation of believers for not giving assent to *any* complex and exclusive
theological system must be grossly misguided and wrong. We may wish to know
the details of religious practice; but metaphysics should never impose intricate
methods or conclusions. Imam al-Juwayni (d. 1085), one of the great theologians of Islam, insisted that 'Should we be asked to define which formulations
should be judged to be unbelief [*kufr*] and which would not, we would say that
this is an unfulfillable wish, for it consists of a remote goal reached by a difficult
road.'² Religious movements that seek to impose a cramped definition of correct belief are usually doing no more than proclaim their own insecurity and
arrogance, and therefore their decadence. A few simple beliefs which are clear
from revelation require assent; but the details, and the manner of theological
exposition, may legitimately vary; and this can only enrich and enliven the religion, and make it a home for every human type.

What characterised the teachings of both Jesus and Muhammad was an
almost complete indifference to the niceties of theology; and a powerful compassion in many forms, whether we remember their loving presences at
marriages, celebrations and funerals, or their persistent gentleness towards
sinners. A love and appreciation of women. Above all, a quiet but almost ruth-
less sidestepping of spiritless ritualism and priestcraft, including the notion of
blood-sacrifice. It seems that they only came to teach one thing: love (*mahabba*),
compounded and guided with understanding and compassion. 'We have sent
you only as a mercy to all the worlds,' says God (sura 31:107), and the Prophet
confirmed, 'I am sent only to perfect the noble qualities of character'.³ And
again: 'You will not enter Paradise until you have faith, and you will not have
faith until you love one another. Show mercy to those who are on earth, and the
one who is in Heaven will show mercy to you.'⁴ And as he summed up his teaching: 'Be joined to those who would cut you off; give to those who deprive you;
and forgive those who wrong you.'⁵

Both Jesus and Muhammad knew that God is over all, and that evil and with it
the ability to acquire our own actions form part of the Divine intention. There
are two paths (*najdayn*), each open to free choice, one of beauty and goodness
and the other of sin and death. Think of the Prodigal Son (Lk 15:11-32). Both
paths bring experience through which a person might, in the end, find God. In
fact, so many of the people Jesus lifted before God were sinners in pitiful and
traumatic conditions; think also of the Companions like Umar who had persecuted the Prophet, only to have their hearts melted so that they became his most

devoted defenders. God offers both ways, because He offers us the ability freely to acquire (*kasb*) our actions. The alternative is the doctrine of compulsion (*jabr*), a vision of a race of humans who are no more than automatons, so that goodness is not meaningfully good at all.

One aspect of the reality of evil is that our physical world may teem with spirit forces, many of them malignant. Anyone with psychic ability is conscious of them. Jesus and Muhammad, like all the prophets, were well aware of the whisperings in men's hearts, of the human urge to do wrong. They believed in evil spirits, and exorcised them, and knew that Satan represents a very real agent of trial sent by God. But does the notion of eternal damnation of weak humans in the kingdom of the devil make sense?

It is certainly a very convenient weapon for threatening recalcitrant congregations. However one can surely see the difficulty of the notion that one of the comforts of the saved in Heaven will be to contemplate the torture of the damned in Hell. The damned are frequently our loved ones, our sons and daughters who have gone wrong. If our hearts bleed, can we really imagine that the All-Compassionate God (al-Rahman) will enjoy their eternal torture?

Certainly there is Hell, and those pitiful, lonely, agonised, mentally tortured souls who have abandoned God are, in a sense, there already. There may well be worse to come for those who die in such sorry states, where they may indeed find much 'weeping and wailing, and gnashing of teeth', as Jesus put it. But this is not what God urged upon them, and surely it will not be a permanent state in a sense which we could understand, since that will be a time out of time. He is ever waiting for the prodigal in the gutter to repent and turn to Him; the Blessed Prophet will intercede for the damned even after their entry into Hell.[6] In the Qur'an we learn that the rewards of Heaven and punishments of Hell are only without end, *if God wills*.[7]

Jesus and Muhammad never taught the crude doctrine that Hell is God's revenge on us: 'In flaming fire taking vengeance on them that know no God, and that obey not the gospel of our Lord Jesus Christ; who shall be punished with everlasting destruction from the presence of the Lord, and from the glory of His power' (1 Thess 1:8-9). It is not God's punishment for human bad behaviour – He forgives that – but the outcome and sign of separation and torment for those who find themselves separated from God's presence because they refused to accept His grace, His offer of forgiveness. Many appalling sinners have averted Hell altogether because they repented and were genuinely griefstricken, and sought forgiveness before the end of their days.

We must know and realise that each action we take here in our lifetimes has the potential for timeless consequences; and that we have the responsibility of responding to God's initiative. Some believers burdened with a naive idea of predestination think that no matter what they do, they will end up in Paradise because God has destined this for them; while others are born destined for Hell. But if the warning purpose of revelation is to have any meaning, we must affirm that our eternal fate is *not* sealed at the time of our physical birth, only at our 'new birth' at the time of our physical death.[8] So long as we have not hardened our hearts to the point where we can no longer acknowledge the compassionate love of our Creator, we are capable of receiving His gift of eternal *falah* (well-being), and of turning from our sins, and leading a new life. If a change in our destination were not possible, the Blessed Prophet would not have urged us to pray, or to seek the good-pleasure of God by reforming ourselves.

The gate of repentance is always open; but no prophet has ever given the impression that the way to Heaven will be easy. As Jesus said: 'The way is narrow, and those who find it are few.' It involves struggle, hardship, sacrifice and self-denial, as well as faith in God.[9]

Jesus and Muhammad tried to show us how to love and how to live; Trinitarianism taught a theological system – that the death of Christ upon the cross, and *only that death*, bought salvation for us. Works were all very well, and faith was an essential; but the thing that mattered, now and forever, was the hanging upon Calvary of the emaciated figure of a God-man who was the Only Son of his Father and himself a part of the Creator of the Universes, with blood oozing from his pierced hands and side and thorned brow. By implication came also the inescapable insight that Judas Iscariot was doing a service to the whole human race when he betrayed his master and friend, as otherwise that master would not have died to save what was his own world anyway from his own wrath!

Yet the living Christ seems never to have thought these things. Jesus taught that people are not saved by creeds, lists and definitions, holy scholars hurling anathemas at each other about exact meanings, or daring to define the exact limits of God's mercy. Jesus taught that God showed compassion without measure – that lovely image of the generous market trader selling his bowls of grain 'heaped up and running over' (Lk 6:38).

Let us just take a cold, hard look at the implications of the doctrine of the Trinity for ideas of salvation. Firstly, can it be true that the millions of the human race fell from grace, or from some fantastic condition, graceful or disgraceful, through the solitary sin of a single man?[10] Secondly, can we really believe that for all time, to the end of the world and the judgement, every man, woman and child lies under the vengeful condemnation of a jealous God, and would have to spend an eternity in a hell of flame had not Jesus descended from Heaven to Earth and offered himself up as that blood sacrifice which alone could absolve humanity?

Lastly, most incomprehensibly of all and without any support of evidence or even common sense, why should this supposed salvation from the sin of Adam not be brought about by any thought or action of any human being – not even by the desire to be saved, but only be achieved by God's quite arbitrary 'predestination' or 'election'?

We have no hint that Jesus, the benign Jew of Palestine, would have had any patience with such 'Spirit-guided dogmas', debated with so many anathemas and blastings, or that he would have anathematised or condemned to death those who dissented. Jesus was, in fact, opposed to the whole idea of vicarious atonement. Like Muhammad, he was a protagonist *par excellence* of self-responsibility and the dignity of personhood. For the author of the letter to the Hebrews, 'without shedding of blood there is no remission' (Hebrews 9:22). 'If the blood of bulls and goats, and the ashes of a heifer sprinkling the unclean shall sanctify the purifying of the flesh, how much more shall the blood of Christ ... ?'

Yet Jesus, far from making a blood sacrifice on the cross the cornerstone of his teaching, never made reference to it. He insisted that God desires mercy and not sacrifice. If redemption by blood sacrifice had been the vital core of Christ's teaching, why do we find him saying instead: 'Neither do I condemn thee; go and sin no more', or 'Thy faith hath made thee whole', or 'Forgive us our trespasses as we forgive them that trespass against us'?

Jesus never believed he had obtained eternal redemption for us, or paid our price. If we are to accept what he taught, we must free ourselves from the idea that one man (who was actually God) had to die for the sins of all people, and also from the assertion that the tragedy of Calvary was unique, and that there had never been anything like it before and never would be again. Noble deaths of martyrs are ten a penny.[11] We must also shed the belief that this 'unique event' was linked with a Chosen Race or Elect People, or that it had been prophesied in the Jewish scriptures.

Next we must abandon the belief that the man who died was part of or coequal with God the Creator of the Universes, and himself therefore the creator of those universes; and that this saviour had to give himself to placate himself because of his wrath against those human souls he had himself brought into being, and so bring about a reconciliation to himself. [12]

In the twenty-first century, on our little earth, lost in the galactic immensities, it is inconceivable that this death on a cross in first-century Palestine could be regarded as God's plan for universal salvation. Spinning on our planet amongst one hundred thousand millions of planets and suns, knowing little about ourselves and almost nothing about the other planets, even our nearest neighbours in our solar system, how can we cling to exclusive and grandiose schemes of salvation? Surely there is no distinction between God's messengers? The liberation they all promise is true liberation; unless God is monstrously arbitrary and unjust.

'Those who believe (in the Qur'an), and those who follow the Jewish (scriptures), and the Christians and the Sabians – any who believe in God and the Last Day, and work righteousness, shall have their reward with their Lord; on them shall be no fear, nor shall they grieve.' (Sura 2:62; 5:72; 22:18.)

It is important to realise, however, that the Christians commended here by the Qur'an are not the Trinitarian worshippers of a Divine Son, but those monotheist followers of Jesus who still clung loyally to the original faith, the spiritual descendants of the Jerusalem Church under James, and the zealot Nazoreans of Qumran. These were the ones who heard the message delivered through Muhammad with joy, and believed. [13]

Qur'anic Christians are those whose fundamental submission to God, whose *islam*, was undertaken within the context of following the prophet Jesus.

> To him had God vouchsafed a revelation that, given its divine origins, could not be inconsistent with God's culminating revelation in the Qur'an. Qur'anic Christians guarded this revelation in its pristine purity, keeping themselves free from the eventual dogmatic aberrations of their coreligionists. Scripturally anticipating the advent of God's final prophet, they stood ready to acknowledge him (Muhammad) as the fulfilment of that same divine graciousness that had sent their earlier Prophet, Jesus. For Qur'anic Christians there was not, nor could there be, any incongruity between the two prophets, Jesus and Muhammad. Those who had faithfully followed the former would necessarily be eager to welcome the latter. [14]

To the surprise, perhaps, of the Trinitarians, this species of Christian never died out. Such people persisted, and one example of this category of Christian from the present day, I humbly submit, is my own self. Like many seekers after the truth, I had become 'muslim' in my mind and heart long before I had heard anything about Islam: simply from my own love and interpretation of the figure I regarded as the real Jesus.

Essential to the concept of pure monotheism is the insistence on the consistent stream of Divine Revelation, the Qur'an being its most recent manifestation. Looking for the true meaning behind the words, it is an easy matter for monotheist followers of Jesus and his Way to 'adjust their minds' so that the formula of witness that brings entry to the Kingdom of Heaven is no longer 'in the name of God, the Father, the Son, and the Holy Spirit' but 'in the name of God, *the One*, the Compassionate, the Merciful.'

For that compassion and mercy promise a forgiveness that is direct, and total, and overwhelming.

Appendix

THE GOSPEL OF BARNABAS

HE GOSPEL OF Barnabas (not to be confused with the Acts of Barnabas, or the Epistle of Barnabas, which are recognised as early Jewish Christian works), has long been thought to be a very late forgery, anathematised and forced out of circulation for its alleged heresy, a work produced by a priestly convert to Islam who wished to rewrite the Gospel record according to his new-found Islamic point of view. [1]

The text has a very elusive past, and the claims made for it do not rest upon adequate scholarly documentation. However the discovery of the Dead Sea Scrolls has made some scholars look at it again, because of the abundance of Qumran terminology to be found in its text. There are striking similarities of belief also. If this Gospel was a late forgery from beginning to end, it is interesting that it is so rich in the Qumran terminology of Jesus' time, including terms and expressions not known to the Western world until the disinterment of the Dead Sea Scrolls in 1947.

The present author is by no means convinced that the Gospel of Barnabas is *not* a Muslim forgery; however, whatever the truth, it is a beautiful and interesting document, written with considerable skill, and some very interesting phrases and variant teachings.

To get the flavour of it, here is a long extract, parts of which will be immediately familiar to New Testament Gospel readers, but with some interesting differences of words or emphasis.

> You ask me to tell you what God will give us in Paradise. Truly, I tell you, that those who think of the wages do not love the Master. A shepherd who has a flock of sheep, when he sees the wolf coming, prepares to defend them; while the hireling when he sees the wolves coming leaves the sheep and flees.

I will speak to you a parable so that you may understand. There was a king who found by the wayside a man stripped by thieves, who had wounded him to death. He had compassion on him, and commanded his slaves to bear that man to the city and tend him, and this they did with all diligence. The king conceived a great love for the sick man so much that he gave him his own daughter in marriage and made him his heir. Now assuredly this king was most merciful; but the man beat the slaves, despised the medicines, abused his wife, spoke evil of the king, and caused his vassals to rebel against him. When the king required any service, he would as usual say: 'What will the king give me as a reward?' Now when the king heard this, what did he do to so impious a man? They all replied: 'Woe to him, for the king deprived him of all, and sternly punished him.' Then said Jesus: 'O Priests and scribes and Pharisees, and you High Priest that hear my voice, I proclaim to you what God has said by His prophet Isaiah: 'I have nourished slaves and exalted them, but they have despised me.'

The king is our God, who found Israel in a world full of miseries, and gave him therefore to His servants Joseph, Moses and Aaron, who tended him. And our God conceived such love for him that for the sake of the people of Israel he struck Egypt, drowned Pharaoh, and discomfited a hundred and twenty kings of the Canaanites and Madianites. He gave him his laws, making him heir of all that land wherein our people dwell.

But how does Israel bear himself? How many prophets has he slain? How many books of the prophets has he contaminated? How has he violated the law of God? How many for that cause have departed from God to serve idols, through your offence, O priest! And now you ask me, 'What will God give us in Paradise?' You ought to have asked me, 'What will the punishment be that God will give you in hell, and then what you ought to do for true penitence in order that God may have mercy on you; for this I can tell you, and to this end I am sent to you.' (Barnabas 68).

Another example is the passage where Peter 'recognises' Jesus as Son of God. Trinitarian Christians should note how the verses familiar in the Synoptics are reinterpreted:

Jesus departed from Jerusalem after the Passover, and entered into the borders of Caesarea Philippi. There, the angel Gabriel having told him of the sedition which was beginning among the common people, he asked his disciples, saying: 'What do men say of me?' They said: 'Some say you are Elijah, others Jeremiah, and others one of the old prophets.' Jesus asked: 'And you, what do you say that I am?' Peter answered, 'You are the Messiah, the Son of God.' Then Jesus was angry and rebuked him, saying: 'Begone and depart from me, because you are Satan and seek to cause me offence! Woe to you if you believe this [...] if our God willed not to show Himself to Moses his servant, nor to

Elijah whom He also loved, nor to any prophet, do you think that God should show himself to this faithless generation? But know you not that God has created all things of nothing with one single word, and all men have their origin out of a piece of clay? Now, how shall God have likeness to man? Woe to those deceived of Satan!' (Barnabas 70)

One example given to prove the 'obvious forgery' is the fact that Jesus is said by this text to have kept Muslim prayer times. The Jews seem to have prayed three times a day (see Psalm 55:17 and Daniel 6:10), whereas the Gospel of Barnabas mentions five prayers. The Dead Sea Scrolls have now revealed that the Qumraners also prayed five times a day, with an extra midnight prayer, like the Muslims. Here is an extract from the Qumran Manual of Discipline:

> Day and night I offer my praise; and at all the appointed times which God has prescribed. When daylight begins its rule [the Muslim dawn prayer – *fajr*]; when it reaches its turning point [=*zuhr*: midday]; and when again it withdraws to its appointed abode [= *'asr*]; when the watches of darkness begin [=*maghrib*: evening]; when God opens the storehouse thereof, when He sets that darkness against the light [= *'isha*: night]; when it reaches its turning point [=*tahajjud*, the voluntary midnight prayer], and when it again withdraws in the face of light [dawn again].

All these hours of prayer crop up unselfconsciously in the Gospel of Barnabas: 'Then said John, 'Teach us, for love of God, of the faith.' Jesus answered, 'It is time that we say the prayer of the dawn.' Whereupon they arose, and having washed themselves, made prayer to our God' (Barnabas 89). 'When he had made the midday prayer, Jesus, as he went out of the Temple, found one blind from his mothers womb' (Barnabas 146). The other prayer times can be found in Barnabas 100, 133, 131 and 182.

The Qumran term 'holy one of God' occurs 36 times in the Gospel of Barnabas, but only twice in the Greek gospels (Luke 4:34 and Mark 1:24). The phrase 'elect of God' recurs 23 times in Barnabas, but only 7 times in the Synoptics.

The twin concept of Faith and Works (*Iman* and *'Amal* to Muslims, or *Hesed* and *Zedek* in the Dead Sea Scrolls) feature regularly as the Ways of Piety and Righteousness.[2]

It is important to realise the extent to which the terminology of Ebionism (the way of the Poor) and its synonyms also penetrated Qumran literature. Ebionism, *'Ani* (the Meek), and *Dal* (the Downtrodden) are interchangeable terms in the Scrolls. For example, chapter 6 of the War Scroll has: 'by the hand of the Poor Ones whom You have redeemed by Your power and the peace of Your mighty wonders [...] by the hand of the Poor Ones and those bent in the dust, you will deliver the enemies of all the lands and humble the mighty of the peoples to bring upon their heads the reward of the wicked and to justify the judgement of Your truth on all the sons of men.'

In the Habakkuk Pesher the Ebionim are the rank and file of the community led by the Teacher of Righteousness. In the Qumran hymns, the title *ebionim-hesed* (the Poor Ones of Piety) combines Ebionism and Hassidism, and there are abundant references to them. The 'poor ones' occur no less frequently in the Gospel of Barnabas. The point is that the Jerusalem church saints were also known as 'the Poor' (see Gal 2:10 and Jas 2:3-5). 'Remembering the Poor' meant bringing a proper amount of monetary contribution back to Jerusalem.

What is known about the disciple Barnabas? In the New Testament, he was identified as the uncle of John Mark, an eminent Levite with a house in Jerusalem. He became a great missionary teacher, and was the companion for some time of Paul. According to the Clementine Recognitions, Barnabas was said to have also been called Matthias. Matthias was the man chosen to be the new 'twelfth apostle' after the death of Judas Iscariot. [3]

The Acts of Barnabas stated that when Barnabas went to Cyprus, he took with him documents he had received from the Apostle Matthew, 'a book of the Word of God and a narrative of the miracles and doctrines.' We are further told that in the synagogue at Salamis the Apostle Barnabas unrolled the scrolls he had from Matthew, his fellow labourer, and began to teach the Jews the authentic gospel of Jesus.

The Church Fathers agree that the Apostle Matthew compiled an account of the life and ministry of Jesus in Hebrew. Papias (CE 144) stated that 'he compiled Oracles in the Hebrew language, and that each interpreted them as he was able'. The suggestion is that it was from the scrolls written by Matthew and those in his own hand that Barnabas compiled his account in the Hebrew tongue.

M. A. Youssef [4] offers several interesting ideas in this connection. One is that the martyr Stephen was not a Nazarene but a Hellenised Jew enthused with the new saviour-mythology, for unlike the monotheist Nazarenes, he was accused and stoned for blasphemy. Peter and John had both been up before the Sanhedrin, but although they were chief spokesmen for the Nazarenes, and preached boldly and very publicly within the Temple precincts, they were never charged with blasphemy. Paul, of course, was at this stage very much a monotheist.

Youssef suggests that following his conversion Paul was sent to be trained at the Nazarene desert headquarters at Qumran ('Damascus'), and kept at first to the Nazarene teaching (see p. 51 above). It was said that he had hopes of marrying the High Priest's daughter, but was turned down. Could it have been the *alternative* High Priest, James, that he approached, his rebuff giving a clue as to his later bitterness towards him?

When word reached the Apostolic governing body in Jerusalem that some of the 'new' Jesus worshippers in Antioch were preaching their saviour-doctrines and being dubbed 'Christians', they quickly dispatched Barnabas, perhaps with some assistants, to counteract the propaganda (Acts 11:22): 'For he, Barnabas, was a righteous man.' His efforts paid off, and many joined the Nazarene movement. It was at this time that Barnabas met Paul, and it seems that they worked together for a whole year, assembling a body of believers in the authentic Gospel of Jesus.

The Nazarene community at Antioch included people gifted with spiritual insight: Symeon Niger,[5] Lucius of Cyrene, and Manaean, possibly the son of the famous Menahem the Essene, who had been much admired by King Herod; Manaean had grown up as the 'syntropos' or 'foster-brother' of Herod's son Antipas.

It was not until Barnabas and Paul reached Paphos that they encountered the Hellenised Jewish sorcerer Bar-Jesus (also called Elymas). He was an associate of the proconsul Sergius Paulus, whom we are told sent for Barnabas and Paul to have them explain the teachings of Jesus to him. The sorcerer countered their teaching, and prevented the proconsul from becoming a believer (13:6-8). At this point, in Acts 13:9, Saul changed his name to Paul.

Now, this name change had nothing to do with Paul being a Roman citizen – he was born a Roman citizen, and appears to have been quite happy until then with the name Saul. But it may indicate Paul's change from Nazarene to Nicolaitan. From then on, the composer of Acts demotes Barnabas. He no longer features as the leader of the missionary team. Paul's name now appears first: 'When Paul and his party set sail from Paphos, they came to Perga in Pamphylia; and John (Mark) departing from them, returned to Jerusalem' (Acts 13:13).

Eventually there was 'sharp contention' between Barnabas and Paul (which is not adequately explained in Acts 15:36-39), and he parted from him, taking Mark to Cyprus.

Youssef now argues that Barnabas, using Matthew's work, probably compiled his gospel at this stage. He considers it to have been the work seen by the Egyptian Christian professor Pantaenus, who mistakenly assumed it was the sole work of Matthew. Pantaenus took a copy of it back with him to Alexandria. The misconception that Matthew was the sole compiler of the authentic gospel history of Jesus was also found in the 'Acts of Barnabas'; that document stated, moreover, that upon the martyrdom of Barnabas, the manuscripts in his possession were secretly placed in a cave with his remains.

The relics of Barnabas were apparently discovered in Cyprus in the fourth year of the Emperor Zeno (CE 478), and there was indeed a copy of the Gospel 'of the Apostle Matthew' lying on his breast. Thus, we see how the gospel compiled through the joint efforts of Matthew and Barnabas was taken as the sole work of Matthew. This was a quarter of a century before the mass alteration of the early gospels in the sixth century, which entrenched the Nicolaitan doctrines in the Christian world. It had survived only because it rested undisturbed in the apostle's tomb. Other copies were probably made from this work for Nazarene usage prior to Barnabas' demise, which survived the Nazarene flight into Pella, which would account for the copy Panteanus found in 'the east'. Unfortunately for those who like to see things properly checked out, this document is no longer extant for us to see, and to identify it with the Gospel of Barnabas can be nothing more than conjecture.

As the background history to this document is so obscure, the following are the fullest details I have been able to find.

Two important ancient documents mention it: the *Decretum Gelasianum de libris recipiendis et non recipiendis* (The Galatian Decree of books to be received and not to be received), which is a list of gospels which were in existence in the sixth century CE. The Gospel is also mentioned at the end of the list of sixty books in the *Codex Barocc.* 206, dated to the sixth or seventh century CE. The Christian scholar M.R. James dismissed the evidence of these lists in his important work *The Apocryphal New Testament* (1924), claiming it was 'a fifteenth century forgery by a Christian renegade to Islam'. However, he offered no evidence supporting this belief. James Hastings, in his *Dictionary of the Apostolic Church* (1952) wondered whether an ancient Gnostic Gospel of Barnabas might have been the basis for this Muslim (Italian) Gospel of Barnabas.

John Toland in his book *Nazarenus* (London, 1718) describes an Italian manuscript of the Gospel, mentioned in the 206th manuscript of the Baroccian collection in the Bodleian Library. He found that the 39th Baroccian manuscript contained a fragment that was an Italian equivalent of a Greek text.

Reland in *De religione Mahommedica* (1718) discovered that the Gospel also existed in Arabic and Spanish. The Spanish edition was a translation of the Italian edition, carried out by one Moustafa de Aranda. Details about it were given by George Sale, who translated the Qur'an in 1734. He possessed a copy of the Spanish version, which had been lent to him by Rev. Holme, the vicar of Hedley. The preface of this Spanish edition contains the story about the monk Fra Marino.

According to this account, Fra Marino read in the writings of the early Church Fathers, including Irenaeus (c130-202), an argument against Paul on the authority of the Gospel of Barnabas. He hoped to find a copy of this in the library of his friend Pope Sixtus V (1521-90). One day they were together in the Pope's library, and while the Pope dozed Fra Marino took up a book to read; and amazingly enough, it chanced to be the very gospel he was seeking. The unscrupulous fellow hid it up his sleeve, and sneaked it out of the Vatican; after reading it, he became a convert to Islam.

Another Spanish version existed in England in the eighteenth century. The Rev Joseph White in the Bampton lectures[6] transcribed some chapters from the Rev Monkhouse's Spanish copy.

Extracts may be found in *Fabricius' Codex Apocryphus Novi Testamenti* (Part 3, Hamburg, 1743, pp. 365-394). The Italian manuscript ended up in the Imperial Library of Vienna, among the books of Prince Eugene.

In 1905, Lonsdale Ragg obtained a transcript of the document, and he and his wife Laura brought out a translation in English, now on sale in many Muslim bookshops.

NOTES

~

¹ Most scholars conclude that John's Gospel, from which the most ambitious christological sayings come ('I and the Father are one'; 'No-one comes to the Father but by me'; 'He who has seen me has seen the Father') is a late work, of multiple authorship, in its final stage a profound meditation probably expressing the Ephesus interpretation of Jesus; hence we should not attribute these sayings to Jesus himself.

² Matthew, Mark and Luke are called the 'Synoptic' gospels because their outline of the events of the life of Jesus follows more or less the same synopsis.

³ The name 'Q' comes from the German word *quelle*, meaning 'a source'. This document has never been seen, and it is not certain whether it was a gospel, a letter, or a collection of teachings. By definition, Q consists of verses common to Mt and Lk which are not in Mk. For a reconstruction see Professor Burton Mack's *The Lost Gospel*. See chapter 14 below.

⁴ See, for example, Lk 4:24; 7:16; 8:33; 4:19, where Jesus is called a prophet; Lk 3:13,26; 4:27,30, where Jesus is called a servant of God; Acts 2:22, where Peter calls Jesus a 'man approved of God'; see also 1 Timothy 2:5 where the author (probably not Paul) says 'There is one God, and one mediator between God and humanity, the *man* Jesus Christ.'

⁵ Sura 2:256.

⁶ J. Hick, 'Jesus and the World Religions', in *The Myth of God Incarnate* (London, 1977), p.179.

⁷ D. Cupitt, 'The Christ of Christendom', article in *Myth*.

¹ J. Hick, 'Jesus and the World Religions', p.175.

² As in Job 1:6; 38:7; Genesis 6:2 etc.

³ It is an indication of the fabulous wealth of these four families that the office was kept within their ranks, with very few exceptions, until the fall of Jerusalem in 70 CE. Some individuals were able to buy their terms of office more than once. Joseph Caiaphas, the son-in-law of Annas and the president of the Sanhedrin that tried Jesus, actually managed to fend off all other bidders for 18 years, from 18-36 CE!

⁴ Pesach fol 57a.

⁵ Herod, for example, made Simon Boethus (a priest of Alexandria in Egypt) High Priest in Jerusalem when he married his daughter Mariamne (the successor to the ill-fated Hasmonaean princess of the same name).

⁶ The Sanhedrin was the Jewish High Court, consisting of two thirds Sadducees and one third Pharisees. The High Priest himself was a Sadducee.

⁷ R. Eisenman, *James the Brother of Jesus* (London, 1997), p.45.

⁸ B. Avodah Zarah 8b; B. Sanhedrin 41b; B. Shabbat 15a, et al.

[9] M. Sanh 4.1.

[10] M. Sanh 4.1.

[11] T. Sheruot 3.8; T. Sanh 11.1.

[12] T. Sanh 11.1.

[13] B. Sanh 8b and 80b; T. Sanh 11.1.

[14] T. Sanh 11.6. The capital offence of blasphemy was not what we nowadays innocuously call 'swearing'. It consisted of actually pronouncing the *Shem Hammephorash*, the Hidden Name of God (M. Sanh 7.5; B. Sanh 56a). This Divine Name was only allowed to be uttered once a year, by the High Priest, in the Holy of Holies, on the Day of Atonement. For anyone else to utter it (if they had managed to find out what it was!) it *was* blasphemy, and a capital offence; but there is no evidence that this is what Jesus had done.

[15] The 'apocryphal literature' denotes all the texts and gospels not included in the present New Testament. The word means 'covered' or 'hidden'.

[16] Sanh 4.2.

[17] Sanh 4.1.

[18] Sanh 4.1.

[19] Sanh 37a; Ab. Zar. 8b.

[20] Sanh 1.5.

[21] Tosefta Sanh 7.5.

[22] See p. 13.

[23] After the debacle in 70 CE, when the Jewish Revolt failed and the Temple at Jerusalem was destroyed, a new court was very swiftly established at Jabneh, a court modelled on and certainly regarding itself as the successor of the old national council. In the Mishnah we possess what it has become customary to describe as to the *corpus iuris* of Judaism, dealing in the greatest minuteness with every legal enactment. This work codifies all sorts of details, works out general principles, interprets and explains difficulties, and presses home to their logical conclusions every item of the Mosaic legislation. The section ('tractate') entitled 'Sanhedrin' deals entirely with the Jewish supreme court of law, its constitution, authority and method of procedure. It is to this document that recourse has been made to test the regularity and legality of the proceedings described in the Gospels. (Cf. H. Danby, 'The Bearing of the Rabbinical Criminal Code on the Jewish Trial Narratives in the Gospels,' *JTS* 21, 1920.)

[24] For example Eisenman suggests, regarding the writing of the New Testament books, that we have a composite recreation of facts and episodes relating to a series of Messianic pretenders in Palestine in the first century, familiar from the works of Josephus, interlaced or spliced into a narrative of a distinctly Hellenistic or non-Palestinian, pro-Pauline case. This includes some light-hearted, even intolerant, satire where events in Palestine are concerned. R. Eisenman, *James, the Brother of Jesus* (London, 1997), p. xxiv.

CHAPTER 2

¹ The four gospels in the New Testament are named as being 'According to Matthew, Mark, Luke and John'. Many theories and disputes have arisen concerning the authorship of these documents. For simplicity's sake, when speaking of these four gospels, they will simply be referred to in this text as Matthew (or Mt), Mark (or Mk), Luke (or Lk), and John (or Jn). It is virtually certain that Matthew and John were not written by the apostles of that name; most accept that Luke was written, in whole or in part, by the Greek doctor and friend of Paul who also wrote the Acts of the Apostles; while we are not completely certain about Mark. It may have been written by the nephew of Barnabas the Levite, who lived with his mother in Jerusalem, and was an eyewitness to some of the events, drawing most of his material from Peter (who was an apostle, and a most important eyewitness).

² Tosefta Sanh 9.11; Mishnah Sanh 7.2b; J. Sanh 24b; B. Sanh 41a.

³ Mishnah Sanh 2.3; T.B. Sanh 48b.

⁴ Mishnah Sanh 5.2; T.B. Sanh 9b, 41a.

⁵ Jos. Ant. xiv.9.3.167.

⁶ Wars 6.215.

⁷ Talmudic tradition actually offers two alternative dates for the moment when that jurisdiction ceased. One strand, found in both Babylonian and Palestinian versions, suggests that capital jurisdiction had been taken away from the Jews forty years before (B. Avodah Zarah 8b; B. Shab 15a; B. Sanh 41b; J. Sanh 18a, 24b). A contrary tradition states that it ceased in 70CE (B. Sanh 52b; B. Kethub 30a; Mekilta of Simeon bar Yohai, Shemot 21.14). The first reference is most interesting since it was somewhere around this year that Jesus was condemned. Unfortunately, we cannot know for certain whether this evidence backs up John's Gospel or not, since we do not know for sure the year of Jesus' trial. Moreover '40 years' is not necessarily meant literally; it is a phrase often used as an idiom by Semitic people to mean 'a long time', and may well refer back to the changes brought about in the administration in 6CE, when the procuratorship was introduced.

⁸ Jos. Wars 6.126.

⁹ A.N. Sherwin-White, 'Roman Society and Roman Law in the New Testament'.

¹⁰ Jos. Ant. 21.9.1. Eisenman suggests that the supposed stoning of Stephen actually referred to a confrontation with James, which he survived, interwoven with elements of James' actual death. Op. cit., pp. 445-453.

¹¹ We shall see that this is frequently the case, despite the consensus that this gospel was written very late. It seems highly likely that it was written in more than one stage, and the earliest strand was indeed the account of an eye-witness: the unnamed Beloved Disciple (whose truth was vouched for by other editors in Jn 19:35, 21:24, and who was connected with the priesthood).

[12] See C.H. Dodd, *New Testament Studies* (Manchester, 1968).

[13] For example, Josephus records that Varus crucified 2,000 Jewish fighters on one occasion in 4BCE. *Ant* 17.10.10; Wars 2.5.2.

[14] C.K. Barrett, *Jesus and the Gospel tradition* (London, 1967), p.54.

[15] Paul Winter, *On the Trial of Jesus* (Berlin, 1961), p.45.

[16] Acts 21:31 later names one such chiliarch as Claudius Lysias, the man in charge of the Antonia Fortress in Jerusalem in 57CE. But does the use of the word *speira* or chiliarch necessarily indicate a Roman force? It did in such passages as Acts 10:1, 21:31,33, but there are several other passages where the same words refer to a Jewish band and not a Roman one. For example, the *speira* in Mk 15:16 was Jewish, and likewise in Jos. *Wars* 2.205, 318 et al.; Judith 14:11; 2 Macc 8:23, 15:26, where the *speira* was actually commanded by one of the Maccabees. In Jos. *Ant.* 17.214 we learn of a Jewish *speira* commanded by a chiliarch under the orders of Archelaus.

[17] In Hebrew, *hiskir-otho* means 'betrayed him'.

[18] The incumbent from 18-36CE.

[19] Shab 6.4.

[20] The prediction of the Temple's destruction was in any case not a capital crime, but a matter of prophecy. Josephus gives us an account of a later and persistent foretelling of just that event by another Jesus (Jesus ben Ananias), shortly before it actually did fall.

[21] Incidentally, a relic believed to be this very placard still exists, kept at the Church of Santa Croce in Rome, the church built by the Emperor Constantine to house the relics brought back from the Holy Land by his pilgrim-mother Helena. The most interesting feature of it is that not only did the writer put the Hebrew words from right to left, as is normal for that language, but the Latin and Greek inscriptions also, which is decidedly not normal. See D. Sox, *Relics and Shrines* (London, 1985), p. 172.

[22] Pilate did, in fact, survive the shake-up after the fall of Sejanus, and stayed in office long enough to arrest yet another Messiah, a Samaritan, and have him executed, this time without any trial at all, in 36CE. It was because the furious Samaritans lodged complaints against him for unlawful action that Pilate was recalled from office at that stage.

[23] Philo, *In Flaccum* 1; Eus. *H.E.* 2.5.

[24] Jn 18:28,33,38, 19:4,9,12,13.

[25] Muhammad Ata ur-Rahim suggests that this Barabbas was really Barnabas, the Levite friend of Paul and uncle of Mark. See *Jesus, Prophet of Islam*, London, 1977, p.53. See also p.244 of the present work.

[26] There is a papyrus of c85CE containing the protocol of a trial before G. Septimius Vegetus, Governor of Egypt, which reveals that he once gave up a prisoner according to the will of the populace, but there is no evidence that this person had been convicted of a capital crime, or, for that matter, that this could have any bearing on any Passover practice in Palestine.

²⁷ This is an example of how important it is to pay attention to jots and tittles in a text: there is only a tittle of difference between the Hebrew letters for B (Barabbas) and K (Karabas).

²⁸ H. Cohn, *The Trials and Death of Jesus.*

²⁹ M. Sanh 7.50.

³⁰ Form criticism of parallel passages suggests gross confusion here. In Lk 22:63-64 the offensive abusers have become 'the men holding Jesus', and in Jn 18:22-23 it is a particular individual, one of the High Priest's officers, who strikes Jesus with his hand, and there is no mention of the unseemly spitting. It may be possible that the whole unsavoury scene really belongs to the arrest sequence, when Jesus was mocked and hurt by the battalion of Roman soldiers in the praetorium (see Mk 15:19; Mt 27:27-31; Jn 19:2-3). . In Luke's version it is the soldiers of Herod Antipas who perform the torture (Lk 23:11). In John's version the blow is presented as a rebuke to Jesus for abusing the High Priest, which was forbidden under the law of Exodus 22:26, a situation that had a close parallel to the case of Paul in Acts 23:2-5. In Jesus' case, the blow was provoked by his refusal to give a direct answer to the question in Jn 18:19, which was taken as deliberate evasion. Jesus then protested that he was not being evasive, since he was willing to have witnesses called!

³¹ Mt 5:10.

CHAPTER 3

¹ Acts 2:46.

² Acts 15:1,5; 16:3; 21:21; Gal 2:3-5.

³ A Nazirite was a person specially consecrated to God, whose vows included the complete avoidance of alcohol and of cutting the hair. Famous Old Testament examples were Samson and Samuel. (Exodus 13:2; Judges 13:5, 16:17; I Samual 1:20.) Jesus' brother James was a Nazirite, and there were hints that John the Baptist and Jesus were too. Mk 1:24 gives us an early example of word-play: 'What do you want with us, *Jesus the Nazarene*? [...]We know who you are, the *holy one of God*'(synonymous with Nazirite).

⁴ Acts 6:7; 15:5; 21:20.

⁵ S. Sandmel, *We Jews and Jesus* (London, 1965), p. 139.

⁶ B. Sanh 43a: a Tannaitic tradition included in the Gemara to Sanh 6.1.

⁷ *Contra Celsum* 11.4.5.9.

⁸ I. Wilson, *Jesus, the Evidence* (London, 1996), pp. 52-53.

⁹ 'The earliest rabbinic stories about Jesus and his followers come from about the same time as Josephus' *Antiquities* or slightly later. One distinguished rabbi, Eliezer, of the generation that flourished from about CE 70-100, is said to have been arrested as an old man on the charge of being a Christian. He submitted his case to the Roman gover-

nor's discretion, was pardoned, and later explained his arrest by the admission that once in Sepphoris, a city of Galilee, a Galilean had told him some heretical teaching 'in the name of Jesus the son of Pantera' to which he had assented. The story goes on to make him confess his guilt in transgressing the rabbinic ordinance prohibiting any intercourse with heretics. This is suspicious; the ordinance may be later than the confession. Subsequent versions of the story cite the saying attributed to Jesus: 'From filth they came and to filth they shall return,' and a legal conclusion is drawn from it: the wages of a prostitute, if given to the Temple, could be used for building privies. The saying may be early, since it resembles many of the Q sayings in being antithetical, general, and oracular, while the legal conclusion was probably drawn by some second-century rabbi.' (Morton-Smith, *Jesus the Magician*, London, 1978, p.46.) 'If Rabbi Eliezer approved of any other teachings of Jesus ben Pantera, no trace of the fact has been preserved in the tradition. However, he probably did refer, in a discussion of Sabbath law, to Jesus' magical practices. The question was whether one who cuts (tattoos?) letters on his flesh during the Sabbath is guilty of violating the law prohibiting labour on that day, and it names Jesus as both Ben Pandira and Ben Stada. Rabbi Eliezer declared him guilty, but most others thought him innocent. Rabbi Eliezer said to them, 'But is it not [the case that] Ben Stada brought magic spells from Egypt in the scratches of his flesh?' They said to him, 'He was a madman and you cannot base laws on (the actions of) madmen.' Was he then the son of Stada? Surely he was the son of Pandira? Rabbi Hisda (a third-century Babylonian) said, 'The husband was Stada, the paramour Pandira.' (But was not) the husband Pappos ben Judah? His mother was Stada. (But was not) his mother Miriam (Mary) the hairdresser? (Yes, but she was nicknamed *Stada*) – as we say in Pumbeditha, '*s'tat da* (i.e. this one has turned away) from her husband.' ' (Morton Smith, p.47.)

[10] References to infant baptism, the command to 'love one another', and the Communion meal.

[11] 'Lucan, a Roman poet who conspired against Nero and was forced to commit suicide in 65, the year after the fire, has left a lurid picture of a witch who would not worship the gods, but devoted her life to the cult of the powers of the underworld (to whose company, Jesus, an executed criminal, was thought to belong). An important element of this cult was cannibalism. Lucan's witch was not content to call up a soul from the underworld. She forced it to reenter and revivify its dead body so that the entire man was raised from the dead (as the Christians claimed Jesus had been). In her prayers at the beginning of this rite, addressed to the gods of the underworld, and among then the nameless 'ruler of the earth' (a role often assigned to the Jewish God in gnostic documents), she makes much of her cannibalism as a meritorious service by which she has deserved attention, 'If I call on you with a mouth sufficiently evil and polluted, if I never sing these hymns without having eaten human flesh [...] grant [my] prayer.' She was not unique; accusations of cannibalism and related, equally revolting,

crimes are frequent in Roman descriptions of witchcraft.' (Morton Smith, p. 52.)

[12] See Jn 1:19; 2:18; 6:41, 52; 7:1; 8:48; 9:22; 18:38.

[13] His wife Procla (Claudia Procla; she is not named in the gospel) also received this distinction. There is one reference to her in Mt 27:19, where she tries to have Jesus' trial stopped because of a disturbing dream she had experienced. Claudia Procla was said to have been an illegitimate daughter of the third wife of the Emperor Tiberius.

[14] Justin Martyr, *Apol.* xxxv and xiviii.

[15] *Apol.* xxi.

[16] Later tradition, however, was not so generous to Pilate. Eusebius reports that he committed suicide in the reign of Gaius Caligula. Other legends place his death in the reign of Tiberius. The most fascinating legend concerns the miscellaneous travels of his accursed corpse, which at first, after he had committed suicide to avoid execution, was tied to a millstone and flung into the Tiber. There it attracted so many bothersome demons that it was fished out again and taken to Vienna. Subsequently it was buried near Lausanne, and more demonic disturbance followed. The corpse was finally thrown into a lake surrounded by mountains, where its awful presence continued to provoke diabolical activities. This legendary material was claimed to have been written in Latin by Albinus, and centuries later was translated by Jerasmus Jared, a bishop of the Orthodox Church of Zahleh in the Lebanon. It may have been nothing more than a historical novel. However, a later bishop vouched for 'Gerasimus Yarid' and said that he had composed the book using an ancient document as his source, but helpful details of this source were, sadly, not forthcoming. Gerasimus' work, which was published in New South Wales in 1893, may have been based on 'Pontius Pilate's Account of the Condemnation of Jesus Christ and his Own Mental Suffering', a pamphlet which was reprinted in 1879 and seemed to have been used not only by this bishop, but also by a Revd W.D. Maham in 1879 for his *Report of Pilate*, and Anatole France for his novel *The Procurator of Judaea* in 1891. Maham also lifted a vast quantity of material from General Wallace's highly successful novel *Ben Hur*, resulting in a court case and General Wallace's own personal investigation into his purported facts. His book was required to be withdrawn from circulation, but was still being reprinted up to 1927, along with the statement that it had been found in the Vatican Library in 1887, despite several pained disclaimers from that quarter. There are extant 'Letters of Pilate to Tiberius', and a 'Report of Pilate to Tiberius' that date from the fourth or fifth century, which have been published in Volume 16 of the Edinburgh edition of the Ante-Nicene Library; but these are of a colouring very different to Maham's version.

[17] The *Acta Pilati* name him as Longinus.

[18] *H.E.* 1.9.2-10.

CHAPTER 4

¹ Herod changed his will several times before he died. His penultimate will had named Herod Antipas as his sole heir, but the final will divided up his kingdom. Antipas received the provinces of Galilee and the Peraea across the Jordan; Archelaus received Judaea, with the capital city of Jerusalem; while Herod Phillip received the Trachon across the Jordan (Ituraea, Trachonitis, Auranitis and Batanaea). The region of Samaria was given a Roman Governor. Herod had wanted Archelaus to rule as king, but Caesar Augustus only granted him a trial period. After ten years of impressive ineptitude and cruelty, he was deposed.

² Hasmonaean was the name of the Jewish royal family, the House of Hasmon. They were also known as the Maccabees, from the nickname earned by the warrior-prince Judas Maccabeus: 'the Hammer'.

³ In Jn 18:40 Barabbas is called a *lestes*, and his crimes are said to have been insurrection and murder. However when Jesus raided the Temple and declared that the corrupt priesthood had made it a den of *lestai* (Mk 11:17; Mt 21:13; Lk 19:49), or when the unwary traveller in the parable of the Good Samaritan fell among *lestai* (Lk 10:38,44), there is no need to assume that *lestai* in these passages meant anything more than that they *were* thieves and bandits, and not members of the Zealot party. Jesus himself angrily rebutted any suspicion that *he* was a thug or bandit. In Mk 14:48; Mt 26:55 and Lk 22:52 he asks: 'Have you come out as against a *lestes* with swords and staves, to seize me?' His accusers obviously lacked any evidence of this nature at his trials, or they would have used it.

⁴ It has been suggested that Zealots were not unlike the Afghan mujahidin rebels fighting the Russians in the 1980s, or the Shi'ite popular uprising in support of Imam Khomeini that dethroned the Shah of Iran in the 1970s. Such men and women were prepared to die for their uncompromising opposition to the 'great Satan': the powerful forces of secularist intrusion represented in the twentieth century by atheistic Western-style government, and in the first century by Rome and anything that smacked of Baal-cults and Triadism.

⁵ Eisenman suggests that this slaughter of 'the innocents', Jews who threatened his throne, formed the basis of the Christmas story of the murdered babes of Bethlehem.

⁶ Jos. *Ant.* 17.10.10; *Wars* 2.5.2.

⁷ Simon ben Kosebah, who also rebelled against Rome in 132 CE, was almost certainly a Hasmonaean. Eusebius records a tradition narrated via Julius Africanus that the family and the descendants of Jesus came from 'the Jewish villages of Nazara and Cochaba' (*EH* 1.7.14).

⁸ Or Bar-Tholmai. This was a surname. All the lists of the twelve apostles link Philip and Bartholomew, and do not mention a Nathanael (Mt 10:3; Mk 3:18; Lk 6:14; Acts 1:13).

⁹ See also p.90.

¹⁰ The Synoptic Gospels are not specific about Jesus being Son of God. This has led to the theory of the 'Messianic Secret', that this knowledge was deliberately held back from people. However it does seem strange that Jesus does not even reveal his true identity to his chief disciple, Peter, not even just before the Transfiguration (Mk 8:29-30). Even though at the Transfiguration a voice from heaven declares of Jesus: 'This is My beloved son, listen to him' (Mk 9:7), throughout the whole narrative Jesus refers to himself as *Son of Man* (eg Mk 8:31, 38; 9:9,12,31 etc). In the Fourth Gospel, Jesus' sonship is explicit from the start, and all his miracles are deliberate 'signs' of it. Muslim scholars point to Jn 1:51, and comment that the reference to a Son of Man does not necessarily mean that Jesus was speaking of himself. 'You shall see greater things than these. Truly I say to you, you will see heaven opened, and the angels of God ascending and descending upon the son of man.' This could be a prophecy of the later ministry of Muhammad. Geza Vermes has persuasively argued that 'son of man' (in the Aramaic, *bar nasha*) is a reflexive circumlocution denoting 'myself'; but many scholars conclude that it may also denote another human being. (G. Vermes, *Jesus and the World of Judaism*, London, 1983, pp.89-99; J. Fitzmyer, 'Another View of the Son of Man Debate', *JSNT* 4 (1979), pp.58-68.)

¹¹ Eisenman suggests that when Herod killed all the 'Jewish children' who sought to replace him (cf Mt 2:17) this refers to his killing of his own sons by Mariamne his Hasmonaean wife, and her relatives, and ultimately herself.

¹² See my previous book *The Separated Ones: Jesus, the Pharisees and Islam* (London, 1991).

¹³ As documented in Jos. *Ant.* 18.6-10.

¹⁴ Jos. *War* 6.312-314.

¹⁵ Jos. *War* 1:10; 2:4,8-419.

¹⁶ The other version of his name, Simon Zelotes, certainly suggests a connection between Zealots and 'Cananaean'. It is argued that the term for 'Zealot' in Aramaic is not *Kananaois* but *qan'an*, but the only example we have of this term is in the Aramaic Targum on Exodus 20:5, where God is described as *qan'an*, which means 'jealous'. Where Jewish literature in Aramaic speaks of zealots such as those who defended Jerusalem against the Romans, it calls them *qanna'im* or *qanna'in* (in the singular *qanna'i*). So it is very likely that the 'Kananaios' of Matthew and Mark was originally 'Kannaios.' Kamal Salibi, however (*Conspiracy in Jerusalem*, London, 1988, pp.97-98) suggests simply that this disciple possibly came from the village of Ze'lota, near another village, Qinan; both places still existing today.

¹⁷ Muhammad Ata ur-Rahim suggests that unlike the Pharisees, who kept the people of the land (*Amme ha-aretz*) at arm's length, Jesus took them under his wing and encouraged them. He further suggests that many were of the Essene community, and were zealots. A large number probably made an allegiance with Jesus and were trained

in the wilderness, all being known as Baryonim, or even Bar-Jesus. *Jesus, Prophet of Islam* (London, 1977), p. 33.

[18] See H. Schonfield, *The Authentic New Testament*, p. 84, note 8.

[19] Mk 11:1-6.

[20] 'A man called Barabbas was then in custody with the rebels who had committed murder in the rising.' Mk 15:7. We do not have any information as to when this insurrection took place. I suggested on p. 244 that it may refer to Jesus' commotion in the Temple.

[21] Jos. *Ant.* 18.3.3.

[22] The Old Russian Josephus was first discovered by modern scholars in 1866, and was published in 1924-7. For Eisler's works see the Bibliography.

[23] That this criticism of niece marriages was also an Essene preoccupation has been revealed by the Dead Sea Scrolls. The sin is categorised as *zanut* or 'fornication', a word cognate with the Qur'anic *zina*. People could marry cousins, but uncles or aunts were in the forbidden decrees (Leviticus 18:12-14; sura 4:22.)

[24] *Letter of Claudius to the Alexandrians.*

[25] Suetonius, *Claudius* 25.4.

[26] Dio Cassius, *Hist.* 40.6.

[27] Acts 17:6-7.

[28] Acts 24:5.

[29] Muslims may compare it to the massive veil that drapes the Ka'ba. For the symbolism of the Meccan 'veil' see Charles-André Gilis, *La doctrine initiatique du pèlerinage á la Maison d'Allâh* (Paris, 1982), pp. 43, 5.

[30] For example, the Ebionites were dismissed as 'of poor intelligence' by Eusebius.

[31] In Mark's Gospel, the centurion says 'a Son of God'; in Lk 23:47 the centurion only praises God and declares that Jesus was innocent. Jn 19:34 mentions a soldier spearing Jesus in the side, and a comment that this fulfilled Zechariah 12:10.

[32] 'Baal' means 'Lord' or 'Master'. It was the title used of many of the gods denounced in the Old Testament. These gods were usually 'divine sons' in a Trinity consisting of Father, Mother and Son, and were generally connected with the earth's seasonal and agricultural cycles.

[33] A leading expert here is Gerd Lüdemann, professor of New Testament at Tübingen in Germany. The brave professor has experienced ostracism for his frank criticisms of many of the 'unholy' themes of the Bible. See his book *The Unholy in Holy Scripture*, pp. 85-9 for the anti-Semitic Gospel accounts of the Parable of the Wicked Husbandmen. On p. 89 Lüdemann concludes that 'the synoptic evangelists are clearly concerned to interpret the death of Jesus in anti-Jewish terms.'

[34] See S. G. F Brandon, *The Trial of Jesus of Nazareth* (London, 1968); A. Richardson *The Political Christ* (London, 1973).

[35] Jn 11:50.

CHAPTER 5

¹ What had particularly disturbed the 'rebel' priests was not only a priesthood that had no legitimate claim, but also the 'pollution of sacrifices', the offerings made on behalf of 'polluted' persons, including the Herodian family and the Roman authorities. These compromised the purity of the Temple itself, and were the first things to stop when the Resistance priesthood managed to over-run the Temple.

² Lk 4:16-30 records Jesus' sermon in his home synagogue at Nazareth, and his rejection there.

³ Mk 3:31-35. Notice that there is no mention of a father. Scholars generally assume that Joseph the Carpenter was dead.

⁴ Jn 7:2-5.

⁵ Mark 6:3.

⁶ For example, we have Mark Antony's two daughters called Antonia. To avoid confusion, the 'number names' Prima, Secunda, Tertia, etc were often used.

⁷ Peter was the first; the second was said to have been a British man, Linus or Lleyn, the brother of Caractacus; and the third was Clement. Paul wrote to this Clement, and gave his full name as Titus Clemens.

⁸ Eus. *H.E.* 2.23.5-7.

⁹ He named the 'seven Jewish sects' as the Pharisees, Sadducees, Essenes, Sampsaeans, Galileans, Hemerobaptists and Masbutheans. The mysterious Masbutheans almost certainly became the Iraqi sect still called Sabaeans, from the Syriac root *sabu'a* which means 'washed ones' (*masbuta* = 'bathing'). To this day, the Mandaeans of that region call their priests Nasariyah (ie. Nazarenes). See also p. 167.

¹⁰ Surely this means the High Priesthood according to the Essenes and/or Qumraners, and not the Herodian nominees?

¹¹ T.Yoma 1.6.180.

¹² Ezra 2:61-62.

¹³ I Chron 24:3-10; Lk 1:5.

¹⁴ Nehemiah 12:12,17,26.

¹⁵ This group is discussed further below, p. 167.

¹⁶ There were Hasmonaean princes who rebelled against their fathers and died fighting.

¹⁷ Lk 24:13-33, and see Origen, *Contra Celsum,* 2.62.

¹⁸ Some scholars believe the Heirs were active writers. Jewish sources and Epiphanius credited Simeon bar Cleophas with no less than three books, the Hebrew Matthew, the Hebrew 'Acts' (by which is probably meant the 'Ascents of James') and the Hebrew 'Book of John'- possibly the first section of the New Testament Apocalypse. The New Testament Epistles of James and Jude might not have been written by Jesus' two brothers of these name, but by Jude's grandsons.

[19] I Corinthians 15:7.
[20] Eus. *H.E.*3.32.7-8.

CHAPTER 6

[1] Cf. Deut 23:24-25. For a full discussion of this and other examples, see Maqsood, *The Separated Ones*, pp. 52ff.
[2] Technically, it is one of *the sunan al-'adat*, not the *sunan al-'ibadat*.
[3] Muslims recognise two principal types of prayer. Firstly there is *du'a'*: the everyday, general supplications, praise, personal requests and so forth, that are familiar to Christians; and secondly there is *salat*, the five regular formal acts of worship involving Arabic litanies and the positions of bending, kneeling and prostration to Almighty God. One can pray *du'a'* anywhere, anytime, with or without the *wudu* ablution.
[4] Acts 15:20. Compare with Sura 5:4 and 6:145-147. 6:146 overrules Leviticus 11:3-6: whatever had parted hoof and was cloven footed, and chewed the cud was lawful, but the camel, coney (rock hyrax) and hare were not. Leviticus 7:23 ruled they should not eat the fat of the ox, sheep or goat, which were the portions given to priests (Lev. 7:3-6).
[5] It does *not* mean they are not allowed to sit and eat with non-Muslims (see Sura 5:6). The dietary principles are not designed to be socially exclusionary.
[6] Neither, six centuries later, was the prophet Muhammad. He did not *found* Islam, for it was the same faith in the same God Who had been revealed by all the prophets. Muslims regard Muhammad as the *last* prophet, and final seal of all that had come before.
[7] Eisenman, *op.cit.* p.67.
[8] Tacitus, *Annals* 2.85 and 15.44.
[9] Pliny, *Letter to Trajan*, 97.
[10] Many Bible scholars have suggested that Galileans were lax in their Judaism, their conclusion being based on passages drawn from the Gospels, the works of Josephus and Rabbinic literature. However, where the interpretation of the law in Galilee differed from that in Jerusalem, it was often stricter. (See L.A.Schiffman, *The Galilee in Late Antiquity*, pp.143-56.) The Gospels depict a peaceful, Hellenized countryside, with saintly Roman officers, and the Herods as bumbling but well-meaning dupes, and present Jesus as politically disinterested, otherworldly, and preaching something essentially congenial to the Romans. On the contrary, the Jewish Zealots of Galilee were quite prepared to die rather than break their faith: they were committed to absolute purity, unbending 'righteousness' and uncompromising integrity.
[11] *Christos* was a Greek term, and they found their own word 'Messiah' quite adequate.
[12] Nobody seems ever to have referred to Muslims as Meccans or Madinans.

¹³ See Isaiah 11:1, and Genesis 21:12 which gives the promise 'Through Isaac shall your seed be named', picked up in the New Testament by Romans 9:7, Hebrews 11:18 and Galatians 3:16.

¹⁴ The Rechabites refused to drink the wine set before them, because they obeyed the voice of Jonadab the son of Rechab, their father, in all that he commanded: 'You shall not drink wine, neither you nor your sons, for ever; you shall not build a house; you shall not sow seed; you shall not plant or have a vineyard; but you shall live in tents all your days.' Jeremiah 35:6-8.

¹⁵ At the time of the Prophet Muhammad the Christians were still called *Nasara* or *Nasiriyyah*. In Arabic, the word has the meaning of giving help, and it is interesting to note that the Muslims of Madina who rushed to volunteer help and support to the emigrants from Mecca (the Muhajirun) were always known as al-Ansar, a Qur'anic term for Jesus's Apostles (sura 3:52, 59:9,9:100).

¹⁶ Epiph. *Oan.*29.1.3 − 5.3.

CHAPTER 7

¹ One might compare Jesus' utterly Muslim words in Jn 12:49-50: 'I do not speak on my own authority; the Father who sent me has Himself given me commandment what to say, and what to speak. And I know that His commandment is eternal life. What I say, therefore, I say as the Father has bidden me.'

² Muslims do not regard the first five books of the Hebrew Bible as being identical to the Tawrat. They hold that it is no longer the Law as originally revealed to the Prophet Moses, but is a text that has been added to, censored, and edited by anonymous authors with various agendas, as any scholarly book of Old Testament background studies candidly reveals.

³ 'Be heedful of a light precept as of a weighty one, for you do not know the grant of reward for each precept.' Aboth 11.1.

⁴ P. Kiddushin 61d. Exactly equivalent in Islam is the story of the murderer who wished to change his ways, and was directed to go to a certain city where he would be forgiven. He died on the way, and the angels came to measure whether he was closer to the old life or the new. When God noted that the dead man was exactly in the middle, He shifted the entire earth so that the measurement would be in the sinner's favour.

⁵ A 'jot' was the letter *yod*, the smallest letter in the Hebrew alphabet. A tittle was a small decorative flourish that might shape a letter and alter the entire sense of a passage.

⁶ Much depends on how the word 'Law' is defined. Does it just denote the clear commands from God, or does it also include the mass of 'hedging' traditions, scholarly opinions, interpretations, and so forth?

⁷ See the hadith: 'Not one of you shall enter Paradise by his works.' 'Not even you, O

Messenger of God?' they asked, and he replied, 'Not even me, unless that God shall encompass me in His mercy.' Many other hadiths make this point. The rules do not save, they provide a pattern of life that helps us to work on our inward lives so that we may become candidates for God's grace.

[8] Galatians 3:19 and Romans 5:20.

[9] *Tos. Sabb* 15:17. Passages such as this might well have been provoked precisely because of Paul's attack on the adequacy of the Torah.

[10] E.P. Sanders, 'Patterns of Religion' in 'Paul and Rabbinic Judaism', *Harvard Theological Review* 86, 1973.

[11] It was one of the leading reasons for Zealot hatred of the naked athletics in the New Hellenistic gymnasium which revealed immediately if a man had been circumcised or not. Paul provocatively also spoke of living the Christian life in terms of runners at the stadium (I Corinthians 9:24-26). There was no new command concerning circumcision in the Qur'an, but it remained a fundamental part of Islam and a sunna. However, according to some schools of *fiqh* adult male converts coming into Islam are not obliged to undergo circumcision.

[12] It was that accepted by such influential and profound writers as Weber, Schurer, Bousset, Bultmann and Billerbeck.

[13] S. Schechter, *Aspects of Rabbinic Theology* (London, 1961), p.18.

[14] J. Hick, 'Jesus and the World Religions', in Hick, *Myth*, pp.170-171.

[15] *Shirk* is the Qur'anic term for dividing the One-ness of God, and considering that God has partners, sharers, internal divisions or 'family' relations; or that any other entity, person, substance or superstition has power to alter the will of God.

CHAPTER 8

[1] *T. Kidd* 1.15. The Parable of the Labourers in the Vineyard (Mt 20:1-16) illustrates this precisely. A householder hired labourers at different times during the day, some at the eleventh hour, yet they all received the same wages, which greatly annoyed some of those who had worked longer. The parable taught not fair employment terms, but God's compassion and generosity.

[2] Assuming, of course, that he is able to do this. Abu Hamid al-Ghazali, *The Remembrance of Death* (Cambridge, 1989), pp.198-9. Compare *Sifre Ahare Pereq* 8.1.

[3] *Hadith qudsi* ('Hadiths from the Divine Presence') are revelations from God to the Prophet that were not directly given as part of the Qur'an, so he was free to express them in his own words.

[4] Professor Sandmel, in his illuminating book *We Jews and Jesus* (London, 1965), p.40, makes a statement with which all Jews and Muslims would surely agree: 'Sin as condition of Man is as unintelligible to us as sin as act is intelligible; the atonement which the person makes periodically, either on the Day of Atonement or whenever a person is

moved to make it, roots that act of atonement within the lifetime of each individual, and we readily understand it. We do NOT readily understand an act of atonement external to the lifetime of any individual. We do not believe that a person needs baptism to wash sins away; we believe that every person must make their own atonement, not have atonement wrought for them.'

5   Mt 12:33.

6   In the developing Christian church the same problems arose as real social power became vested more and more in the hands of a priestly hierarchy, who alone could administer the sacraments, declare marriages valid, excommunicate, and appoint other clergy. It is hard to believe today that people were tortured and executed for trying to make the words of the Bible available to people in their own languages by clergy. One cannot resist the temptation to assume that this was partly because they *knew* that what the church taught was not Biblical.

7   M.D. Hooker, *The Signs of a Prophet* (London, 1997), p.91.

8   Paul may actually have been the person who started off the idea of a sacramental meal. Previously Christians had broken bread together, but Paul claimed that he 'received from the Lord the teaching' that he passed on: 'that the Lord Jesus, on the night he was betrayed, took a piece of bread, gave thanks to God, broke it, and said, 'This is my body, which is (given) for you. Do this in memory of me.' In the same way, after the supper he took the cup and said: 'This cup is God's New Covenant, sealed with my blood. Whenever you drink it, do so in memory of me.' This means that every time you eat this bread and drink from this cup, you proclaim the Lord's death until he comes.' (I Corinthians 11:23-26)

In the Gospels (written after the time of Paul), Jesus' Last Supper was recorded in: Mk 14:22-26, which leaves out Paul's comment and adds that Jesus said he would not drink again of the fruit of the vine until the day he drank it new in the Kingdom of God; Mt 26:26-29, which has virtually identical words and is therefore copied from Mk; Lk 22:14-20, which adds a second cup after supper (often dropped to a footnote, as in the Revised Standard Version); and the Fourth Gospel which does not mention the meal of body and blood at all, but has five chapters of teachings. Some scholars suggest that the teaching in Jn 5 on Jesus being the 'bread of life' is a replacement to the institution of the sacrament.

9   Followed by D.Daube and D.Carmichael; see Daube's 'He that Cometh' on the Significance of the Afikomen; Wine in the Bible'; and D.Carmichael on 'The Eucharist and the Passover Seder.'

10   The Gospels state that Jesus was executed at Passover time, but the waving of palms at Jesus' entry into Jerusalem is actually more reminiscent of the autumn festivities of the Day of Atonement, when people did cut and wave palms (known as *lulabs*), and marched in triumph to the Temple.

11   Leviticus 16:7-10, 21-22, 34.

[12] Hebrews 10:12,14.

[13] V.A.Holmes-Gore, *The Distortion of Christianity* (London, 1980), p.58.

CHAPTER 9

[1] Paul's accuracy in describing this event varies in the reporting: see Acts 9:3-9; 22:6-16; 26:12-18.

[2] Gal 1:20. Paul was rather sensitive about being accused of lying, as we shall see.

[3] Presumably Paul's letters predate Luke's Book of Acts. In any case, Luke does not appear to have used them as a source of information for his book.

[4] Professor Eisenman suggests that the 'We' narratives in the Book of Acts could actually have been specific letters reporting back to James, and that all overseas teachers required letters of introduction or certification from James and were required to send him back periodic reports of their activities. Eisenman, p.78.

[5] When the Gospels refer to the three chief disciples, they pick out Peter, James and John. In the Book of Acts, the James referred to as one of the 'three pillars' of the church is not the brother of John, but the brother of Jesus.

[6] 'The poor' did not necessarily mean 'people with little wealth'; it more likely referred to the Jerusalem community, who, like the Essenes of Qumran, favoured the epithet 'the poor' for themselves.

[7] In the terminology of traditional Islam, Paul had no *ijaza*, and was not part of a *silsila*.

[8] Let us consider a few of the problems raised by comparing Acts 15 and Galatians 2. Those who had caused trouble for Paul are anonymous in Acts, whereas Gal 2:12 specifically identifies them as 'certain men from James.' In the Galatians account, Paul somewhat provocatively took Titus – an uncircumcised Greek – with him to Jerusalem, and according to Gal 2:3-5 was not obliged to have him circumcised. The version in Acts 15, however, only mentions circumcision in passing, as one of several reasons for the Council, and does not mention Titus at all!

The Acts narrative is supposed to be following a chronological sequence of events, in which Galatians 1:18 seems to be the parallel of Acts 9:26, Paul's first visit to Jerusalem after his conversion. 'I visited Cephas [Peter] and stayed with him fifteen days. I saw none of the other Apostles except James the Lord's brother ... (In what I am writing to you, before God, I do not lie!) ... I was still not known by sight to the churches of Christ in Judaea; they only heard it said: 'He who once persecuted us is now preaching the faith he once tried to destroy'.

The account goes on to tell that when Paul 'had come to Jerusalem he attempted to join the disciples; and they were all afraid of him, for they did not believe that he was a disciple. But Barnabas took him and bought him to the apostles, and declared to them how on the road he had seen the Lord ... So he went in and out among them at

Jerusalem, preaching boldly in the name of the Lord. And he spoke and disputed amongst the Hellenists, but they were seeking to kill him. And when the brethren knew it, they brought him down to Caesarea and sent him off to Tarsus.' (Acts 9:26-30.)

Now, Galatians 2:1 states that the occasion mentioned next was Paul's second visit, and that it took place fourteen years after the first visit. It was for a private conference with church leaders, and after reaching an understanding, Paul promised to keep the material needs of 'the poor' in his mind. No other restriction was placed upon him.

Was this the visit of Acts 11:30, a trip Paul and Barnabas made to Jerusalem for charitable purposes, apparently after Herod Agrippa's death in 44? (See Acts 12:20-25.) It does not seem very likely that Acts 11:30 and Acts 15 could be two variant accounts in the same book of the same meeting; but it is quite conceivable that Gal 2 is referring to Acts 11 and not Acts 15.

In Luke's chronology, after the Acts 11 visit he records a missionary journey in chapters 13 and 14, then goes on to describe the visit to Jerusalem to take public issue over the question of circumcision in chapter 15. Paul and Barnabas had been summoned to consult with the original Apostles at the Jerusalem headquarters.

9 Sanh 56 a-b.

10 The author of the Gospel According to Mark. It is believed that Barnabas was killed in Cyprus, and Mark in Alexandria. In the ninth century CE, when the mad caliph al-Hakim was taking building materials from various churches for his palace, Mark's body was taken to Venice, where the great St. Mark's Cathedral was built to receive it. The story is both fascinating and macabre: Mark's corpse was replaced by that of St Caecilia, whose shroud was taken off to wrap him up in. His body was then concealed in a barrel of pork, so that the Muslim port officials would not investigate and discover it. In 1968, his head was returned to the Copts, crowds massing at Cairo airport to receive it. See D. Sox, *Relics and Shrines* (London, 1985), pp. 48-9, 55.

CHAPTER 10

1 John's brother James was executed by Herod Agrippa, Acts 12:2.
2 Mk 6:3; Mt 12:46-50; 13:55-58; Lk 4:16-30; Jn 2:1-12; 7:1-10; 19:25-27.
3 He also proposes the theory that Simon Cephas the Apostle should probably be identified with Simon son of Cleophas.
4 Take the list of his sufferings that Paul gives in his second letter to the Corinthians (11:23;27). This list included several imprisonments whereas Acts gives us only one (16:23); five beatings by the Jews – none in Acts; three beatings by the Roman rods – Acts 16:22 mentions only one at Philippi; one stoning – Acts 14:19, at Lystra; and three shipwrecks – Acts gives only the final one, which was obviously yet another occasion from the three mentioned in the letter. Paul's letters to Corinth show that his

relationship with the Christians was much more complicated than Acts suggests. I Cor 15:32 and 2 Cor 1:8 suggest that Paul was in great danger at Ephesus, but this is not revealed in Acts 9:31f.

5 The Muslim suggestion is that the Spirit of Truth that was to come, that would guide people into the path of Truth, was the Blessed Messenger Muhammad. (See p. 163.)

6 Ernest Renan, *The History of the Origins of Christianity,* Bk III (followed by the theologians Baur and Volkmar).

7 Eus. *H.E.* 3.28-29.

8 In Islamic terms, *ibaha.*

9 Hipp. *Haeres* 30.3.3-5 on the Ebionite/Sabaean/Elchesaite 'Adam'.

10 Eus. *H.E.* 4.22.

11 See Michael Golder, 'The two roots of the Christian myth' in *Myth*, pp. 66f.

12 Justin, 1. *Apol.* 26.

13 Suetonius' comment about Jesus calls him *Chrestus*, not Christus. See p. 50.)

CHAPTER 11

1 Pope Gregory I was a famous example of a Christian leader who actively encouraged the trend of using peoples' existing customs and beliefs rather than try to antagonise them with a new faith. He was most accommodating. If a group of people worshipped a tree, or the spirit abiding in it, rather than cut it down he urged priests to consecrate it to Christ and allow them to continue their worship.

2 See Genesis 32:19,34; I Samuel 19:13,16.

3 The famous sanctuary at Mecca had deviated so far from the worship of One God in the time of the Prophet Muhammad that it housed a veritable museum collection of some 360 cultic objects and statues, and tribesmen came for hundreds of miles to reverence their gods there. Just as Abraham's first act on being called was to destroy his father's idols, so Muhammad's first act on the capture of Mecca was to destroy the Ka'ba idols.

4 For example, Jehovah's Witnesses do not celebrate Christmas, on the grounds that it is a pagan festival.

5 A Muslim, who tries to spend all waking moments conscious of God, will never pray at the exact times of sunrise, noon or sunset, for the very reason that those moments are so intimately linked to the symbolism of Baalism.

6 From the Nicene Creed, 325 CE.

7 St Nicholas had nothing to do with Christmas either: he was the Bishop of Myra in Turkey. His relics still exist, having been moved to Bari, where Muslims might be surprised to discover an eleventh century marble floor in front of his tomb decorated with the words of the *Shahada*!

8 For some of these images see the Plates.

9 *Praeparatio Evangelica* v.xvii.

10 The NT Greek *tekton*, usually translated as 'carpenter', in fact means something closer to a 'master-builder'.

11 One Gnostic Christian relief actually showed an ass suckling its foal with the figure of the crab above, and the inscription 'D.N.INVS.XPS' – which means 'Dominus Noster Jesus Christos'. See A. Robertson, *Jesus, myth or history?*

12 Complete details are given in A.S.K. Joommal's *The Bible: word of God or word of man?*, pp.147-9, which he took from the January 1922 issue of *Quest*. Joommal also listed 16 saviour-gods including Krishna, Indra, Bali, Iao, Wittona, Prometheus and Quirinus as well as the ones dealt with above.

CHAPTER 12

1 Thus, al-Lah, or Allah, is to be understood as the same God who has revealed Himself throughout all prophecy, identical to the Jehovah or Yahweh of the Jews, and God the Father of the Christians. Arab Christians, to this day, still refer to God simply as Allah.

2 They are frequently referred to in the Qur'an: see Suras 6:100; 19:92; 61:57; 53:19-20.

3 These three goddesses were the subject of the infamous book by Salman Rushdie, *The Satanic Verses*. The issue was whether or not it would have been possible for the Prophet to have been deceived by the devil, so that verses were briefly included in the Qur'an which were not true revelations from Allah. It is claimed that in Sura 53:19, the Prophet recited the words: 'Al-lat, al-Uzzah and Manat are the exalted birds (*gharaniq*), whose intercession is desired indeed.' These words delighted the Meccans, who believed them to be the daughters of Allah, and with this concession to their beliefs, they were prepared to accept Islam and bowed down. Then the Prophet was told by God that these words were inserted by the devil, and formed no part of the Revelation, whereat the Meccans also withdrew their support for Islam. The story is entirely absent from the earliest history of the Prophet (Ibn Ishaq), but appears in the third-century works of Tabari and Ibn Sa'd, so that God knows best the truth of the matter.

4 Kamal Salibi, a Lebanese Christian, historian and specialist on the Modern Middle East, has used his detailed knowledge of the geography of Arabia and his study of Biblical texts to put forward some very interesting theories. His three books, *The Bible Came from Arabia*, *Secrets of the Bible People*, and *Conspiracy in Jerusalem*, propose that the Bible narratives actually describe people and places from the west coast of the Arabian peninsula, and that it was Israelites from this region that colonised Palestine.

5 Salibi suggests that there was more than one Abraham, this one being the Abraham of Genesis 15.

[6] Salibi, pp. 163-165.

[7] The practice of keeping special gardens to produce the special food of god's representatives or priests was still in force at the time of the Prophet Muhammad; his critics expressed surprise that if he was a genuine prophet, he did not keep a special garden (Sura 17:89-91 and 25:7-8); the anti-prophet, Maslama of Najd, certainly did. The Qur'an actually speaks of the 'gardens' (plural) of Eden in eleven references. Maslama's garden was called *Hadiqatu'l-Rahman*: al-Rahman (the 'merciful One') being the name of the One God in some pre-Islamic Arabian monotheistic cults. (*The Bible Came from Arabia*, p. 178.)

[8] One example is the Sulubbah, the defenceless tinkers and entertainers of the Syro-Arabian desert. In Hebrew, the name Cain (*qyn*) also means 'smith' or 'tinker'. The Sulubba are distinguished to this day from other desert people by a tattooed mark.

[9] Albert van Drandem, *Les Inscriptions Thamoudeenes*, Paris, 1950, pp. 59, 69. The inscriptions referring to this god are listed as HUB 48, HUB 57 (10); EUT. 87.

[10] This was the conclusion drawn by Salibi.

[11] Salibi, *Conspiracy in Jerusalem*, pp. 167-8.

[12] Some have suggested that the Lazarus of the Fourth Gospel narrative was actually James, the brother of Jesus, who was famous, amongst other things, for being a life-long virgin. Indeed, the doctrine of the perpetual virginity of Mary might originally have applied to him, and not to her!

[13] Matthew's version presents the event as an actualisation of Old Testament prophecy concerning the Messiah, and misquotes Zechariah 11:12-13, which he wrongly attributes to Jeremiah: 'Then what the prophet Jeremiah had said came true: "they took the thirty silver coins, the amount the people of Israel had agreed to pay for him, and used the money to buy the potters field".' Mt 27:3-10.

[14] In the Egyptian system, Osiris is betrayed and killed by his brother Set.

[15] See p. 128.

[16] There is an interesting suggestion in Muhammad Ata ur-Rahim's book *Jesus, Prophet of Islam*, that the Beloved Disciple was Barnabas, who was known to have been a Levite and to have had a sister with a house in Jerusalem where Jesus was guest at the Last Supper, and which became a headquarters for the first Christians. He further suggests that Barnabas could be the same man as Joseph Barsabbas Justus, a candidate for election as the twelfth apostle (to replace Judas Iscariot); one of the qualifications of the new apostle was that he had to have been with Jesus ever since his baptism by John the Baptist.

CHAPTER 13

[1] Basilides claimed that he had received his knowledge from Glaucias, one of Peter's interpreters; while Valentinus claimed his secret teachings from Theodas, a disciple of

Paul. According to Hippolytus, Naassenes (Nazarenes/Ossenes), held traditions from Jesus' brother James which he had delivered to a certain Mariamne, from whom they had received them. In the Nag Hammadi texts, the second Apocalypse of James changes 'Mariamne' to a certain 'Marieme', one of the priests, a person closely associated with a man called Theuda, the father or brother of James the Just. Celsus mentions both a Mariamne and a Salome, and they are referred to many times in the Apocryphal literature. It is much too simplistic to claim that these persons were complete inventions of the fertile Gnostic imaginations; they *may* have been, but we can never be sure.

2   One suggestion was that this was the most suitable because everyone knew the earth had four corners!

3   Or was this the Injil copied by Waraqa?

4   Eus. *H.E.* 4.22.8

5   Vir *Inl.* 3.

6   Eus. *H.E.* 3.25.5

7   These ideas are central to the Epistle of James.

8   Origen, *De Princ.* 4.11.

9   In a sense this made Jesus also Baryonah – son of a dove.

10   *Panarion* 30.16f.

11   Eusebius , *H.E.* 3. 32. See Schonfield, *According to the Hebrews,* 1937. Simeon was said to have died at the age of 120.

12   Eus *H.E.* 6.17.

13   See Salibi's theory, p. 105.

14   Eus *H.E.* 3.39.11.

15   Some of Papias' teaching is strongly reminiscent of the Jewish Apocalypse of Baruch (c70 CE). Another writer, Andrew of Caesarea, reported that one of Papias' pieces of information concerned God conferring on specific angels the task of administering the earth, after which the angels betrayed this trust. This was certainly a doctrine of Jewish-Christian origin, and it reappeared in Athenagoras, Irenaeus and Gregory of Nyssa. Irenaeus, like Papias, recorded other fragments of data that he attributed to 'the Elders', such as the translation into Paradise of the physical bodies of Elijah and Enoch, and speculations about the nature of Paradise.

16   *Stromateis* 6.7.61.

17   That is, living before the Council of Nicaea in 325 CE.

18   Some think Trypho was a pseudonym for the famous Rabbi Tarfon, who had been a leading opponent of Trinitarian Christianity in his day (Sabb. 116a).

19   'Behold, I send my messenger to prepare the way before Me, and the lord whom you seek will suddenly come to his Temple; the messenger of the Covenant in whom you delight, behold, he is coming, says the Lord.' (Mal 3.1). 'Behold, I will send you Elijah the prophet before the great and terrible Day of the Lord comes. And he will

turn the hearts of the fathers of their children, and the hearts of the children to their fathers, lest I come and smite the land with a curse.' (Mal 4:5)

20 'Did you go out to see a prophet? Yes, I tell you, and more than a prophet. This is he of whom it is written – Behold, I send my messenger before my face, who shall prepare thy way before thee [. . .] all the prophets and the Law prophesied until John; and if you are willing to accept it, he is Elijah who is to come. He who has ears to hear, let him hear.' (Mt 11:11-14. See also Mt 17:10-13, for the same connecting inference.)

21 The Hebrew text of Lk 3:22 adds: 'Thou art my beloved son; *this day* have I begotten thee.' The latter phrase remains in the Revised Version of the Bible just as a footnote. Justin also claimed that the pre-human Jesus was a 'created angel' who was other than 'the God who made all things.' Jesus the man was inferior to God, and 'never did anything except what the Creator willed him to do and say'

22 *Dialogue* 8.10.32.

23 *Dialogue,* 67.2.

24 *C. Cels,* 2.xiii and 2.27.

25 See p. 21 above.

CHAPTER 14

1 Professor Burton L. Mack is but one of many modern New Testament scholars who have worked on this ancient document. Mack's 1993 work *The Lost Gospel* is an attempt to reconstruct Q, and draw conclusions from it as to the nature of the beliefs of the earliest followers of Jesus.

2 The verses given in Mark after 16:8 are an appendix added later.

3 Mack, *Lost Gospel,* pp.4-5

4 Mack argues that the idea of a vicarious human sacrifice was anathema to Jewish culture, but could be traced to the strong Greek tradition of extolling a noble death: when for example, the warrior 'dies for' his country, its laws, or its people. Socrates was a prime example of a philosopher-teacher who died for the truth of his vision for the very people who condemned him to death. In the Graeco-Roman world, the Socratic ideal was the prime model for ethical integrity.

The notion of resurrection from death, on the other hand, offended Graeco/Roman sensibility, whereas this *had* been put forward by Jewish philosophers struggling with the question of vindicating God's justice in a world which was patently unjust. Many Jewish wisdom stories follow an age-old narrative plot: an innocent Jewish victim-hero is charged with disloyalty to a tyrannical king and condemned, later to be rescued or vindicated when his wisdom and beneficence are realised. Biblical examples include the Joseph story, and the Esther and Daniel sagas. Apocalyptic projection gave the vindication of the righteous one a new twist; even though he was killed, he would still be vindicated after death in new circumstances. Various views of transformation were possible at this point, including immediate ascension and/or eventual resurrection from the dead. These wisdom stories and martyrological literature figured in Hellenistic-Jewish writings from northern Syria to Alexandria.

5 Mack, 16-7.
6 See David Frederich Strauss, *Life of Jesus* (1835); Albert Schweitzer, *The Quest of the Historical Jesus* (1906); Rudolf Bultmann, *History of the Synoptic Tradition* (1921); B.H. Streeter, *The Four Gospels:A Study of Origins* (1930).

CHAPTER 15

1 Quoted by Dupont-Sommer, *The Essene Writings from Qumran*, pp. 37-38.
2 Ibid.
3 J. Allegro, *The Sacred Mushroom and the Cross* (London, 1970).
4 Eisenman and Wise, *The Dead Sea Scrolls Uncovered* (Shaftesbury, 1992).
5 J. Allegro, *The Dead Sea Scrolls* (London, 1956), p.45.
6 Allegro, op. cit. p.48.
7 M. Baigent and R. Leigh, *The Dead Sea Scrolls Deception* (London, 1991).
8 De Vaux also concluded that the monks were reclusive and peace-loving!
9 Incidentally, the Qumran graves have long remained a mystery because they are not aligned towards the east like other Jewish graves, but north-south (like the Islamic graves of the region). This may be 'proof' of a connection with Sabaeans, who prayed towards the middle of the dome of heaven at its highest place (al-Biruni, *Chronology of Ancient Nation*, 8.10-23.) Both al-Biruni (973-1048) and his predecessor, known as Ibn al-Nadim (c995), recorded the Sabaeans as originating in the Jewish tribes who remained in Babylon and in northern Syria around Harran, and further east in Adiabene. Benjamin of Tudela noted that there was still a Jewish 'Elchesaite' synagogue in Mosul (Adiabene) when he visited that city in 1164 CE.
10 Driver, *The Judaean Scrolls*, p.211.
11 Josephus, *Wars*, 6.6.
12 Baigent, p.171.
13 Josephus, *Wars*, 2.8.
14 *Adversus Octaginta Haereses* II, *Haeres* xx.
15 Baigent, p.174.

CHAPTER 16

1   Eisenman suggests that the author of Acts is guilty of presenting *disinformation* , and that the story of Stephen really refers to the first attack on James on the Temple steps (see p.962).
2   See above, p. 12.
3   Damascus Document xv. 12-14; Vermes, *Jesus the Jew*, p.42.
4   Origen, *Contra Celsum*, 1.47; 2.13.
5   *Habb. Comm* 8.1f (Vermes p.287).
6   Allegro, pp.124-135. For a more recent translation see Vermes, *Dead Sea Scrolls in English*, 197-9.
7   Allegro, p.139.
8   From Allegro, p.40.
9   Josephus, *Wars*, 11.i.
10   Eisenman, pp36-7, p.90, n164; p.98 n179.
11   Josephus, *Wars*, 11 xxii.
12   Mt 1:2-16; Lk 3:23-38.

CHAPTER 17

1   Two of his closest disciples were the brothers James and John, whom the Gospels of Luke and John refer to as the 'sons of Zebedee' (Ar. Z.b.d) as in Mk 1:20 and Mt 4:21 etc). It is possible that Zebedee was *not* the name of their father, but of their native town or village. There was a village of Zubaydah (written zbydh), 32 kilometres south of Ta'if in the same region where Wadi Jalil ('Galilee') and the tribe of Nazirah are said to be located (Salibi p93). In Aramaic, the 'son of Zebedee' would be *Bnay Zbida*. Mark says they were actually surnamed Boanerges (the Greek transliteration of *Bnay Rgas*: Son of Thunder). The simple explanation is that their father was not Zebedee but Rgas, in Arabic vocalised as *Rajas*. However, the more common Arabic word for thunder is *ra'd*, and the name Ibn Ra'd is relatively common.
2   We have already looked into the problems connected with this on page 6.
3   Did he really mean Cephas (Simon Peter) or Cleophas, or Simeon bar Cleophas?
4   Paul's home town, in Turkey.
5   It is fascinating to compare the slow progress, trials and tribulations faced by early Trinitarian missionaries, and their general failure to attract the masses, to the almost instantaneous success of Islam when it was preached in the region. It is nonsense to suggest that this was because people who didn't accept it would be put to death, or threatened in any way. The Muslim rulers allowed each person their own beliefs, and guaranteed the protection of people of other religions under their sway, so long as they gave their word for political peace and support of the taxes. One needs to disentangle the warfare and conquests of Muslim leaders from the matter of the acceptance of the

faith by the masses. The speed of conversions was because people readily accepted monotheism, and found the dogmas of Trinitarianism difficult to believe.

6   For example, his wife's cousin Waraqa ibn Nawfal; his own cousin Ubaydallah ibn Jahsh; Salman the Persian; the Negus of Abyssinia, and many others.

7   al-Rawd al-Mi'tarfi khabar al-aqtar, ed. Ihsan Abbas, Beirut, 1984, p. 573.

8   Elsewhere, the Qur'an says the pregnancy was announced to her by 'angels' (3:45-47).

9   This was when shepherds would have been in the fields guarding their flocks by night (Lk 2:8); in December (the Baal-cult birthday of the Sun-god) the sheep would have been under cover.

10   This would fit better with the Dead Sea Scrolls' 'Teacher of Righteousness', who seems to have lived and worked a long time before the New Testament period.

CHAPTER 18

1   Introduction to sura 19; F. Malik and Maududi, on the authority of Umm Salama.

2   It is not often realised that today most of the population of Ethiopia is Muslim.

3   Muslims will spot this immediately, for the story of Hagar, or Hajar, is intimately connected with the Hajj to the Great Sanctuary, where pilgrims recall her desperate search for water when she ran to and fro between mounts Safa and Marwa, followed by the Standing before God at Mount Arafat.

4   The Qumran community had the notion of a Messianic 'pair' – the priestly Messiah of the House of Aaron, and the royal Messiah of the House of David, who was less important.

5   It is amazing to compare this with the 'wicked' household of Herod, who insisted that when their princesses married outside the Jewish nation, their husbands were all to be circumcised first!

6   The verses only in Matthew are referred to as M, and those only in Luke are referred to as L.

7   Especially the 'I am' sayings.

CHAPTER 19

1   Professor 'Abdu'l-Ahad Dawud is an example of a scholar with knowledge and competence who presents many extremely interesting theories on this topic in his book *Muhammad in the Bible*. The Professor himself is an interesting witness, for he was formally a Christian, the Catholic Bishop of Urmiah in Iran: the Reverend David Keldani, BD.

2   The New Testament references to the 'one to come, who will speak all that he hears' is discussed later in the chapter.

³ Notice how the prophecy concerning Isaac's descendants broke into the narrative, and took place while Abraham was asleep.

⁴ Dawud, p. 32.

⁵ Hagar was an Egyptian, possibly of the royal house, and not just a 'servant'.

⁶ Seir is usually identified with Petra.

⁷ It can surely hardly be a coincidence that of all the names on earth his pagan relatives chose the very name Muhammad. In linguistic terms, Muhammad is cognate with the Hebrew passive particle of what is called the *pi'el* form of the verb *hamad*, and the passive participle of the second derived form of the Arabic *hamida*: its meaning being: 'praise and praiseworthy, celebrity and celebrated, glory and glorious.'

⁸ See above, p. 84.

⁹ Dawud, pp 23-24, 144-145.

¹⁰ 'Spirit of truth' (*Ruh al-haqq*) is one of the Prophet's titles of honour.

¹¹ Of like substance, similar but not the same.

¹² Of the one and the same substance.

¹³ Dawud, p. 67.

¹⁴ Eisenman, op cit. p. 836.

¹⁵ Appalling atrocities have been committed by Crusaders, inquisitors and other enthusiasts who were convinced that they were following the Spirit.

CHAPTER 20

¹ W. Löhr, *Basilides und seine Schule* (Tübingen, 1996).

² The story occurs in the 'Gospel of Barnabas'.

³ Because they regard their founder Ghulam Ahmad as a Prophet, whereas Islam maintains that Muhammad was the *last* prophet.

⁴ The Subcontinent is full of tombs of Middle Eastern saints and prophets who never went within a thousand miles of India. The region contains several thousand 'tombs' of Shaykh Abd al-Qadir al-Jilani alone!

⁵ See also Tertullian: *De Spectaculis* 30 (Tr T. R. Glover, Loeb Classical Library).

⁶ British Museum Oriental MS 6804.

⁷ For example, when Lazarus died his sister Martha appealed to Jesus for help, and said: 'I know he will be raised up on the Last Day', Jn 11:24.

⁸ Critics who disbelieve in the physical resurrection of Jesus point out that he seems to have come through walls – or at least a locked door – and dematerialised rather than taken his polite leave of his friends.

⁹ Other relevant passages are Daniel 12:1-4; Maccabees 7:9-36; 14:46; and the post-Jesus rabbinical synagogue liturgy, Eighteen Benedictions 2. In all these texts the resurrection refers to ordinary human corpses, and is certainly not intended to prove

divinity, but simply the power of a Merciful God over life and death.

¹⁰ The Pharisees taught that a tiny human bone, the Luz, survived even cremation, and was the basis on which God would recreate each person's flesh and bone.

CHAPTER 21

¹ D. Sox, *Relics and Shrines* (London, 1985), p. 168-9.

² Another fascinating relic stolen at the same time was the Holy Prepuce: the 'foreskin of Christ', which had been preserved along with his umbilical cord in a crucifix filled with oil and was kept in the private papal chapel of the Lateran. It turned up thirty years later at Calcata, from where it was stolen again in 1984, but returned safely. There is another 'foreskin of Jesus' in 'Pepin's Reliquary' at Conques: Pepin being the father of Charlemagne.

³ From 'Veronica and her Veil', Maurus Green, *The Tablet*, December 31, 1966.

⁴ In case this is thought to be far too odd to be true, compare it to Acts 5:15 where sick people were laid out for Peter's shadow to fall on them and cure them; Mk 5:28, where a sick woman said 'If I touch even the hem of his garments, I shall be made well'; Mk 6:56, where 'as many as touched the fringe of his garment were made well'; and Acts 19:12, where Paul touched handkerchiefs and aprons that were then taken to the sick to cure them.

⁵ Lk 22:44.

⁶ I. Wilson, *The Turin Shroud*, London, 1978.

⁷ Noel Currer-Briggs, *The Holy Grail and the Shroud of Christ* (Maulden, 1984).

⁸ This notion has been argued by those who believe that Jesus certainly did leave descendants, and the theory is connected with the strange history of Montsegur in France.

⁹ The crown of thorns, which came to France in 1239, is kept in the Sainte Chapelle of Notre Dame de Paris. It consists of plaited rushes bound by other rushes, which is often considered very odd since it is supposed to be made of thorns! However, attached to it are some twigs of the very spiny *zizyphus spina Christi* plant, and it was from these that many thorns were detached over the centuries and sent to various shrines. Interestingly, the Shroud of Turin does not reveal evidence for the usual type of thorny band tied around Jesus' brow that we see in so many crucifixes and paintings: on the contrary, it suggests that it was more a 'hat', shaped rather like a thorny thatched roof, and this was presumably held in place by some sort of band. Those who have tried playing with zizyphus twigs will know how difficult it is to bend and twist them into shape. The Shroud depiction has a far more authentic feel to it, and there is theoretically no reason why the 'crown' in the Sainte Chapelle should not be the band used to hold the object in position.

¹⁰ The lance had been broken into two parts: the spearpoint and the shaft. A spear-

point alleged to be the original was kept in Constantinople, then given to the fearsome St Louis and kept with the crown of thorns in the Sainte Chapelle, where it disappeared during the French Revolution. The 'shaft' was also at Constantinople, and in 1492 the Turks sent it to the Pope as a gift. *Relics and Shrines*, p. 167.

[11] Reported by the Rome correspondent of the *Daily Telegraph*.

[12] Holger Kersten and Elmar Gruber conclude that it has been known since medieval times that the Shroud had wrapped the body of a living person. Their book *The Jesus Conspiracy* (Shaftesbury, 1992) is just one example of modern work that takes up this theme. Without going into all the details, one interesting sidelight was the question of why the Cathars were so viciously persecuted, and why the Knights Templar were excommunicated by the Church and tortured to death. Kersten and Gruber assume it was because they knew the image on the Shroud proved that Jesus had not died from his crucifixion: the Shroud-body was a living man. The Templars were also suspected of being much too in sympathy with the Muslims (whom they ought to have been fighting, as Crusaders!).

The most sensational accusation against the Templars was that they worshipped a mysterious idol or 'Head', before which they would bow their heads to the ground with shouts of 'Yallah'. It was also said that the priests at their services read Psalm 67, which has the repeated cry of 'selah'. Could this have been mistaken for 'Yallah'? Muslims will instantly recognise the prayer-position of *sujud*, and the cry 'Ya-Allah!' with the sense of 'In Your Name, O God!' or 'Here's to You, O God!' This was also the Saracen warcry. *Salah*, of course, is the usual Muslim word for formal prayer, and is repeated during the Call to Prayer.

Is this the origin of the cry of 'Alleluia' at revivalist services, when the congregation finds a statement particularly appealing? 'Alleluia' could easily be a version of '*Ya-Allah-Hu!*' or 'O Allah, You are He (or the One).' The source of most of our information about the Templar idol came from the interrogation of individual knights by the Inquisition. Only the most senior members of the Order attended ceremonies at which the 'Head' was exposed for worship. There were copies of it kept in chests and coffers in many places, including at least four in England (one at Templecomb in Somerset).

Brother Pierre d'Arbley said the 'idol' had two faces (recalling the back and front of the Shroud image?), and Guillaume d'Arbley said the *real* idol was only exhibited at General Chapters. Hugues de Pairaud said the 'Head' had four feet, two in front on the side of the face, and two behind.

Currer-Briggs concludes that this idol was nothing less than the folded Shroud, which was taken out and displayed fully on certain special occasions.

[13] M. Guscin, *The Oviedo Cloth* (Cambridge, 1998).

[14] Guscin, 64.

¹⁵ Jn 19:40.

¹⁶ Shabbat 23.5; Ketub 20b.

¹⁷ J. Neusner, *Jews and Christians* (London, 1991).

¹⁸ It was also one of the most important remedies against infectious diseases in the Middle Ages.

¹⁹ Perhaps called Essenes from the Aramaic *assaya*, 'healers'.

²⁰ 'Vinegar' simply means sour wine, the sort of rough red wine mixed with egg yolk that soldiers drank, known as *posca*.

²¹ Another possibility is that the Roman javelin or spear was called *hanith* in Hebrew. There is a very similar word, *kaneth* which means 'reed' (the ton kana in Galilee was famous for its strong reeds which were used for spear-shafts). Reed may well have been a colloquial expression for a spear: it is a word for spear in Arabic.

²² Sanh 43a.

²³ The only bleeding is the natural downward flow due to gravity. This is the obvious reason why animals slaughtered by the *halal* method are then hung upside down: for the blood to flow out. If a corpse is left for long before burial, the blood collects at the underside of the corpse. A wound made on top of a corpse lying horizontally would not bleed. Interestingly, some Shroud critics have used this very argument as proof that the relic is a false one, missing the possibility that it suggests that Jesus was still alive.

²⁴ J. Ketubot 12:3; J. Terumot 8:10.

²⁵ Muslims will know that male corpses are traditionally wrapped in three such cloths, and women in five pieces.

²⁶ There is one exception: the modest placement of his hands over his genitals. This would only be possible for a dead person if the wrists were tied together.

CHAPTER 22

¹ See Gerd Lüdemann, *The Great Deception* (London, 1998).

² Josephus, preface to *The Jewish War*. My italics.

³ See A. Bridge, *Theodora* (London, 1978), p. 88.

⁴ It is sometimes claimed that the first Christian Emperor was not Constantine but the Arab, Marcus Julius Philippus (ruled 244-249). The theologian Origen wrote letters to him. His status as Christian is not clear; it is certain that he did not adopt Christianity openly (*Oxford Classical Dictionary*).

⁵ See W. H. C. Frend, *The Donatist Church*, p. 226.

⁶ In Greek, Jesus was *homoi-ousios* and not *homo-ousios*.

⁷ One of the 'highlights' for this author was the saintly St Nicholas of Myra (our Santa Claus), losing his temper while denouncing Arius and punching him on the jaw!

CHAPTER 23

¹ So far, the search for lost gospel materials has only been successful in retrieving Christian writings which were of later composition than the canonicals. They shed light on numerous heresies but contribute little to the understanding of the Jesus of history

² The most important of these works is the Gospel of Thomas, Codex III, which can probably be dated to the 4ᵗʰ century CE. The original, however, goes back much earlier, and this codex is either a translation or an adaptation in Sahidic Coptic of a Greek work of around 140 CE, which itself was probably based on even more ancient sources, undoubtedly Jewish-Christian.

The Gospel of Truth is probably the most famous extant Gnostic Gospel, written by Valentinus, as was mentioned by Irenaeus (*Ad.Haer.*3.11.9). It is a tortuous esoteric extravaganza, using all four canonical Gospels but allegorizing the meanings.

³ A complete translation of the Didache is given in an appendix to J.M. Robertson's *The Jesus Problem*.

⁴ Incidentally, there was a Jewish tradition of a female person being more compassionate than God and therefore able to influence Him on our behalf: Rachel, the beloved of Jacob (see Mt 2:18).

⁵ Prince Hassan of Jordan, *Christianity in the Arab World* (London, 1998), p. 34.

⁶ See M. Green and C. Butler, *The Truth of God Incarnate* (London, 1977).

⁷ Nestorian missionaries were active throughout the fifth to thirteenth centuries, and Nestorian Christians could still be found in Asia as far east as China, India and the Indian Ocean coast of Africa.

⁸ *Theodora*, p. 141.

⁹ Meanwhile the Nestorians took their own reading of Christianity to many parts of the Indian Ocean basin. When the Portuguese conquered the island of Socotra in the sixteenth century they found Monophysites established there. A Jacobite communion remains in India to this day.

¹⁰ From *Myth*.

¹¹ See *Christianity in the Arab World*, pp. 33-42.

¹² Critics of Islam will instantly be able to show a few comparable incidents in Islamic history; but it is clear that minorities were always far better protected in the Islamic world than in traditional Christendom.

¹³ Donovan Joyce, *The Jesus Scroll* (London, 1973), p. 26.

¹⁴ Kirsopp Lake, *Landmarks in Early Christianity* (London, 1920), p. 55.

¹⁵ Hugh Schonfield, *The Pentecost Revolution* (Shaftesbury, 1985), p. 16.

CHAPTER 24

1   There are so many relevant passages one could choose to confirm the point: 'God does not accept your beliefs if they are not expressed in deeds; and your deeds are worthless if they do not back up your beliefs.' (Hadith); 'He is not a believer who eats his fill while his neighbour remains hungry by his side' (Hadith); 'If you do not give up telling lies, God will have no need of your giving up food and drink (in fasting). There are many who fast during the day and pray all night, but they gain nothing but hunger and sleeplessness.' (Hadith).

2   Midrash Tannaim 15:19.

3   *Forty Hadith Qudsi* (Ezzedine Ibrahim and Abdul Wadud Johnson-Davies, eds.), Beirut, 1980.

4   Col 1:19-22.

5   This is the main ceremony of the Hajj. Without the *wuquf*, performed at the appropriate time, the whole Hajj is invalid and becomes an *umra* or lesser pilgrimage.

CHAPTER 25

1   A.N. Wilson writes: 'While the West tries to dub the followers of Islam fundamentalist lunatics, increasing numbers of men and women turn to the Koran and find what a sizeable proportion of the human race has always craved: a moral and an intellectual acknowledgement of the lordship of God without the encumbrance of Christian mythological baggage in which almost no-one really believes.' (*The Daily Express*, 21 October 1999.)

2   Imam al-Haramayn al-Juwayni, cited in Habib Ahmad Mashhur al-Haddad, *Key to the Garden*, 72.

3   Narrated by Imam Malik.

4   Narrated by Bukhari.

5   Narrated by Khara'iti.

6   Imam al-Haddad, *The Lives of Man*, 65.

7   Sura 11:105-108.

8   The *khatima* (the 'Sealing State') is at the end of life, not at its beginning.

9   This idea is in total opposition, incidentally, to that presented by the Deuteronomic editor of the Old Testament, who taught that those with whom God was pleased would enjoy success in their earthly lives and be protected from harm and misfortune, while the wicked would be punished. That this is incorrect seems so obvious now, but that editor worked in his opinions throughout the books of Torah, misleading many.

10   The usual Christian position is defined by the Council of Trent as follows: 'If anyone does not profess that the first man Adam immediately lost the justice and holiness in which he was constituted when he disobeyed the command of God in the Garden of

Paradise; and that, through the offence of this sin, he incurred the wrath and the indignation of God, and consequently incurred the death with which God had previously
threatened him ... And if anyone asserts that Adam's sin was injurious only to Adam
and not to his descendents ... or that ... he transmitted to the whole human race only
death and punishment of the body but not sin itself [the Muslim view] which is the
death of the soul; let him be anathema.' Cited in John Hick, *The Metaphor of God
Incarnate* (London, 1993), pp. 115-6. The quotation is given by Hick in a chapter which
shows the moral unattractiveness of the original sin and atonement ideas.

11 As I write this, three Christian nuns have just been slaughtered for their faith by
ignorant Wahhabi 'Muslims' in the Yemen: today's martyrs.

12 Readers of the SCM Press booklist are already quite familiar with the fact that
many of today's Christian thinkers are already well-travelled down this path.

13 This is made clear in many passages: 'Woe to those who write the Book with their
own hands, and then say "This is from God", to traffic with it for a miserable price! Woe
to them for what their hands do write, and for the gain they make thereby [...] but
those who have faith and work righteousness, they are Companions of the Garden;
therein shall they abide for ever.' (Sura 2:79,82)

'They do blaspheme who say "God is Christ the son of Mary". Christ had said: "O
children of Israel! Worship God, my Lord and your Lord". They do blaspheme who say
God is the third of three: for there is no God except One God. If they do not desist,
surely a grievous penalty will befall the blasphemers among them. Why do they not
turn to God and seek His forgiveness? For God is Oft-Forgiving, Most Merciful.' (Sura
5:75-77)

14 McAuliffe, op. cit., p. 28

APPENDIX

1 The Epistle of Barnabas dates between 70-100 CE and was actually included by
some of the early fathers in the canon of New Testament scripture. Origen (185-254)
and Eusebius (265-340) both knew it, and it is included in the Codex Sinaiticus, one of
the earliest and most authoritative of complete Bible manuscripts, dated to the fourth
century. However, it is not to be found in any version of today's Bible.

2 See also the Epistle of James, and Josephus' *Antiquities* 18.116: 'righteousness
towards men and piety towards God'; also *Ant* 15.375, and *Wars* 2.128ff. See also Mt
22:37ff; Lk 10:27 (love God and love your neighbour).

3 A surviving Jewish tradition indicates that Jesus had five close disciples, named as
Matthai, Naki, Netser, Buni and Todah.

4 *The Dead Sea Scrolls, The Gospel of Barnabas, and the New Testament,* American Trust
Publications, 1990.

5   Could this be Salibi's 'bar Nagara' again?
6   Oxford, 1784, XXXIII-XXXVII, LVIII.

BIBLIOGRAPHY

Abrahams, I. *Studies in Pharisaism and the Gospel*. Cambridge: CUP, 1917.

Allegro, J. *The Dead Sea Scrolls*. Harmondsworth: Pelican 1956.

—— *The Sacred Mushroom and the Cross*. London: Hodder and Stoughton, 1970.

Ashe, G. *The Virgin*. London: Routledge, 1978.

Ata ur-Rahim, M. and Thomson, A. *Jesus, Prophet of Islam*. London: Ta-Ha, 1996.

Baigent, M. and Leigh, R. *The Dead Sea Scrolls Deception*. London: Cape, 1991.

Banks, R. *Jesus and the Law in the Synoptic Tradition*. Cambridge: CUP, 1975.

Barrett, C.K. *Jesus and the Gospel Tradition*. London: SPCK, 1967.

Bernheim, P.-A. *James the Brother of Jesus*. London: SCM, 1997.

Black, M. *An Aramaic Approach to the Gospel and Acts*. Oxford: OUP, 1967.

Blinzler, J. *The Trial of Jesus*. London: Mercier Press, 1959.

Blunt, A.W. *Epistle to the Galatians*. Oxford: Clarendon Press, 1955.

Brandon, S.G.F *The Trial of Jesus of Nazareth*. London: Batsford, 1968.

Bridge, A. *Theodora*. London: Cassell, 1978.

Bultmann, R. *Primitive Christianity in its contemporary setting*. London: Thames and Hudson, 1956.

—— *The Theology of the New Testament*. London, 1952.

—— *The History of the Synoptic tradition*. Oxford, 1963.

Burkitt, F.C. *Church and Gnosis*. Cambridge: CUP, 1932.

Carmichael, J. *The Death of Jesus*. London: Gollancz, 1963.

Carrington, C. *The Primitive Christian Calendar*. Cambridge: CUP, 1952.

Catchpole, C. *The Trial of Jesus*. Leiden: E.J.Brill, 1971.

Cohn, H. *The Trial and Death of Jesus*. London: Weidenfeld and Nicolson, 1971.

Crossan, J.D. *Jesus: A Revolutionary Biography*. San Fransciso: Harper SanFrancisco, 1994.

Currer-Briggs, N. *The Holy Grail and the Shroud of Christ: The Quest renewed*. Maulden: ARA Publications, 1984.

Cupitt, D. 'The Christ of Christendom,' in *The Myth of God Incarnate*, ed. J. Hick, London: SCM, 1977.

Danby, H. 'The Bearing of the Rabbinical Council Code on the Jewish Trial Narratives in the Gospels,' *J.T.S.* 21 (1920).

Danielou, J. *The Theology of Jewish Christianity*. London: Darton, Longman and Todd, 1962.

Danziger, E.A. *Forerunners of Christianity*. London: Dutton, 1903.

Daube, D. *The New Testament and Rabbinic Judaism*. London: Athlone Press, 1956.

Davies, W.D. *Christian Origins and Judaism*. London: Darton, Longman and Todd, 1962.
    Paul and Rabbinic Judaism. London: SPCK, 1972.

Dawud, Abdul-Ahad (David Keldani). *Muhammed in the Bible*. Doha: Shariah Courts
    and Religious Affairs, 1980.

Derrett, J.D.M. *Law in the New Testament*. London: Darton, Longman and Todd, 1970.

Desmond, S. *Jesus or Paul?* London, 1945.

Dodd, C.H. *Apostolic Preaching and its Developments*. London: Hodder and Stoughton,
    1936.

—— *New Testament Studies*. Manchester: Manchester University Press, 1968.

Driver, G. Rolls-. *The Hebrew Scrolls*. Oxford: Oxford University Press, 1951.

Dunn, D.G. *The Parting of the Ways*. London: SCM, 1991.

Dunkerley, R. *The Unwritten Gospel, Ana and Agrapha of Jesus*. London: Allen and Unwin,
    1925.

—— *Beyond the Gospels*. Harmondsworth: Pelican, 1957.

Dupont-Sommer, A. *The Essene Writings from Qumran*. Oxford: OUP, 1961.

Edersheim, A *Life and Times of Jesus the Messiah*. London: Longman 1883-6.

—— *The Temple*. Edinburgh: T. and T. Clarke, 1959.

Eisler, R. *The Enigma of the Fourth Gospel*. London: Methuen, 1938.

—— *The Messiah Jesus and John the Baptist*. London: Methuen, 1931.

Eisenman, R. *James the Brother of Jesus*. London: Faber and Faber, 1997.

Eisenman R. and Wise M. *The Dead Sea Scrolls Uncovered*. Shaftesbury: Element, 1992.

Eusebius, *Ecclesiastical History*. London: Macmillan, 1954.

Finkel, A. *The Pharisees and the Teacher of Nazareth*. Leiden: E.J. Brill, 1964.

Flusser, D. *Jesus*. London: Herder and Herder, 1969.

France, R.T. *Jesus and the Old Testament*. London: Tyndale Press, 1971.

Frend, W.H.C. *The Donatist Church*. London: Clarendon, 1985.

Funk, R.W. *Honest to Jesus: Jesus for a New Millennium*. New York: Harper Collins, 1996.

Funk, R.W. and Hoover, R. *The Five Gospels: The Search for the Authentic Words of Jesus*.
    New York: Macmillan, 1993.

Gartner, B. *The Temple Community in Qumran and the New Testament*. Cambridge: CUP,
    1965.

Gilis, C.-A. *La doctrine initiatique du pèlerinage à la Maison d'Allâh*. Paris: Editions de
    l'Oeuvre, 1982.

Green, M. and Butler, C. *The Truth of God Incarnate*. London: Hodder and Stoughton,
    1977.

Golder, M. 'The Two Roots of the Christian Myth' in J. Hick, *The Myth of God Incarnate*,
    London: SCM, 1977.

Goulder, M.D. *Midrash and Lection in Matthew*. London: SPCK, 1974.

Graves, R. *The Nazarene Gospel Restored*. London: Cassell, 1953.

Guscin, M. *The Oviedo Cloth*. Cambridge: Lutterworth, 1998.

Guilding, A. *The Fourth Gospel and Jewish Worship*. Oxford: Clarendon, 1960.

Al-Haddad, Imam Abdallah ibn Alawi. *The Lives of Man*. Louisville: Fons Vitae, 1998.

Hanson, A.T. *Grace and Truth*. London: SPCK, 1975.

Hennecke, E. *New Testament Apocrypha*. Vol. 2. London: Lutterworth, 1963.

Holmes-Gore, V.A. *The Distortion of Christianity*. Scythians, 1980.

Hooker, M.D. *The Signs of a Prophet*. London: SCM, 1997.

Hick, J 'Jesus and the World Religions' in Hick (ed.), *The Myth of God Incarnate*. London: SCM, 1977.

—— *The Metaphor of God Incarnate*. London: SCM, 1993.

Ibrahim, Ezzedine, and Johnson-Davies, Abdul-Wadud. *Forty Hadith Qudsi*. Beirut: Dar al-Kitab al-Lubnani, 1980.

James, M.R. *The Apocryphal New Testament*. Oxford: OUP, 1924.

Jennings, P. *Face to Face with the Turin Shroud*. London: Mowbray, 1978.

Jeremias, J. *Jerusalem in the Time of Christ*. London: SCM, 1969.

Joommal, A.S.K. *The Bible: Word of God or Word of Man?* Islamic Missionary Society, 1976.

Josephus. *The Jewish War*. Grand Rapids: Zondervan, n.d.

Joyce, D. *The Jesus Scroll*. London: Sphere, 1973.

Kersten, H, and Gruber, E.R. *The Jesus Conspiracy*. Shaftesbury: Element , 1992.

Koester, H. *Ancient Christian Gospels: Their History and Development*. Philadelphia: Trinity Press International, 1990.

Lake, Kirsopp. *Landmarks in Early Christianity*. London: Macmillan, 1920.

Layton, B. *The Gnostic Scriptures*. London: SCM, 1987.

Löhr, W. *Basilides und seine Schule*. Tübingen: JCB Mohr, 1996.

Lüdemann, G. *The Great Deception*. London: SCM, 1998.

—— *The Unholy in Holy Scripture: The Dark Side of the Bible*. London: SCM, 1998.

Maccoby, H. *Revolution in Judea*. London: Ocean Books, 1973.

—— *The Mythmaker*. London: Weidenfeld, 1996.

Mack, B.L. *The Lost Gospel: the Book of Q and Christian Origins*. Shaftesbury: Element, 1993.

—— *Who Wrote the New Testament? The Making of the Christian Myth*. San Francisco: Harper SanFrancisco, 1995.

—— *A Myth of Innocence: Mark and Christian Origins*. Philadelphia: Fortress Press, 1988.

Maqsood, R. *The Separated Ones: Jesus, the Pharisees and Islam*. London: SCM, 1991.

McAuliffe, J.D. *Qur'anic Christians*. Cambridge: CUP, 1991.

Metzger, B. *The Text of the New Testament: Its Transmission, Corruption and Restoration*. 3rd ed. Oxford: Oxford University Press, 1992.

Moore, G *Judaism in the first centuries of the Christian Era*. Cambridge (Mass): Harvard

University Press, 1954.

Morton-Smith *The Secret Gospel*. London: Gollancz, 1974.

——*Jesus the Magician*. London: Gollancz, 1978.

Neusner, J. *The modern study of the Mishnah*. Leiden: E.J.Brill, 1973.

——*From Politics to Piety*. New York: Prentice Hall, 1973.

——*The Development of a Legend*. Leiden: E.J.Brill, 1976.

——*Jews and Christians*. London: SCM, 1991.

Nickell, J. *Inquest on the Shroud of Turin*. New York: Prometheus, 1983.

North, R. 'Chenoboskion and Q', *Catholic Biblical Quarterly*, Vol xxiv, 1967.

Parkes, J. *Jesus, Paul and the Jews*. London: SCM, 1936.

Pike, J.A. *If this be Heresy*. New York: Harper and Row, 1967.

Pliny *Letter to Trajan*. Warminster: Aris and Phillips, n.d.

Reynolds, A. *Jesus versus Christianity*. London: Cambridge International Publishers, 1988.

Richardson, A. *The Political Christ*. London: SCM, 1973.

Richardson, N. *Was Jesus Divine?* London: Epworth, 1979.

Riddle, D.W. *Jesus and the Pharisees*. Chicago: University of Chicago Press, 1928.

Robertson, A. *Jesus, Myth or History?* London: Watts and Co, 1940.

Robinson, A.T. *The Pharisees and Jesus*, London: Duckworth, 1920.

Robinson, J.A.T. *Redating the New Testament*. London: SCM, 1976.

——*The Nag Hammadi Library*. 3rd ed. San Francisco: Harper and Row, 1988.

Salibi, K. *The Bible Came from Arabia*. London: Jonathan Cape, 1985.

——*The Secrets of the Bible People*. London: Saqi Books, 1988.

——*Conspiracy in Jerusalem*. London: Tauris & Co, 1988.

Sanders, E.P. *Paul and Palestinian Judaism*. London: SCM, 1977.

——*Jesus and Judaism*. London: SCM, 1984.

——*The Historical Figure of Jesus*. London: Allen Lane (Penguin Books), 1993.

Sandmel, S. *We Jews and Jesus*. London: Gollancz, 1965.

Schechter, B. *Some Aspects of Rabbinic Theology*. Black, 1961.

Schiffman, L.A. *The Galilee in Late Antiquity*.

Schofield, G. *In the Year 62*. London: Harrap, 1962.

Schonfield, H.T. *The Authentic New Testament*. Hamilton, 1962.

——*According to the Hebrews*. Duckworth, 1937.

——*Saints Against Caesar*. Macdonald, 1948.

——*The Jew from Tarsus*. Macdonald, 1948.

——*For Christ's Sake*. Macdonald and Jams, 1975.

——*After the Cross*. New York: Barnes, 1981.

——*The Pentecost Revolution*. Shaftesbury: Element, 1985.

Sheehan, T. *The First Coming: How the Kingdom of God became Christianity*. New York: Random House, 1988.

Sherwin-White, A.N. *Roman Society and Roman Law in the New Testament*. Oxford, 1963.

Sox, H.D. *File on the Shroud*. London: Coronet, 1978.

—— *The Gospel of Barnabas*. London: Allen and Unwin, 1984.

—— *Relics and Shrines*. London: Allen and Unwin, 1985.

Tacitus *History*. Harmondsworth: Penguin, 1975.

Talal, Prince al-Hassan ibn. *Christianity in the Arab World*. London: SCM, 1998.

Van Drandem, A. *Les Inscriptions Thamoudéenes*, Paris, 1950.

Vermes, G. *Jesus the Jew*. Collins, 1973; London: SCM 1985.

—— *The Dead Sea Scrolls in English*. Fourth edition, Harmondsworth: Penguin, 1995.

Wilson, A.N. *Jesus*. London: Flamingo, 1993.

Wilson, I. *Jesus, the Evidence*. Weidenfeld, Nicolson, 1996.

—— *The Turin Shroud*. London: Gollancz, 1978.

Wilson, R. Mcl. *The Gnostic Problem*. London: Mowbray, 1958.

Winter, P. *On the Trial of Jesus*. Berlin: Walter de Gruyter, 1974.

Youssef, M.A. *The Dead Sea Scrolls, the Gospel of Barnabas, and the New Testament*. Indianapolis: American Trust Publications, 1990.

Zeitlin, S *Who Crucified Jesus?* New York: Harper Bros, 1942

—— 'The Origin of the Pharisees re-affirmed', *Jewish Quarterly Review* 59, 1969.

The Qur'an. Yusuf Ali interpretation in English. Leicester: The Islamic Foundation, 1988.

Encyclopedia Judaica. 16 vols. Keter Publishing House Ltd, 1972.

The Babylonian Talmud, ed. Isaac Epstein. London: Soncino Press, 1963.

The Revised Standard Version of the Bible. London: Collins, 1952.

INDEX

Aaron, 44, 71, 138, 148, 149
Ab Beth Din, 16
Abgar of Edessa, 182
Abijah, 44
Abraham, 77, 100, 160, 168, 172
Absalom, tomb of, 44
absolutio, 3
Abu Rahm, 100
Abu Sarghis, 145
Acha, 59
Acts of Barnabas, 234
Acts of Pilate, 24-25
Adah, 102
Adam, 91, 101, 211, 216, 267-8
al-'Adhr, 104
Adiebene, 259
Adonis, 95
Adoptionism, 30, 114, 118, 119
afikomen, 70
Agrippa, 15, 16, 134
Ahmad, 147, 162, 163
Ahmadiyya sect, 170
Akeldama, 105
Akhira, 220
Alabastron, 30
Alexander, 28
Alexandra, 28, 195
Alexandria, 15, 36, 111, 197, 203
Aloe vera, 188
Allat, 100
Allegro, J., 126
Alphaeus, 40, 41
al-'Alyan, 100
Amos, 68
Amram, 148
Andrew of Caesarea, 257

angels, 2, 161, 190, 258, 261; and see
    'Gabriel'
Ananias, 143, 153
Ananus, 10, 43, 134, 135
Annas, 2, 11, 12, 13, 237
Antigonus, 28
Antioch, 50, 53, 78, 143, 195, 203, 205,
    233; council of, 200
antinomians, 88-9, 114
Antipas, 233
antisemitism, 19, 37, 38, 63, 246
Antonius Felix, 134
Aphrodite, 96
Apocrypha, 193-4
Apollinaris, 203
Apollo, 95
Apostolic Constitutions, 202
Arabia, 75
Arabic Infancy Gospel, 144, 145
Arabs, 162
Arafat, 162, 217, 261
Aramaic, 32, 34
de Aranda, M., 235
d'Arbley, 264
Archelaus, 27
Aretas, 129
Aristion, 117
Aristobolus, 28
Arius, 195, 197-8, 265
Armenian Church, 205
Ascension, 147, 170, 173, 176, 259
The Ascents of James, 42, 114
Asclepius, 119
Ashmunaith, 145
Ashur, Ashurbanipal, 98
Ashteroth, 209